Sound Tracks

Sound Tracks

Uncovering Our Musical Past

GRAEME LAWSON

THE BODLEY HEAD

LONDON

1 3 5 7 9 10 8 6 4 2

The Bodley Head, an imprint of Vintage, is part of the Penguin Random House group of
companies whose addresses can be found at global.penguinrandomhouse.com

First published by The Bodley Head in 2024

Copyright © Graeme Lawson 2024

Graeme Lawson has asserted his right to be identified as the author of this
Work in accordance with the Copyright, Designs and Patents Act 1988

Every effort has been made to contact all copyright holders. The publisher will be pleased to amend in future
editions any errors or omissions brought to their attention.

penguin.co.uk/vintage

Printed and bound in Great Britain by Clays Ltd, Elcograf S.p.A.

The authorised representative in the EEA is Penguin Random House Ireland,
Morrison Chambers, 32 Nassau Street, Dublin D02 YH68

A CIP catalogue record for this book is available from the British Library

ISBN 9781847926876

Penguin Random House is committed to a sustainable
future for our business, our readers and our planet. This book
is made from Forest Stewardship Council® certified paper.

Contents

Contents

Contents

Preface

It takes the average adult about four minutes to read and absorb a thousand words of text, so if you try to read this book from cover to cover without a pause, it will keep you busy for just under seven hours – almost a whole working day. In that time you'll have delved back through more than three million years, criss-crossing the known world; you'll also have had a brief brush with the future and you'll even have soared out into distant regions of outer space. But as any traveller knows, even a simple journey demands careful preparation, and if it's to be anything more than a whistle-stop tour, it also requires a leisurely pace, giving you time to absorb and find meaning in new experiences and surroundings. So as we set out to voyage back through time in search of music's origins, you may be pleased to hear that leisure is one of the principles at the heart of *Sound Tracks*.

Navigation is another. The path we're about to take, from the twenty-first century back to the dawn of humankind, is in very large parts untrodden. And like any expedition into the unknown, we're going to need a map and some kind of itinerary to help us negotiate the terrain, to avoid hidden pitfalls and to draw our attention to important features that we might otherwise miss. For our particular journey, that guide is going to be provided by archaeology, which will supply the material framework and inform our understanding of the things and the people we'll meet. As we engage with the astonishing diversity of our material musical heritage, some encounters, like the dazzling assemblage of chimes from the tomb of Marquis Yi in China, will speak eloquently for themselves. Despite the passage of two and a half thousand years, their magnificence and near-perfect state of preservation will leave us open-mouthed at the sheer audacity of their engineering, and the splendour of the music and drama that they served. A rusted fragment of perforated steel from the Alamo in Texas, on the other hand, will seem so small and insignificant that we might easily have trodden on it, or kicked it out of the way. Yet it will prove to bear witness to a common aspect of life on the front line of conflict: making music to pass a weary soldier's spare time. And somewhere in between these two extremes will be the spectral trace of a once-cherished lyre found in an Anglo-Saxon royal burial-mound in Essex, a dark shadow being almost all that remains of a magnificent instrument that's been slowly turning to dust over the last fifteen hundred years.

Archaeology is a curious practice. It's also a practice for the curious. It's nosey, it's never satisfied, and it's messy. It operates in mud, in graves, under the sea and at scenes of natural disasters and human-made calamities. It inevitably has to deal with a certain randomness: its objects of study are thrown up by chance and are subject to all the vicissitudes of time. It investigates them with a cool and clinical eye; but it also takes into account their contexts which, when interrogated carefully, can tell us as much about their origins and uses as the material objects themselves. Many of the magnificent musical relics we see in museums have been detached from their original circumstances. To gain a more intimate view of the people who loved and used them, and to discover how they played them, we need to place them back within their social settings.

With music's origins as our theme and archaeology as our guide, the book takes an unusual direction: we go backwards rather than forwards in time. A more conventional treatment of musical history might have started at the beginning and worked forward to the present day. But that's not how archaeology works. When we excavate a many-layered deposit, we naturally begin at the top, with the layer that's closest to the surface; from there we proceed downwards, which means reversing the order of time. What's more, to begin at the beginning rather presupposes that there is a beginning to start from, as well as a coherent and even purposeful direction of travel; it may suggest that our present-day world is the journey's destination. But in terms of music's evolution – and perhaps even our own – that's not the case: it's just where we are now.

Going backwards in time also happens to be the way that I myself joined the quest, first by exploring the world's music today and the rich archaeological finds of the medieval and post-medieval world, before applying what I'd learned to the more remote and in some ways less well-evidenced archaeologies of Classical Greece, Rome and Egypt. Only then did I dare to venture into Prehistory. Yet before we begin to probe first the brighter and then the dimmer reaches of music's dreamtime, we need to gain some sense of what music looks like when it's become archaeology. Or to put it another way: if archaeology is to be our lens, then first we have to understand its optics.

Prologue

The Present and Remembered Past

It's a fine, calm summer's evening during a warm spell in the last Ice Age, and someone is sitting in the mouth of a limestone cave in southern Germany, fingering elaborate tunes on a long slender pipe of swan bone. The haunting sounds drift out across the valley, to lose themselves among the trees and the birdsong, and the endless clamour of the river far below. Fast forward around thirty-seven thousand years and in central China a gorgeously attired crowd circles a huge open tomb, looking on as the body of their dead king is solemnly lowered into his grave. The year is 433 BC, and amid the splendour of the equipment that's going to be buried with him we see drums and stringed instruments and flutes of various kinds, while a vast lacquered timber scaffold supports a carillon of sixty-four magnificent heavy bronze bells. We skip another two thousand years, and see a beautiful violin sink to the bottom of the Baltic Sea, where it joins the other wreckage of a naval battle that erupted in the late morning of 1 June 1676. And today, still shrouded in the deep cold darkness beneath the ice of the Weddell Sea in western Antarctica, rest the instruments and gramophone records abandoned by Sir Ernest Shackleton's Imperial Trans-Antarctic Expedition, when their ship *Endurance*, crushed by the pack ice, foundered on a November evening in 1915.

Shackleton's musical memorabilia are still to be recovered, but all these other instruments have been excavated, and form parts of an extraordinary musical jigsaw puzzle that archaeologists are now piecing together around the world.

Music's archaeological records are a uniquely human achievement. It's true that animals also make music, or patterns of sound that we hear as music, and that their sound-making may sometimes leave a material trace. A hollow tree branch or a telephone pole may bear the scars where a woodpecker has been drumming. A rainforest floor may briefly preserve the performance space, or 'court', of a Wilson's Bird-of-Paradise. But for the most part the sounds that animals make are transitory. If the songs and performances of birds have any physical substance of their own, it's embodied in their anatomies: in the syrinx within a songbird's airway that allows it to sing, in the whistling wing feathers of a flying swan, in the buzzing tail feathers of a sky-diving snipe. Storks clatter their beaks together. Cranes dance. Anatomical and cognitive adaptations have enabled the elaborate calls and gestures of lemurs, howler monkeys, wolves, whales, frogs and cicadas. But while all these forms of communication are intense and, to our minds, deeply redolent of the beauty and drama of the natural world, they exist entirely in the moment. When the song or dance is over, it's over.

We humans are different. We've evolved ways of giving our voices, our words and our music a more permanent physical existence: through the ingenious systems we've devised to record and recreate them, and through the elaborate hardware we've developed to express our musical abilities and preferences. Through time this materiality has left behind a distinct archaeological trail; and to begin to make sense of it we could do worse than start with some instructive examples from our most recent past.

Capturing sound

The first must be the humble piano-roll. It wasn't by accident that our ancestors developed the means of harnessing sound and preserving its memory: it was quite deliberate. Many centuries ago, they began to represent music in words by attaching names to lengths and pitches of notes, and by writing them down as symbols on parchment, papyrus and bamboo, or engraving them in stone.

Dots and undulating lines would sometimes be traced to capture the rise and fall of melodies. And then, much more recently, we began to develop mechanical means of capturing the physical sound directly onto wax cylinders, or by recording a keyboard player's keystrokes and stamping their shapes into punch-cards. To play back these old, fossil-like recordings today on a wind-up Phonograph or a Player-piano is to eavesdrop on history in a particularly magical and intimate way.

A wax cylinder of the sort that Thomas Edison devised and produced is an extraordinarily tactile object. The original sound waves, collected and focused by a cone-shaped microphone, have been transferred directly to a sharp cutting stylus. The stylus has then scored the rotating wax surface, leaving behind an undulating analog groove that, when it's played back, will recreate (more or less) the original sound. You can even play it with your fingernail.

By contrast, the Phonograph's competitor, the Player piano, uses a 'digital' system, first developed in the early eighteenth century to speed up the industrial weaving of textiles. When the roll is fed into the mechanism and it's set in motion, its perforations interact with a vacuum pressure system to cause selected hammers to strike the strings in the order in which they appear on the recording, sustaining each note for exactly the right length of time. Its unique attraction as a playback system is not just that it reproduces an echo of the original performance, it's that it does so with an authentic piano sound. In spite of its complex playback mechanism, a Player piano is still a real piano, with hammers and strings. It therefore replays without any of the surface noise, rumble or hiss that besets the wax cylinder. To all intents and purposes it sounds exactly like a live performance.

Today the piano roll's remarkable technical possibilities have been largely forgotten, but briefly, for a period of just thirty-five minutes on 17 September 1988, the technology once again came under the spotlight. That evening, the BBC's 'Last Night of the Proms' featured a live but decidedly ghostly performance by the Australian pianist Percy Grainger, playing Edvard Grieg's Piano

Concerto in A Minor. It was by then twenty-five years since Grainger had died, but the motions of his fingers lived on in the piano roll. Accompanied by the BBC Symphony Orchestra and masterminded by Rex Lawson, a champion of the piano roll, the performance astonished and thrilled Promenaders and viewers around the world.

We take solid-state memory of this sort for granted these days, but little more than a hundred years ago it must have seemed nothing short of magical that voices and music could be preserved and manipulated in that way. For the first time in human history, people could listen to a musical performance or a speech that wasn't being delivered in the present. It may have taken place hours, weeks, months, even years before.

We're often told, in an attempt to define it, that music, like the other performance arts, is essentially transitory and ephemeral. It's certainly true that for the casual listener it passes leaving only a memory. It can't be held in our gaze in the way that a painting or a sculpture can. But that doesn't mean that it's always disembodied. As the cutting stylus of the Phonograph recorder follows its helical path around the surface of a fresh wax cylinder, it leaves behind a sound recording, for sure, but it's also a track. Like the tyre trails of a Jeep travelling across desert sand, or a snowmobile in winter, the sound has imparted the invisible character of its passing, the shape of its past journey, into the visible matrix of wax. Unwind a typical piano roll and you'll find a similar passage of time stretching out before you. The first movement of the Grieg concerto would probably extend for about thirty metres, the rectangular perforations wandering across the width of the unrolling paper like so many little footprints.

The power of amplification

Another example has to be our fascination for loudness. One of the great technological advances of our time has been the invention of signal amplification. In the twentieth century the development of the thermionic-cathode valve and the semiconductor transistor allowed the creation of the electronic amplifier, and gave us the ability to harness the power of music and amplify it to previously unimaginable levels. As we begin our search for music's ancient origins, it might seem a little improbable that a modern electronic device like that could provide a clue to the route we should take, but in a roundabout way it may. The clue lies not so much in the electronics that provide the power, impressive though they are, but in the effects such systems have on us, and what they tell us about our musical habits and preferences.

In particular they seem to reveal something about our appetites for three strong musical forces: for high levels of resonance, for very high- and low-level frequencies, and for extreme volume of sound. Since time immemorial, reverberation has held a constant allure, from the six-second echo in the Cathedral of Notre Dame in Paris to the smoothing effect of the piano's sustaining pedal. The high notes of a coloratura soprano and the deep rumble of a sixty-four-foot organ stop provide their own powerful frissons. And at least as far back as 600 BC, thunderous blasts from Bronze Age trumpets were already shaking the forests and plains of Northern Europe. While we often imagine loudness to be a modern musical preoccupation, it clearly isn't. But what exactly is its attraction?

We sometimes use volume of sound to display our status and power, whether as individuals or as groups and institutions. With the aid of ever larger loudspeakers we broadcast our voices and music in attempts to impose ourselves on our environments. Football crowds chant at the tops of their voices to express their collective identities and intimidate their opponents. In the sixteenth century, one of the things that most impressed the Aztecs about their Spanish invaders was the sound of their muskets and cannons; and we still witness cannonades on state occasions like the 124-gun salute that marked the Platinum Jubilee of the late Queen Elizabeth in 2022. It seems that loudness and power often go hand in hand.

But it's equally capable of giving pleasure. It's not to everyone's taste, of course, but to many people part of the joy of being exposed to loud music, especially dance music, seems to be the feeling of immersion that it can bring, and the sense of separation from everyday normality that comes with it. Sometimes that separation can be quite extreme. Its power can best be exemplified in experiments by surgeons in the eighteenth century, which showed that the sudden beating of drums and the violent discharge of firearms could benefit a patient during dental extractions and other painful procedures – provided that the drum beats and the discharges were sufficiently close and unexpected to shock and distract the patient's wits (and provided, of course, that the surgeon was able to work quickly).

Green music

At the other end of the spectrum of technology, another core element of music can be found among a group of the most insubstantial of all musical instruments in use today. They come under the general heading of 'tree-bark flutes'. If you've never seen one in a music shop, there's a very good reason for it. It's a question of biology: they can only be made at a particular time each spring when, with the warmer weather, the sap begins to rise in deciduous trees. Throughout the cold months the bark on each of last year's new twigs has been stuck firmly to its wooden core, but now in certain species it loosens its grip and for a short time it can be slid off in one piece, as a length of thin, leathery tube. With the addition of a small sounding-hole at one end, and a short piece cut from the core to create a mouthpiece, the result is one of the sweetest, most magical instrument sounds you'll ever hear.

Sadly, it's only ever a matter of days or even hours before a bark flute dries out, shrinks and cracks. But in that brief moment it reveals one of music's deepest and most universal characteristics. It's embodied in the instrument's simple, economical form. There are no finger holes to help shape its tuning. Instead the length and narrowness of the tube, the 'air column', enables an altogether different way of playing. It invokes what's called the 'harmonic series': a precise sequence of notes, or overtones, that forms a very particular gapped scale. The harmonic series is a phenomenon that answers only to the laws of physics and it comes to life spontaneously whenever air is excited within a tube. The rising scale of notes produced by increasing the air flow through the tube is always the same, and it's quite immutable. It's always been and will always be with us. It emerges as if by magic from the very fabric of the physical universe; and it carries with it a powerful implication.

If you've ever wondered how or why humans more or less agree to make and share our tunes within octave frameworks, based on intervals more or less the size (and sum) of tones and semitones, here's a first clue: they represent elements of the harmonic series. And the bark flute has one more surprise in store for us. Place a fingertip over the further end of the tube while you blow into the mouthpiece, and a second series of overtones will emerge, different from the first. By alternately opening and closing the tube a new combined scale is formed, which is both more tuneful and more versatile. It's not one of our usual major or minor keyboard scales, or modes; it has a raised fourth note and a lowered seventh. But it's wonderfully expressive, and it's a scale that's well known from traditional musics the world over. We may well begin to wonder for how long humans have been exposed to its influence.

Because by its very nature tree bark quickly decays in humid earth, almost no trace of these flutes has ever been found by archaeologists. But what we do know is that making them was once widespread. Indeed, from Scandinavia to Scotland, and from Siberia to Turkey, it's persisted at least until the twentieth century, so that in our grandparents' day it was not unusual in an Anatolian village in springtime to hear a chorus of willow whistles echoing like birdsong from the waterside places where children were playing. So, on the one hand, the bark flute, with its simple elegance and economy, remains an object lesson in how a primitive-seeming tool might unlock unexpected beauty and creative potential; on the other, it leads us to consider how the influence of even a childhood pastime may have contributed to our ancestors' developing perceptions of sound and music.

The bark flute traditions of the world are just one example of what my Swedish colleague, the prehistorian Cajsa Lund, calls *Grön Musik* or 'Green Music'. Such living traditions may not be able to tell us directly how music was made in our remote past, but their fragility offers us a timely warning: that the treasures that we're going to encounter in this book, astonishing as most of them are, may represent no more than a small part of humanity's lost music – no more than the exposed tip of a vast metaphorical iceberg. It's a simple matter of survival. Most of the objects that we find have been made from tougher, more resilient materials such as stone and pottery, metal and bone, antler and ivory. To understand those deeper and potentially more representative layers of our ancestors' musical lives, we're going to explore the objects that we have, naturally; but we must also understand their limitations.

Origins and invention

Another kind of evidence that we're going to need to weigh carefully is evidence for the origins of musical ideas and traditions. When we think of innovation in past music technologies, there's a natural temptation to imagine their gradual improvement through time. Prehistorians in particular are so used to charting slow changes occurring in tiny increments through thousands, even millions, of years, that it can almost seem to be the normal, natural order of things. But this is by no means always the case. The modern world shows us that a musical idea may take only a few decades to graduate from conception to becoming one of the world's most popular musical instruments.

In the 1930s, on the Caribbean island of Trinidad, the British colonial administration sought to suppress the popular drumming tradition of *Tamboo Bamboo*, on the grounds that it threatened public order, particularly during Carnival. When the bamboo drums were eventually banned, Carnival goers were forced to look elsewhere for an alternative. By chance a solution lay on their doorstep. Trinidad, famous for its asphalt lake, was already a major oil producer, and in the 1940s was playing a vital part in the British and American war effort. As a result, vast numbers of empty steel oil drums were piling up and, being so obviously resonant whenever they were moved or knocked, they now naturally invited musical experiments. Musicians found that the sawn-off end of such a drum could make an excellent, if slightly unusual-sounding *tambour*, and that it could be made to resonate even better if it was first tempered. Before long they noticed that by stretching the metal into discrete depressions and domes, they could achieve different musical pitches from different parts of just one drum head. From this modest beginning further refinements followed, including the development of different kinds of beater and ways of fine-tuning, giving us the unique steel-drum sound that's now so familiar.

All of this took place within living memory. The first time a steel band appeared in the United Kingdom, as far as I know, was in 1951 when the newly formed Trinidad All-Steel Percussion Orchestra made a sensational debut at the Festival of Britain. From there the pans' rise to prominence and global popularity was little short of meteoric. It seems that although we might expect gradual, quiet change to be the norm in traditional musics, there's also plenty of room for the occasional Big Bang.

Understanding the evidence

There's also room for time and circumstance to play their part in the way we experience and interpret music's physical presence, and nowhere is this more apparent than in the tragic pianos of Pripyat. I don't suppose a calamity like Pripyat can ever be said to be fortunate, and yet the lamentable consequences of disaster can sometimes offer lessons in how music's materiality may make the transition into archaeology. Worryingly, they reveal that not everything can be taken at face value.

When an explosion happened in the early hours of 26 April 1986 at the Chernobyl nuclear power plant, most of the residents of the neighbouring town of Pripyat were asleep. Since the blast itself caused obvious damage only to the plant, some thirty-six hours elapsed before people were told to evacuate their homes. But once they'd left they never returned, and Pripyat became just another human settlement abandoned as a consequence of a sudden and unforeseen change of circumstance. In this case it was the dark shadow of toxic radiation. But a unique feature of Pripyat, and one that makes it different from many other abandoned sites, is that we can now piece together precisely what happened and some of the things that continue to happen there. And there is a strange musical dimension to the story.

It seems that when a city is deserted by its residents, it may not simply be left to nature to do its work. Certainly nature has the major part to play; but so do looting, vandalism and, astonishingly, even tourism. On the face of it, Pripyat would seem a rather unlikely tourist attraction, but right up until the Russian army's invasion of Ukraine in February 2022, officially sanctioned tours were on offer to anyone who wanted to see the disaster site from the comfort of a luxury minibus. Photographs and reports of visitor experiences are still to be found on Tripadvisor. And among the most arresting and haunting images on the Internet are photographs that show the ruined and desecrated interior of Pripyat's music school.

The images reveal the particular fate of two of its grand pianos. One has been brought crashing to its knees, another brutally eviscerated. Together with many of their other moving parts, the keyboards have fallen foul of looters and vandals, leaving the iron frame with some metal strings attached, and an assortment of hammers and dampers. The question for an archaeologist of course is: what lessons should we draw from these once beautiful and cherished instruments? And what can they tell us about our approach to music's more ancient past? Quite a lot, it seems.

Prior to the disaster, professors and students would have touched the smooth ivory and ebony keys each day in exactly the manner for which they were designed. Today it's very different. What little is left of them can still make sounds. Indeed snatched recordings of them have been exploited as a raw sound source by composers of electronic music. Other visitors have tried to play the strings like harp strings, or in the modern tradition of 'prepared piano'. But while these anguished twangs are undoubtedly atmospheric, they bear almost no discernible resemblance to an original piano sound, and they reveal almost nothing of the kinds of music that the instruments could once have served. And this may be one of Pripyat's most unlikely musical legacies. Here we can compare a familiar musical instrument before its demise with what it's subsequently become: comparing the state of a thing as we encounter it with its known historical past. For music's archaeologists the lesson is a powerful one. Interference is always a risk.

Tombs, treasures – and chance

There's another way too in which unseen hands can put their seal on a musical phenomenon: and that's by burying it. In this book we'll often be focusing on the more random aspects of archaeological preservation and discovery – on objects which have been lost or abandoned and even deliberately destroyed. These are a large part of the modern archaeologist's stock in trade. But in our search for music's origins we'll also need to take into account musical objects that may have been deliberately buried or entombed, becoming in effect archaeological time capsules. This will come with its own benefits, and its own special challenges. The biggest and richest of these 'capsules' are provided by tombs, whether the graves of ordinary people or the burial chambers of royalty, and they preserve some of the greatest and certainly the most dramatic of our discoveries. But such things always come with a caveat. An object that's been accidentally lost is probably an honest witness to the way things once were, but objects that we find in tombs have been sent down to us for a purpose. So we must always ask who put them there – and why.

And this is why, on the pilgrimage we're about to make, we're going to be including simple, marginal and forgotten musical acts as well as those of ceremony, within our working definition of 'music'. It's not that we need to draw every last fragment into our purview, or that we need to make the subject relevant to particular communities and interest groups. It's simply a matter of common sense. If we're hoping to answer that most fundamental question, 'where does music come from?', we'll need to come to some appreciation of what exactly music is, and to do that we'll need to keep an open mind.

Like every archaeological museum in the world, this book curates and presents a collection of archaeological evidence. I've selected some of the finds that I've encountered in a lifetime spent trying to make sense of our musical past, and which I think make important contributions to the archaeological story of music's deep origins. Other objects could have been chosen, and other storylines followed: we're spoilt for choice. But I hope that this particular collection will help point the way and in the process offer a new perspective on our ancestors' humanity.

PART ONE

The Archaeology of Familiar Things

The Nineteenth to the Seventeenth Century

A grand piano and an early phonograph; a child's home-made flute and a set of Caribbean steelpans. These and so many other physical expressions of music's diversity still bring joy and meaning to our lives in the twenty-first century. But sooner or later, being material things, they will come to form parts of the archaeology of our time. Becoming an archaeological relic is always just round the corner. And the likely fates of these twentieth- and twenty-first-century objects hold clues that will help us make sense of music's more distant past, even of its ultimate origins. So far we've traced musical traditions and technologies as they stand on the threshold of an archaeological future. Now it's time to step across that threshold and down into archaeology's first layer: the earth immediately below our feet.

This surface layer might be called 'the archaeology of familiar things': *archaeology* because in spite of the modernity of the objects, their evidence emerges directly from archaeological excavation, and *familiar* because the time frame that they occupy is, to all intents and purposes, within our own remembered and recorded traditions. Being familiar in no way detracts from an object's archaeological value or historical interest. In fact it rather adds to it. Certainly, the sense of shared experience that familiarity brings adds a very special dimension, and brings with it important clues to some of the deeper mysteries that lie ahead.

Recent musical traditions reveal something else too. They allow us to see just how environment affects different materials, shapes, surfaces and structures, over known periods of time. It's the vital next step on this journey. If the first step was to address how every-day things become archaeological objects in the first place, the second will show how they are changed and transformed by their surroundings, and how the processes of ageing can preserve – or disguise – their true musical character.

CHAPTER ONE

Music on the move: lost instruments from a shipwreck and a famous siege

England and Texas, nineteenth century

In 2017, about fifteen kilometres off the coast of Sussex, divers recovered a strange musical object from the sea bed. Searching through the wreckage of an unnamed sunken steamship, around twenty-five metres beneath the waters of the English Channel, they noticed a curved, tapering plate made of thin metal, about a metre long, with rows of small neat holes drilled into it. Once they'd carried it to the surface and were able to examine it more closely, they realised it was the brass facing from the neck of a large pedal harp, the kind of harp you might see today on any concert platform.

All the wooden parts had vanished: exposed to seawater they would have decayed soon after the ship sank. But an inscription delicately engraved on the brass plate identified it as the product of the well-known London harp-maker, Érard. It even carried a serial number: 5331. This was the clue archaeologists had been searching for as they tried to put a name to the ship. It led them to Érard's sales ledgers preserved in the Royal College of Music in London, and against number 5331 they found a handwritten note. It told them that the instrument had been made of satinwood, and offered two further snippets of information. It had been built in October 1839 and sold in September 1840 to a customer in Ireland: Samuel J. Pigott's music shop in Dublin. The wreck site was exactly on the course a ship would take when sailing between London and Dublin.

There are still examples of Érard's harps in playing condition, so it's possible to imagine the instrument despite the loss of its wooden parts. The more immediate benefit that the plate provided was to maritime history. When the date in the ledger was checked against records of ship losses, the shape and location of the wreck showed it to be the SS *Ondine*, of Waterford, on the south coast of Ireland. The ship regularly plied between Ireland and London, until 19 February 1860 when she collided with another vessel and sank. There's a twenty-year gap between the sale of the harp and the sinking of the *Ondine*, but instruments were often shipped back and forth for repairs and servicing.

Fine though they are, expensive concert harps like Érard 5331 represent only the very top end of Victorian music technology, and reflect only a small part of the musical experience of their times. At the other end of the scale, so to speak, another category of finds stands out, if not for their beauty then at least for their quantity. At first sight they seem to be no more than bits of rusty iron, without obvious purpose or significance. To the untrained eye their shapes don't seem in the least bit musical. But you've almost certainly been entertained by the charming, sometimes soulful tones of the instrument they belonged to. It's vital to several celebrated musical repertoires: from the folk ballads of Bob Dylan and the electric blues of Little Walter to the concert performances of Larry Adler, John Sebastian and Tommy Reilly. These rusty bits are parts of a mouth organ, a diatonic harmonica, one of the great pocket instruments of the world. And they are important precisely because of their ordinariness. They all belong to the same type of instrument, most likely from the same country of manufacture – Germany – and yet they've ended up at widely separated points around the globe. One of the first came to light in the 1970s at a famous site in San Antonio, Texas.

During the winter of 1835–6, Mexican forces under General López de Santa Anna laid siege to an old Spanish mission known as the Alamo, which had been occupied by a force of Anglo-American rebels fighting for the independence of Texas. Having taken the mission and killed all the rebels inside it, the Mexicans destroyed much of what remained; only the church escaped. Through the Mexican War of 1846 and the Civil War of 1861–5 the United States and Confederate armies continued to use the site as a military base, and with the return of peace commercial development followed. In 1970 excavations began to establish the site's architectural history, and in 1977 archaeologists found a small piece of rusty metal along with a variety of other objects in a layer of yellow sandy earth to the north of the church. These other objects could be dated to the 'Anglo-American' period of occupation and were probably deposited there around 1836. The metal fragment was rectangular and about the size of a matchbox, with parallel slots of slightly different lengths. It didn't take long for a practised eye to make the musical identification: it had been broken off the reed plate of a harmonica.

In vibrating systems, different lengths generate different resonant frequencies, and the fragment seemed to be from the lower end of the instrument's range, as they were progressively longer towards the plate's unbroken end. In the laboratory, the fixture points for the reeds, which had long since corroded away – they would have been wafer-thin – became visible.

The way a harmonica is constructed is ingenious. Having punched out the reed slots with a cutting tool, the maker fixes two tiny leaf springs to one end of each slot, so that their free ends can vibrate up and down within the space. They are rather like tiny springboards, mounted above and below a trapdoor. The fit has to be sufficiently precise to close the trap when stationary but still allow the spring free movement up and down. Forcing air around it will make it rise and fall, creating the harmonica's reedy buzzing sound. For the instrument to be playable, though, three further elements have to be added, to form a kind of sandwich. Above the reed plate sits an open casing of thin pressed metal, to protect the reeds from accidental damage, while below the plate there's a thin wooden board and a second flat metal plate. The wood has slots cut into it, resembling a comb, and once sandwiched between the metals the slots become air ducts, in effect pipes, corresponding to the positions of the reeds and opening along the leading edge of the instrument. Blow into one, or draw a breath through it, and you will activate one or the other reed, making it sound its particular note.

The resulting design is a wonderfully compact little instrument, a diatonic reed organ small enough to travel anywhere with you. Its standard ten pipes enable a series of twenty different notes, and are so closely spaced that it's possible to play two or more at a time to form rudimentary harmonies. But of course this offers only the first hint of the instrument's musical potential in skilled hands.

What kind of music might the Alamo harmonica have played in its day? I guess it could have been practically anything: traditional ballads, popular dance tunes, religious hymns, military marches, well-known operatic arias, sentimental airs – whatever people wanted, in fact. It could have been played either privately, for fun, or for more formal entertainments. In time it would become a signature feature of that ultimate professional entertainer, the one-man band. And of course, it would play an important part in the blues. But most of all, its discovery at the Alamo and at other military sites suggests that it was the instrument of choice for people on the move.

Archaeological finds generally possess two valuable attributes: their immediate local context – the place where they were found and the other things found with them – and the wider background provided by similar objects from other sites. One well-preserved example has been excavated almost intact at a place called Ploegsteert (known to British Tommies as 'Plug Street') in Hainaut, Belgium, lost or abandoned by a soldier of the First World War. Another was unearthed recently at the riverside site of a burnt antebellum mansion at Bluffton, South Carolina. Indeed, the instrument's association with war is a common feature. There's another from Gettysburg and two more on or close to the Civil War battlefield of Antietam. Two virtually intact examples have been recovered from the Wilderness battlefield in Virginia and from Fort McCoy in Wisconsin. By some miracle of preservation,

6

the Virginia find has all its reeds still in place, while the upper cover of the Wisconsin instrument carries the mark of Friedrich Hotz & Co. of Knittlingen, Germany (a firm later acquired by the great Matthias Hohner).

The preponderance of nineteenth- and twentieth-century harmonica finds doesn't mean that the underlying technology is a Victorian invention. Its principles draw on a much wider global technology that powers a number of familiar mechanical instruments: the concertina, the piano accordion, the harmonium and the reed organ, and even (although voiced in a different way) the mouth harp. But that's far from all. More than two thousand years ago, instrument-makers in East Asia were already making the Chinese mouth organ or *sheng*, which produced a closely similar sound. There the reeds were made of slit bamboo but the principle was broadly the same.

The fact that many of the places where bits of harmonicas have been found witnessed dramatic and violent events has facilitated their discovery. If the siege of the Alamo hadn't occupied such an iconic place in US history, historians would have been less likely to enquire and archaeologists to excavate. Indeed, it's remarkable how many advances in music's archaeology have been linked with warfare in one way or another. Outrageous fortune (and the Alamo is surely a case in point) plays a crucial part in the way everyday objects become archaeological relics, and lends them a randomness that contributes so much to their value as historical evidence of our musical past.

So at the end of the day, perhaps the most important lesson that the Alamo fragment brings to music's archaeological table is that, after all, drama and spectacle aren't everything. Finds like the Érard harp and the great musical discoveries in ancient tombs that will be encountered later in this book are undeniably magnificent: the spectacular gold and silver lyres of Ur, the glittering trumpets of Tutankhamun, the towering bells and chimes of Zeng Yi. But the threads that connect such treasures to their everyday past realities are made up of myriad small and largely unexceptional fragments that lie scattered across the world's landscapes or have already found their way into the storerooms of museums. It's the human networking that the little things reveal by small increments which in the end will paint our most compelling portraits of ancient musicianship – which is to say music as ordinary people made and experienced it. In fact, perhaps paradoxically, scattered fragments will be of interest to us precisely because they're *not* exceptional. They are part of the archaeological background. They are the physical remains not so much of music's celebrity as of its grass roots. And the grass-roots story that they tell is going to be the story of all our music.

CHAPTER TWO

All that glisters is not gold: a metal horn from Suffolk

England, nineteenth century

One spring afternoon in 1985 I took a phone call from the curator of a museum in Suffolk. A couple of hours earlier, she said, a member of the public had walked in off the street carrying something tied up in brown paper. It was a large, delicate object that he'd found while metal-detecting in a wood, not far from the coast. Although it was badly damaged, it looked almost certain to be a horn or a trumpet – it seemed to be the funnel-like part that brass players call the 'bell'. She thought it looked extremely old. Its thin sheet metal was coated in a greyish-green crust, and she was curious to discover its true age and likely origin. Could it be prehistoric? Suffolk had already produced its fair share of ancient musical finds, and in the last two centuries, metallic horns and trumpets had been turning up all over Europe. In Britain they included a long, curved horn from Anglesey in North Wales, and a straight trumpet dredged from the River Witham in Lincolnshire. Both instruments could be dated back to the pre-Roman Iron Age, around two thousand years ago. Might this new piece be the beginning of a new adventure in music's prehistory?

The following morning I drove across to the museum to see the object for myself. I was immediately struck by just how badly damaged it was. It was surely a trumpet of some sort, but a large part of it – the slender tube leading to the mouthpiece – was missing, crudely snapped off. The surviving portion had been beaten flat by someone, quite deliberately. They had then tried to roll up the flat-tened remains. Who would have attempted such a thing and why? It was very difficult to make out the instrument's original shape and decide what kind of trumpet it might have been. Back in those days before laser scanning and virtual 3-D modelling the only sure way to reimagine the original instrument was to take careful meas-urements and then plot them on a sheet of graph paper; so this is what I did. It took some time, but when at last the work was done, the instrument's original profile leapt off the page.

There have been many magical moments in archaeology, when a new find has led to a breakthrough and opened up a new and unexpected direction for fresh exploration. This, sadly, wasn't one of them. The drawing revealed that the find was a modern conical-bore instrument of the kind known as a flugelhorn: a bandsman's valved horn popular from the middle of the nineteenth century. Its grey-green crust was a consequence not of millennia underground but of mere decades.

To say that this was a disappointment would be an understate-ment. And yet, as it turned out, the find wouldn't be entirely without value. It came with some interesting features, and in an oblique way it offers an object lesson for anyone setting out to explore music's deeper roots.

In archaeology, first impressions can so easily deceive. Damage and decay take many different forms, because the human, chemical and biological influences that bring them about vary enormously. Different materials respond in different ways and at different speeds to wear and tear, to use and abuse, and to various underground environments: warm or cold, acidic or alkaline, airy or airless, wet or dry. So if we're to extract useful information from an object's surfaces – information about how it's been made and used, and for how long and by whom – it's first necessary to form some estimate of how far those surfaces may have changed through archaeological time, and how far the changes have enhanced or compromised them as sources of evidence. There's a name for its particular study: taphonomy – the study of the way buried things age. Of all the methods used in modern archaeology today, taphonomy is one that most closely resembles the work of forensic science; and as it happens, it's going to hold the keys to more than a few musical mysteries.

The ageing of metals is an area of special interest to archaeologists. It's a complicated business, requiring patience and diligence; but as taphonomists pull together fresh case studies they can begin to build up a picture of how particular metal alloys degrade when they are subjected to different forms of chemical and biological attack. Some of the effects can be surprisingly beautiful. One of the most striking transformations occurs when marine and freshwater silts, low in oxygen, impact old brasses and bronzes over time. When they are first found, still moist from their immersion, their surfaces can seem so bright and perfect that many finders wonder if they've struck gold. Sadly, they haven't: the brightness is merely a wafer-thin coating of pyrite crystals. But it can still preserve a lot of the surface details that are needed in order to understand how the objects were originally handled and used. In common topsoils like sand and loam, on the other hand, the processes are very different, especially if there's been air and moisture in the mix, as there most often is; and the corrosion on the Suffolk trumpet turned out to be typical for this kind of earth.

Nevertheless, there was still something odd and unsettling about the instrument: something mysterious about its deliberate destruction and the manner of its concealment. It was hard not to wonder just how and why it came to be buried in the first place. For archaeologists it's a familiar puzzle. There's always a buzz of excitement when we uncover something that someone in the past has deliberately buried; but whenever we sense deliberation we also need to ask why – and how it might affect the way we read it. In this case it came with a hint of an answer. Why dispose of something like a flugelhorn? And why destroy it first? Let's be clear: there was nothing casual or accidental about it. Whoever smashed it would have needed to use deliberate force. They then had to dig a hole, or at least find a suitable rabbit hole, and fill it in afterwards.

Somehow this didn't feel quite right; and it was to offer us a cautionary message.

Coming across a similar find from the distant past, a prehistorian, classicist or medievalist might be tempted to imagine some ritual or at least some symbolic dimension. In other words, that the deposition was enacted as part of some rite, to satisfy a spiritual need, for instance, or to contribute to a formal religious ceremony. 'Ritual' is a label that was once widely applied in archaeology to make sense of all manner of mysteries. But at a guess, this instrument could have been buried at any time up until the middle of the twentieth century; and as far as I'm aware there's nothing in the records of English brass band music that would lead us to expect any such ritual. So might we be looking at a prank, or malice, or the deliberate concealment of evidence?

When we consider the possible differences in meaning that can flow from different kinds of deposition, and the various motives they might reflect, we begin to realise what an important, indeed vital, role archaeological context is going to play in our scientific understanding of much older musical finds. In this case, regrettably, the finder noticed no clues in the surrounding soil and, because some considerable time had elapsed, he was no longer even certain of the precise find-spot. Objects lacking those kinds of details immediately lose much of their historical significance, becoming at a stroke mere curiosities or at best *objets d'art*. Our horn was in this sense orphaned, separated from any of the background information that might have accrued through the application of due archaeological process. So maybe it's just as well that it was after all no more than a piece of Victorian or Edwardian local history. Had it been something more precious, we might now be wringing our hands.

CHAPTER THREE

Music in miniature: a pipeclay whistle from Trondheim

Norway, nineteenth century

One of the most satisfying ways to get involved in archaeology has always been through the simple act of finding and collecting buried treasures. You only have to dig a small hole somewhere, or watch carefully while someone else is digging, and you never know what might turn up. At any rate, this was how I caught the bug. I made my first discovery when I was about twelve, in a freshly dug rose bed. Most of my treasures were just fragments of old glass and china, but buried with them were some small pieces of delicate white pipeclay tubing. They looked about the size, shape and colour of a discarded cigarette, and in fact they were the Victorian equivalent: broken stems of old clay tobacco pipes, dropped by farm workers perhaps in the days before the houses were built and the land was still open fields. Collecting them became a hobby. Wherever I noticed anyone digging holes I'd go and take a look, and everywhere I looked there seemed to be more of these fragments. Now and then I'd find one that wasn't just a plain tube: it had letters embossed on it, spelling out a maker's name or a motto. Sometimes, with a little luck, it might have the mouthpiece or the bowl still attached. These came with such a variety of fascinating shapes and commemorative designs that they felt instantly collectable. I naturally wondered how old they were. Might their different and distinctive shapes and decoration provide the key?

From flower beds in the local park, my collecting friends and I graduated to construction sites in fields around the edge of town – when the builders had gone home – and as our collecting became more ambitious, we'd cycle further out into the countryside, to see what local farmers had turned up with the plough. We were getting a first taste of some of the essential processes of archaeology: first the washing and inspecting, then sorting things into families of types. Some shapes of clay pipe felt older than others. They had longer, thicker stems and smaller, plainer bowls. From school history lessons we knew that tobacco had been introduced to Europe from America as long ago as the sixteenth century; we also knew from books of old Flemish paintings that pale-coloured pipes of similar shape were popular in the seventeenth. Could our finds really be that old? Our local museum staff told us that, indeed, some of them could. What I didn't dream was that one day I would encounter a clay pipe that was not only very old but had a musical story to tell.

The discovery came some years later, in Norway. By then my attention had shifted from clay pipes to musical finds. I was a graduate student sifting through museum stores in search of small pieces of medieval musical equipment, pieces that had so far escaped their eagle-eyed curators. In this kind of search it makes sense to focus on places where archaeologists have been most active and where they've found the best soil conditions for preserving things, and Bergen and Trondheim ticked both of these boxes. The two cities had historic waterfronts and origins that stretched right back to Viking times. Their deep deposits of foreshore silts and clays preserved soft organics like wood; and by the time of my visit in 1980 they had each hosted large-scale archaeological excavations.

I was hunting especially for fragments of stringed instruments, but in the course of my search I necessarily inspected thousands upon thousands of other objects, of all kinds. In the museums they'd all been cleaned and lovingly set out on open sliding trays in tall moving stacks, and to my delight they were arranged not by material or by type but by context: things that had been found together were grouped together regardless of what they were or might be. This placed familiar domestic items like hair combs and sewing pins alongside large numbers of unidentified objects, and it was these 'mystery objects' that seemed most promising.

The first to catch my violinist's eye was a circular spool of steel wire that looked very much like a fiddle string, and in fact it turned out to be exactly that. There were flutes and whistles of wood and bone, and there were small bells by the score. Then, suddenly, I noticed an old familiar friend: a length of white clay tobacco pipe. Like all clay pipes it had been used and eventually broken, but this one had a surprise in store: some unknown hand had turned it into a tiny penny whistle. It came from the site of the new Trondheim public library, close to the historic waterfront. It was just over four centimetres long, and when I turned it over I saw that close to one end there was a little oval voicing hole, like that of a tree-bark flute. Along the rest of its length were four tiny finger holes, all of them delicately bored with the tip of a sharp knife.

Repurposing is something that's always happened in musical history. In Chapter One we've already encountered Caribbean steelpans made from oil drums. Today, most makers of fine instruments work only with fresh materials, for which they pay a great deal, but in the past few could afford that luxury. Reclaimed wood, bone and metal would be reused wherever possible. Old instruments would be cannibalised. Later in the book there's an encounter with flutes and pipes sourced from animal bones retrieved from cooking hearths and kitchen middens: the long, slender wing bones of large birds such as swans and cranes, or the stronger, stouter shin bones of sheep and goats. People will always find new uses for discarded things.

It so happens that this little clay whistle bears more than a passing resemblance to those earlier bone flutes and whistles – with one notable exception: it's tiny. I found the holes much too close together for my fingertips to manipulate, and the bore was so very slender that I doubted that it could even have worked. If it made any sound at all, it would surely have been a high-pitched whistle. So why make such a thing? Was it just a one-off experiment, a trial piece perhaps? Or could it be something else?

There were some clues. A piece of delicately turned wooden tube found in Norwich, not far from where I'm now writing, appears to be part of another miniature pipe. And from the same part of England we have several very small medieval flutes made of goose wing bone, sharing that same curious anomaly: their finger holes are too close together for an adult's hands. Could this little clay whistle from Trondheim have been made for or by a child? Music has played an important part in childhood throughout the ages, so why shouldn't some archaeological finds turn out to be children's musical toys?

In Norway another charming musical tradition of childhood has left a distinct archaeological footprint: it's the humble 'buzz-bone'. Like the tree-bark flute, buzz-bones were quickly and easily made, usually by children. When we find them we can see that they've been shaped from a small bone extracted from the pot after cooking pig's trotters, a traditional delicacy in Scandinavia. The cooking was generally done in midwinter, when it was customary to slaughter the family pig. We know from Bremanger in the western fjords that on the Sunday before Christmas the children would be given the bones to play with. The ones they preferred were between five and seven centimetres long. The game was to bore a hole through the narrow waist of the bone and thread a length of twine twice through it to form two loops like a figure eight. Holding one loop in each hand, the bone could then be spun round and round so that when the loops were pulled tight it would spin rapidly and make a fine humming or buzzing sound. It was this sound that gave the toy its onomatopoeic folk name: *snørle*. Bones of the same sort have been found in excavations all over north-western Europe. Archaeologists have usually described them as 'toggles', endowing them with a more prosaic purpose, as handles on the ends of cords which they believe were used for binding and carrying bundles. Well, this may be so. But in Norway their traditional musical properties are well understood. Their other dialect names, *snurre* and *hørre, hurre* and *klotr*, echo some of the variety of buzzing, humming and clattering sounds they can be persuaded to make.

But could our small whistle from Trondheim have offered the same kind of reward for the effort of making it? Would it have been capable of making music of even the most childish kind? Might it not be just a token miniature or part of a toy? We know that in some traditional cultures diminutive instruments aren't always meant to be played: they are made to be attached to toy figures and figurines of musicians. There's only one way to solve a puzzle of this kind: you have to try for yourself. You can't play the original instrument, of course, because you might compromise the archaeological evidence. So you have to make and test accurate replicas.

Fortunately, blank clay pipe stems aren't hard to find – especially if, like me, you spent much of your childhood collecting them. With the tip of a sharp knife – preferably not one from the kitchen knife drawer – it's perfectly easy to bore a sound hole and finger holes. Lightly fired, the smooth pipeclay cuts like chalk; and with a small piece of twig inserted to represent the block or 'fipple' of a bark flute, the instrument is complete. All that's needed is a volunteer with suitably small hands, and the rest is, quite literally, child's play. My volunteer, a small cousin, had no trouble articulating the notes. Of course the roughness of the scale made it hard to pick out 'God Save the King' in any form the King would recognise, but the result was a surprisingly pleasing musical sound.

What all this goes to show is that it's never a good idea to leave children out of our archaeological calculations. But it also highlights something else: that we need to remember how easily the identities and purposes of physical objects can shift, and how blurred distinctions can become between types of things. Transformations and ambiguities of this and other sorts have often proved a challenge to museums and scholars alike. Collections depend on careful, systematic storage, and in order for it to function, any system demands definitions. But if something has begun life with one identity or purpose, and later attracted quite another one, in which drawer should we put it? Questions of this kind, questions of attribution and identity, are going to resonate throughout this book. Definitions, especially commonsense definitions, can so easily go on to distort the way we read the past. And the challenges this poses find further echoes in the next chapter, as the focus moves across the Atlantic Ocean to an indigenous community on the lower Mississippi.

Chapter Four

Improving on Nature: a cache of metal jingles from the Natchez Grand Village

Southern Mississippi, c.1700

Around three hundred years ago, the country we now call the United States was home to thriving indigenous communities. Among the most prominent of these groups was a nation whose appreciation of music and dance has left us a distinct archaeological footprint: they were the Natchez of southern Mississippi.

Like most indigenous people through the ages, the Natchez were farmers. Maize was their principal source of food, supplemented with occasional hunting and gathering. They made pottery and wove textiles. But the simplicity of their day-to-day routines masked a complex culture that had evolved through millennia of independent development, in complete isolation from Europe and Asia and uninfluenced by Old World technologies, fashions and ideas. They'd adapted their domestic arrangements to the peculiarities of their geography and climate; and when they came together as a community their prosperity and social organisation enabled them to indulge in some surprisingly ambitious projects. The most impressive of these were architectural. Tucked away in their forests and swamplands along the vast Mississippi River were clusters of large mounds, some with wooden temple structures at their summits – the Mississippian equivalents of the great pyramids of Mexico and Central America. But among the most intriguing objects to have emerged from archaeological digs in their precincts are caches of little tinkling amulets.

The amulets don't look much today, but they must have been important to the Natchez and their neighbours across the southern and south-western United States because they've been found deposited at the sites where they invested much of their cultural capital. One of them was the place that early French explorers called the *grand village* of the Natchez, evidently their most important tribal and religious centre. In the late eighteenth century the Natchez would find themselves evicted from their lands, sold into slavery or forced to seek refuge among their neighbours and beyond; but their abandoned Grand Village or 'Fatherland Site' would survive, albeit forgotten for the time being. It was rediscovered in the late nineteenth century, near the banks of a creek on the southern outskirts of what is now Natchez City. When excavations were carried out between 1930 and 1972, one of the three large mounds, 'Mound C', produced thirteen little brass jingles and thirty-five small spherical bells, thirty-three of them made of brass and two of silver. The brass indicates that they can only have come from the Old World.

Until the arrival of Europeans, seashells had been the Amerindians' first choice for tinkling ornaments. They often chose those of the *Conus* marine snail, attractive little objects that were traded upriver from the warm waters of the Gulf of Mexico.

But by the end of the seventeenth century, new materials were entering the lives of North America's indigenous peoples. Metals were being brought across the ocean by European merchant adventurers to be bartered for the native produce that European markets craved, especially furs. One of the earliest and boldest of these travellers was a Frenchman from Rouen named René-Robert Cavelier, Sieur de La Salle. In the spring of 1682, after some years exploring the Great Lakes, La Salle made his way down the Mississippi by canoe, reaching what would later become Louisiana. After securing a sea passage home to France, he returned to America in the three-mast sailing barque *La Belle*. He and his sponsors, who included the Sun King, Louis XIV, hoped to establish a new French colony somewhere along the Gulf Coast, but when the expedition unaccountably overshot its intended landfall, the mouth of the

Mississippi River, the enterprise began to fall apart. Arguments broke out and in 1687 La Salle was murdered by his compatriots. To complete the disaster, while lying at anchor in Matagorda Bay, between modern Corpus Christi and Galveston, *La Belle* was caught in a severe storm and sank.

For the next three hundred years the remains of the ship lay undisturbed on the seabed, until 1995, when divers discovered it not far out, lying in the shallow water of the bay. Excavation began the following year, behind a coffer dam of steel pilings. Among the cargo in the forward part of the hold were many European goods, including metal pots and pans, but also a large consignment of small 'pellet bells', very similar to those found in the Grand Village. Shaped from sheet brass and ranging in size from a large pea to a small tomato, each has a loose iron 'pellet' inside it, which made it tinkle.

Bells of this sort were common in Europe in the seventeenth century, where they were worn as dress accessories, attached to animal harnesses and collars, or fitted to waggons and sleds: they are the 'jingle bells' of the popular Christmas song. Now Europeans brought them along to America. Some thirty years after the Matagorda disaster, in the 1720s, when the French engineer Antoine-Simon Le Page du Pratz went to live among the Natchez, he reported seeing them wearing French bells on their belts. Might some of them have come from La Salle's expedition? It's perfectly possible. The excavation of *La Belle* recovered vast numbers of them, more than fifteen hundred in all. There were five broad types, each identified by a different maker's stamp and each with its own distinct frequency range. Between them, they covered a couple of octaves, up among the tinkling notes at the top end of a modern piano keyboard.

If bells of this kind were much valued by the Natchez, so were European pots and pans – and not always for cooking. Like the Trondheim clay pipe and the Trinidad steelpans, they repurposed some of them, cutting them up and using the metal to make other things. Among these were the conical jingles found in Mound C.

The imported bells clearly delighted the Natchez. But what fascinates archaeologists is the way they used the new metals to transform their native jingles, manipulating the brass and silver to mimic and even improve on their existing seashell forms. The technical term for this kind of thing is a skeuomorph: something that recreates a natural shape in a different, often man-made, material. My colleague Mark Howell, who's studied the jingles, sees the increasing prevalence of brass jingles as an early indication that Amerindians already saw them as a means of maintaining their cultural identities through sound they made, as they tried to outface growing European influence and political control. It's an idea that's supported by other evidence, notably the traditional dance of the Green Corn Ceremony practised by the Cherokees, which they accompanied with singing and the discharge of firearms. To European ears the effect of the gunfire would have seemed merely cacophonous, violent and threatening. But its role in the dance was in fact quite peaceable: it was simply making use of another European technology to improve on the drumming they'd always used, to simulate thunder.

For Mark and his colleagues, the glimpses supplied by the Grand Village finds, and other discoveries like them, have opened a new way of understanding the musical lives and mindsets of indigenous people living on the very cusp of written history. But there are broader issues too. First, there's the question that has both entertained and tormented musicologists for many years, and which we've already touched upon: what exactly *is* music? How ought we to define it? When does sound-making become 'musical' and when is it just that, a pattern of sounds? If something can be perceived as having elements of 'musical' character or purpose – whether it's tinkling dress ornaments or a piano quintet, a tumbling waterfall or a whale's song – does that bring it within any definition of 'music' that we can all accept?

This hasn't always been seen as a problem. For purists, inclined to take a traditional Western view of music, the answer has been simple enough. Music is sound, organised according to agreed rules that make it satisfying to create or to listen to, or at least that offer us some emotional connection. By rules I mean that music consists primarily of melodic and rhythmic patterns, sound textures and combinations that strike us as agreeable. Inevitably, according to such a definition, some music seems more meaningful than others. It's a point of view that lays claim to quite an illustrious pedigree. For the ancient Greeks, including some of their greatest thinkers, only their own music was true music, and then only the best of it. The rest was just noise. However, it's a theory that no longer stands up to scientific scrutiny. For the modern anthropologist or musicologist exposed to music's extreme diversity in the world today, and to the great range of aesthetic preferences driving it, it no longer fits the evidence; it merely reflects Western complacency. And when the same definition is applied to the archaeological mysteries of the ancient world, it immediately falls apart. The flaw is in its inherent circularity. If our goal is to arrive at better appreciation of what music is, and what it is not, definition can't be our starting point. The answer must emerge from our evidence, not be imposed on it. We have to try to leave our preconceptions behind and listen harder to what the past itself is trying to tell us.

Of course, looking at these jingles and bells, a sceptic might be tempted to ask: so what? Surely this kind of thing can't be compared to great musical discoveries like the trumpets of Tutankhamun? Taking each object individually, it would be hard to disagree. Yet to an archaeologist familiar with the bigger archaeological picture, it's not nearly so straightforward. As we delve into music's ancient past, we see that the bells are part of a hitherto unconsidered pattern: a pattern of small things that by themselves appear to be of no more than passing local significance but which cumulatively reveal how music permeated everyday life through the ages. There are many grand and glittering treasures in music's archaeology, to be sure: rich expressions of music's complexity, of its technological and even its political power, as well as miracles of

archaeological survival. But it's from the quiet industry of archaeologists like Mark Howell, and from small beginnings like his
Natchez bells and jingles, scattered across the world, that a truer,
deeper and more penetrating vision of ancient music is beginning
to emerge.

At the heart of this ongoing endeavour is the growing power of
'grass roots' archaeology to reveal – and situate – the sheer breadth
and depth of music's buried past. It's a story of tips of icebergs, certainly. And nowhere is its potential revealed more vividly than in
the way song and poetry can sometimes be discerned in the arch-
aeologial landscape – as the next chapter reveals.

Chapter Five

Memorial to a lost music: harp tuning pegs from Montgomery Castle

Powys, Wales, *c.*1700

The ruins of Montgomery Castle stand on a tall rocky bluff over-looking the village of Montgomery and the peaceful countryside of the Welsh Borders. The sounds that envelop it today are the singing of songbirds, the cawing of crows, and the faint far-off noises of a modern farming landscape. But if you should ever find yourself strolling up there on a warm summer's evening as the stars begin to open, or early on an autumn morning when the castle walls are still shrouded in mist, be sure to listen carefully. This is a place that hasn't only inspired music and song: musicians and poets now long dead have left their physical traces within its very walls.

The hilltop bears witness to a long and colourful history. It was first fortified against the Welsh in the year 1223, by the English king Henry III. We know that in 1267 Henry himself spent time here, to negotiate a treaty with Llywelyn ap Gruffudd, the native prince of North Wales. But sixty years later in 1330, after the conflicts of the thirteenth century appeared to be over, it fell into decline. It was just strong enough to withstand an attack by the army of Owain Glendŵr in 1402, but in the early 1500s it was in disrepair, and by the close of that century it had lost almost all of its remaining strategic importance. A mansion was built to replace the stronghold as the principal dwelling of its owners, the Herbert family, but in 1649, during the English Civil War, that house too was torn down. By Victorian times, the whole site had become a mere ornament: a scenic destination for tourists and Sunday walkers, the beauty of its ruins praised in guidebooks and its image reproduced on countless picture postcards. But then, in 1967, conservators working to consolidate the ruins uncovered what was to be the first in a series of extraordinary musical finds.

As they were clearing some of the jumbled earth and debris from the footings of the Inner Ward they found a hidden cache of pencil-thin rods of brass. There were twenty-four of them, all neatly made to the same precise specification. Around ten centimetres long, filed to a square cross section at one end with a small drill hole at the other, they were identified as the rotating pins used to tune late-medieval harps: harps of the wire-strung kind that can still be seen in historic instrument collections in Ireland and Scotland.

While the musical character of the pins was quickly identified, their location seemed baffling. It seems that someone has carried them, or perhaps the instrument to which they belonged, up to the desolate stronghold, and there they appear to have concealed them among the already tumbled masonry. Stranger still, this doesn't seem to have been particularly unusual. Metal pegs of similar shape, size and age have been found in equally remote ruins in Ireland and Scotland, sometimes in proximity to other metal fittings. Could these shared circumstances be simply coincidental, or might they be reflecting a distinct tradition?

Remarkably, in Ireland one set of such pegs was still attached to the wooden frame of a harp when it was found in a bog close to Larne, in County Antrim, at the end of the eighteenth century. Indeed, most Irish pegs have been found in bogs, or within the remains of *crannogs* – wooden houses built on timber pilings or on small islands. And there's growing evidence that they were placed there deliberately. In Scotland the type of dwelling where they are found is different, but the emerging story isn't dissimilar. They've been excavated in ruined castles, deposited like the Montgomery pegs when the fortifications were nearing the end of their usefulness or shortly afterwards. Three metal specimens were retrieved during excavations in Finlaggan Castle on the island of Islay, and another was found with fragments of wire nearby, in the ruins of Castle Sween in Knapdale, Argyllshire.

The sense of purposeful burial is enhanced at Montgomery by the lack of any accompanying household or workshop waste of the kind that would indicate abandonment. They've been buried just by themselves. It's as if someone has chosen to consign or even dedicate them to the ruins. But why would they have done something like that?

Whenever metal objects are found cached together in this kind of deposit, archaeologists tend to think of them either as 'votive' deposits – meaning that they've been interred as offerings to gods and spirits – or more prosaically, as hoards of scrap: depots of metal put aside by itinerant metalworkers or traders with a view to recovering and recycling them at a later date. Both are perfectly sensible, practical explanations, yet in this case neither seems to provide a wholly satisfactory answer. There's insufficient metal for them to be general scrap, and it's equally difficult to square their musical character with any known formal religious rite of the time. So what other meaning could they hold?

Without accompanying coins or sherds of pottery, it's hard for us to put a precise date to the act itself, but by comparing the Montgomery pegs' shapes with finds from other excavations now housed in museum collections we can conclude that they most likely originated in the sixteenth century or early seventeenth. This tallies with what we know about the demolition of the castle, and thus raises a new possibility. Could their burial represent ritual of a different, more secular kind? Could it have been prompted by romantic feelings for a lost past? Might it be an expression of nostalgia?

An oblique clue may be provided by the Irish harp found buried in the bog near Larne. Sometimes known as the 'Dalway', the 'Cloyne' or the 'Fitzgerald' harp, its elaborate carved decoration shows that it must once have been a precious and valuable instrument. But there's something else as well. In between the carvings are lines of text. Inscribed on the neck itself are the Latin words *ego sum regina cithararum*, 'I am the Queen of Harps', and on its curved forepillar is a series of evidently connected statements, again in Latin. Although some of the letters are difficult to make out, it seems to say: *plecto vinco rego . . . monstra viros . . . musica Dei donum . . . distractas solatur musica mentes . . . ut sonus . . . transit sic gloria mundi. Vincit Veritas* – 'by weaving I conquer, I rule . . . I show people . . . music, God's gift . . . music is a consolation to distracted minds . . . as a sound . . . thus passes the Glory of the World. Truth will conquer.' And to this the maker has added his signature: *Donatus filius Thadei me fecit, spes mea in Deo* – 'Donatus son of Thadeus made me, my hope in God'.

Thus far the Latin words reflect the instrument's Christian milieu; but now, in a unexpected twist, there follows a series of statements in native Irish. These suggest something rather different: something oddly sentimental. The harp has evidently become a private memorial, for the lines commemorate an entire aristocratic household at Cluain, or Cloyne, in County Cork. The householder appears to identify himself in the first person as the harp's owner, John fitz Edmond, or John fitz Edmund Fitzgerald, the second of that name, and he goes on to list his retainers, with words of appreciation and affection. They include his butlers, his cook and his tailor. Significantly he also names his carpenter or cabinet-maker, Donnchadh Fitz Teigh, who he says has built the harp for him; and this is of course the Irish meaning of *Donatus filius Thadei*. He goes on to describe how his household musician, Giollapatrick Mac Cridan, has helped care for him, perhaps during a period of illness, and gives the year as 1621. So the harp's purpose was not just to make music: it was to commemorate. But why then was it later buried, and by whom? And could their action help explain the Montgomery find?

In a curious way it might. If the Larne find owes its interment to 'John fitz Edmond' or to one of his heirs, at Montgomery too history has left us the names of potential 'persons of interest'. They belong to the Herberts, a family notable for its love of poetry and music and who also owned the castle and the mansion. had famous names: the poets Edward and George Herbert, and with them their friend John Donne. Might their association with the ruins parallel what happened at Larne?

We know of John Donne's intimate connection with the Herberts through his poem 'The Primrose', which carries the subtitle 'Being at Montgomery Castle, Upon the Hill, on which it is situate'. We can't say precisely when he came here, but it's most likely to have been in or shortly after 1596. He knew both the brothers and their mother, the formidable Magdalen Newport, who was his patron and had made him godfather to George. Edward and George had been raised in the mansion built within the crumbling castle ruins. But in 1644, Edward had both the castle and the mansion snatched from him by a victorious Parliament, and in 1649 they were demolished in retribution for his royalist sympathies during the recent Civil War. Could the burial of the objects have been some kind of response to that doleful event? Might he or his heirs have chosen to bury them as a memorial, not just to lost poetry and music, but to a lost way of life? The harp has always been the emblem of poets and poetry – indeed, in both Wales and Ireland it remains the national instrument to this day. Magdalen's lavish tomb in the parish church already shows that the Herberts were capable of elaborate romantic gestures, so their love of poetry, their elevated self-image and their sense of loss would supply credible motives for such a gesture.

As evidence goes, this is all frustratingly circumstantial of course. However much we would like to be able to make such connections, they can be very difficult to prove. The reasons lie in part in the nature of archaeological evidence. While history speaks to us in words, and in eyewitness statements of one kind or another, archaeology's methods and core strengths are more physical. They lie in its ability to situate things and events accurately in geographical space and, within the limits of modern science and technology, in time. They lie too in its ability to preserve and analyse physical evidence in intimate and forensic detail – in the case of Montgomery, evidence of how musical instruments were designed and built, what musical needs they were shaped to serve, how they were played and how they sounded. As a general rule the archaeological record is less good at matching material substance to individuals.

Still, there can be exceptions to even that rule, as we're going to see. And in the meantime the puzzle stands as a warning, or at least a timely reminder: that while human beings generally do things (including burying things in the ground) with a purpose in view, in the highly emotional context of music and poetry it doesn't necessarily follow that their motives must always be strictly practical or, indeed, entirely rational.

PART TWO

Of Ships and the Sea

The Seventeenth and Sixteenth Centuries

Up to now, all the objects we've looked at have been in an obviously corrupted state: that's to say, corrupted when compared to the fine historic instruments curated in musical collections or illustrated in books. Their condition reflects the random circumstances to which they've been exposed in dry and tumbled earth, so hostile to perishable materials like wood or metal. They've been broken and crusted, crushed and corroded, almost beyond recognition. Pieces that are still intact survive mainly because of their small size or their hard mineral composition. But now we're going to see what archaeology can do for music when the odds are stacked more in its favour. Let's follow some familiar forms of music-making down to a deeper level: to a depth that's measurable not in accumulated earth but in cold salt water and marine sediment.

The kind of excavation that this demands will prove to be very different – different in its challenges and methods, and different in its outcomes. From its deep-water explorations a detailed and vivid narrative begins to emerge, of sound and music in a particular kind of community: that of seafaring folk. The stories behind the objects recovered are grim, yet fascinating: they show what happens physically to a small community's musical possessions when their ships – their homes from home – are lost at sea or driven ashore. A visit to Davy Jones's locker will show how an environment that can be so hazardous to life can turn fragile things into pure archaeological gold. The submerged lands around our shores are perilous places, but once the forces of death and destruction have done their worst they can also become surprisingly benign. Hidden in the details they preserve are clues to the kinds of sounds that appealed to people's musical tastes, and how they went about expressing them.

First we're going to sink down into the bottom of the Baltic Sea, to witness the aftermath of a colossal explosion. It was a disaster that cost many people their lives. And yet for us, more than three hundred years later, their misfortune opens a precious window on musical life in eighteenth-century Europe.

CHAPTER SIX

Sounds from the deep: a baroque violin from the Swedish warship Kronan

Öland, Sweden, 1676

Imagine the scene. It's a calm summer's day in 1982 and a dive boat is moored in the Baltic Sea just off the Swedish island of Öland. On deck there's the smell of the ocean and a hint of coffee in the air. Wavelets lap along the hull in the gentle breeze, while seabirds soar overhead, gleaming white in the afternoon sun. Standing or crouching by the rail are technicians and members of the crew, waiting patiently for two divers to return from the seabed with their latest find. It's been another busy day on one of the most ambitious underwater excavations ever attempted – an investigation of the wreck of the seventeenth-century Swedish warship *Kronan*. Now something astonishing is about to be brought back to the surface after three hundred years at the bottom of the sea.

The Swedish maritime archaeologist Lars Einarsson told me this story two years later, as we sat in the conservation laboratory of the County Museum at Kalmar, reliving the moment when the divers broke the surface of the water and their strange and fragile treasure was lifted gently aboard. It proved to be an oblong wooden box, about sixty centimetres long, covered in silt. Lowering it carefully to the deck, the team peered inside. It was full to the brim with seawater, but through it, coated in fine marine sediment, a shape could be made out. And drifting this way and that in the water with the motion of the boat, the archaeologists noticed little black things like beetles' wing cases.

Carried back to the laboratory for further investigation, the ghostly shape revealed itself as an ancient violin. Its wooden parts were saturated but perfectly preserved, their surfaces still bearing a coat of clear varnish. Beside it in the case were a fiddler's necessities, most importantly his bow. The state of preservation was quite astonishing – it was a music historian's dream. And if this wasn't remarkable enough, the beetles' wings proved to be something still more evocative. It turned out that they were bits of print that had become detached from sheet music as the seawater dissolved the paper.

When I visited the museum and met Lars Einarsson and other members of the team, all the wooden parts had been laid out on the laboratory bench in front of us, freeze-dried to preserve their shapes. Wood that's been waterlogged for a long time must be dried out carefully and in a particular way. Immersion can be an excellent way of preserving wooden objects, even the timbers of big ships like *Kronan*, but appearances can be deceptive. While a waterlogged object may appear completely intact, much of the wood's internal cellular structure has dissolved. It's become quite soft to the touch. If we wanted to we could actually squeeze the water out of it, like wringing out a sponge. Although it still feels heavy, the weight is mostly water. So if left to dry out naturally in the air it would collapse in on itself. Abandoned pieces of waterlogged wood shrink and crack in startling ways. Thin boards and strips of wood curl up and split until they look like twisted cracker biscuits. The way to prevent this from happening is either to keep the wood wet, which will make it hard to display, or to freeze it. Once it's deeply frozen, the ice temporarily provides the supporting structure, and if there's an electric fan running to stir the air inside the freezer unit, the ice will slowly vaporise by sublimation, without disturbing the object's external shape. This is what the Swedish conservators had done, and it had worked beautifully.

At that time I'd been working in Portsmouth on some no less astonishing finds: two fiddles from the wreck of the sixteenth-century English warship *Mary Rose*. (We'll return to the *Mary Rose* in Chapter 16.) They too had been found at the bottom of the sea and had gone through a broadly similar conservation treatment; but the completeness and delicacy of the *Kronan* fiddle took my breath away. As I studied it, Lars explained the miracle of its survival. From the smallest wooden objects to the ship's great timbers, the prime factor seemed to be the same conditions that preserved the wreck of the *Mary Rose*. Both ships had quickly become sealed beneath a layer of marine sediments after they sank. But here on *Kronan* another crucial factor had been at work: the Baltic Sea is notable for its very low salinity.

With the exception of Hudson Bay in Canada, it's the least salty sea on earth. In the Atlantic and Pacific Oceans there are typically about thirty-six parts of salt to a thousand of water. But because so many major rivers flow into the Baltic, and because surface evaporation is slowed by the cool northern climate, its salt content is mostly in the region of six parts per thousand. This is barely even brackish: it's all but fresh. It means that most of the marine organisms that would normally destroy wood in the open ocean can't survive. The worst enemy of ships' timbers at sea, the wood-boring shipworm *Teredo* (actually a mollusc) can't tolerate low salinity and is almost entirely absent. The other main menace, the tiny nibbling isopod crustacean *Limnoria* that slowly devours more delicate woodwork, finds the Baltic far too cold. For this reason objects made of wood are always going to survive longer in the Baltic, even without becoming blanketed in silt. And survive the fiddle certainly has.

Things could so easily have turned out differently. It seems that the instrument had come close to destruction on at least three separate occasions. The first had been in the initial catastrophe. It was during the Scanian War between Denmark and Sweden, with the Swedish Army campaigning across the sea in Pomerania, and the Danes trying to prevent the Swedes from sending supplies and reinforcements. On the morning of 1 June 1676, the two fleets had been sailing up the east coast of Öland, and as *Kronan* turned to engage the enemy, she heeled over to port and began to capsize. At that moment the forward powder magazine blew up. The tremendous blast destroyed much of the starboard side and forward end of the hull. The remaining parts of the ship sank rapidly and settled on the bottom in thirteen-fathom water, just over twenty-six metres down. Out of a total of 842 officers, crew and soldiers on board only forty-one men were picked up alive.

The second moment of danger came when, a few years later, the Swedish Navy sent down a diving bell and grapnels to salvage what they could from the wreckage. Some of the 128 valuable cannons were brought up to the surface, yet somehow the fiddle case remained undisturbed. The third and final threat might have come in 1980 when the wreck was discovered. Had the activity not been illegal in Sweden, it could easily have fallen prey to treasure hunters, rummaging and suction-dredging the site for treasures of the more glittering sort. But fortunately none of this happened and now here it was, laid out before us with all its fragile parts intact and gleaming.

Not all violins look the same, especially early violins. It's true that if you've never picked up a fiddle, one tends to look much like any other. Indeed, it takes an accustomed eye, and ear, to tell a good one from a less good one. That's because since the nineteenth century violins have tended to follow a common design. They have much the same outline, they show similar methods of construction, and they are even made from the same types of wood: typically maple for the back and ribs, and for the belly – the all-important sound board – a piece of softwood, usually spruce. They have the same number of strings and tuning pegs. This is equally true of the *Kronan* fiddle. A hundred and twenty years or so before the Swedish ship met her fate, this hadn't been the case. The fiddles found in the wreck of the *Mary Rose*, lost in 1545, belong to an older and more varied family: their sound boxes have oblong, not rounded, outlines and their backs have been hollowed out of solid wood. But by 1676 the violin already matches today's instrument quite closely. It's a true violin. Even so, a modern player would quickly spot some subtle differences.

The most important is in the shape of the neck and fingerboard. For a start, the fingerboard is somewhat shorter than it is today: it's not designed to reach the highest notes of the modern concert repertoire. The neck on which it's mounted is also shorter and attached at a slightly different angle: if we lay the instrument on its back, its neck and pegbox lie level, parallel with the sound box, not angled backwards in the modern manner. This meant that the fingerboard had to be shaped slightly differently, in order that its upper surface – its contact surface – should remain parallel with the strings. And in this respect the fiddle is what music historians would call a 'baroque violin'.

The change of violin design from baroque to classical came about in the eighteenth and nineteenth centuries, in a series of structural modifications that enabled tighter stringing and a stronger, brighter sound. Mostly it was applied to new-built fiddles, but older instruments too were rebuilt, much as late-Victorian railway engines were dismantled and upgraded in the early twentieth century. In both railway engines and violins the new forms swept away the old. Not even the work of the great Italian masters Nicolò Amati and Antonio Stradivari escaped unchanged. Surprising numbers of their baroque violins have survived, many of them still being played, but none retains its original baroque neck. Only one of Stradivari's is sometimes referred to as 'untouched': the so-called 'Messie' Stradivarius in Oxford's Ashmolean Museum. But even the Messie proves to be less authentic than we like to think. Not only have the tuning pegs, bridge and tailpiece been replaced, but so too have the neck and the fingerboard. Except for some rare folk survivals such as the *hardingfele* or Hardanger fiddle in western Norway (of which the earliest dates from about 1650), and some actual baroque violins attached to wooden statues in Freiberg Cathedral in Saxony, all of the 'baroque' fiddles we hear today are either rebuilt originals or modern replicas.

So the *Kronan* instrument isn't just a miracle of archaeological preservation. The miracle is that it's still in its unaltered seventeenth-century condition. It's been frozen, so to speak, at a very precise point in time: at noon on 1 June 1676. Time has taken its toll, for sure; but human interference has not. For music history this has to be one of the glories of the archaeological record, a jewel in archaeology's crown. Like the bodies at Pompeii that lie where they fell and still bear authentic witness to the world in which they lived, the *Kronan* fiddle can be interrogated by us for what it really was, and will reply to our questions directly. So, for instance, when we look at the surface of its fingerboard and see how little wear there is under the strings, we're seeing evidence that the instrument was still quite new when it was lost.

Sadly we don't know whether the owner of our violin survived the explosion and the sinking of *Kronan*. Given the numbers who perished, it seems doubtful. Most likely his remains lie with those who were buried on land, when they were found washed up on the shore, or are among the bones of more than two hundred men so far recovered from the seabed by Lars Einarsson and his team. Like many anonymous musicians of the past, his beautiful fiddle must serve as his monument. Still, as such things go, there could be many worse ways to be remembered.

CHAPTER SEVEN

Hostile shore: a cittern from the Spanish Armada

County Donegal, Ireland, 1588

The fate of the sailors and musicians who lost their lives when the Swedish flagship *Kronan* blew itself to pieces is awful to contemplate; but to survive a maritime disaster and be cast away on a hostile shore could be every bit as terrible. I don't suppose it was a prospect that troubled the officers and men of the magnificent, newly built forty-two-gun Genoese armed transport ship *La Trinidad Valencera*, as she joined the Spanish fleet off La Coruña in June 1588. Captained by the aristocrat Don Alonzo de Luzón, her mission was to ferry more than three hundred troops, part of the army of the Spanish Netherlands, across the North Sea to invade Protestant England. Known today simply as the Spanish Armada, the expedition's title proclaimed that it was *Grande y Felicísima*, 'great and fortunate'. The *Trinidad* was nevertheless doomed to end her days as a wreck in a bay in County Donegal, on the storm-bound shores of northern Ireland. But buried among the wreckage, she's left us an intriguing musical footprint: a uniquely tactile relic of the music of her time. It's the neck and fingerboard of a cittern, a fine Renaissance stringed instrument similar to a guitar or a mandolin. And what's more, locked into its design are the musical scales it was meant to play.

It shows that at least one of the ship's officers was a musician. Was it Don Alonzo himself? Maybe. We just don't know. But what we do know is that the fleet was attacked and scattered by the English fleet in the narrows of the English Channel. Strong south-westerly gales then deflected the survivors further and off course, around the far north of Scotland, and as they approached the coast of Ireland – having so far survived the worst that the wild Atlantic could throw at them – a storm drove the *Trinidad* inshore. Her anchors failed to find a hold on the sandy bottom, and there was only just time for the troops to be ferried ashore in boats. Pounded by the Atlantic surf, she soon began to capsize, and before long, she went to pieces on submerged rocks, barely a stone's throw from land.

If you've ever witnessed a ship break up on rocks in a storm, as I once did when I was in my teens, you'll know that it's a horrible sight. The power of an angry sea on an exposed beach is devastating. The noise is tremendous, the churning strandline littered with broken wood, planks, rails, boxes, cabin furniture, hatch covers, ropes and other debris. And as the *Trinidad* broke up, her cannons and some of the heavier timbers and wooden items – metal-bound chests, barrels, casks – would have sunk, to be slowly swallowed up by shifting sediments on the seabed. It would be another four hundred years before anyone would see them again.

But now we fast-forward to a chilly day in February 1971. On the Inishowen peninsula divers from the Derry Sub Aqua Club are on a training dive in Kinnagoe Bay when one of them notices what appears to be a ship's cannon lying exposed on the seabed, about five fathoms (or nine metres) below the surface. As they inspect the barrel, they notice the Spanish royal insignia and the name of Philip II. More cannons follow, and understanding the significance of their find, they call in archaeological help. It quickly becomes clear that they've found the long-lost *Trinidad*.

In a series of underwater investigations that lasts from 1971 to 1983, they discover more objects of all kinds, preserved in the airless sand and silt of the sea floor. Like the finds from *Kronan*, they include personal possessions such as fine clothes and weapons, but also luxury items such as delicate porcelain bowls from Ming China. There are elaborate navigation instruments too. But as they continue their survey, one piece of waterlogged wood immediately attracts attention. It looks very much like the neck of a guitar. Like a guitar's fingerboard, it's been fitted with frets to form the notes under the player's fingertips. At one end the frets lie closer together, showing that this is the part closest to the sound box; and here is the key to the mystery: its curious shape reveals that it's not been a guitar or a lute or a mandolin – it's a shape unique to the fingerboards of citterns.

Strung with fine wire, a cittern was an elegant parlour instrument, either plucked with the fingernails or strummed with a plectrum. Viewed from the front, its sound box has a teardrop outline, with a flat back, and this combination of features gives it a light and brilliant tone reminiscent of the mandolin, and even of the modern banjo, and like both those instruments today, it became very popular as an accompaniment to song. Because it was compact and robust it was also well adapted to fit into a mariner's sea chest; and this is presumably how it came to be aboard the *Trinidad*.

Whoever owned it was clearly someone with a taste for the finer things in life. We can imagine him in happier times, singing love songs and songs of home, perhaps in a light tenor voice, privately in his quarters or to friends in the officers' cabin. It's a poignant reminder that although archaeology is usually less good than history at naming people, it's extremely good at capturing intimate snapshots of past lives. Of course, lost and discarded property is something that archaeologists deal with every day, but even so, knowing the exact location and the doleful circumstances make this find uniquely personal. The sweet tones of cittern strings, plucked or lightly strummed, contrast starkly not just with the horror of the ship's last moments, but with the fate of many of the survivors. Was the owner one of their number, and if so, did he ever make it back to Spain? Again, it's impossible to know.

But for the crew and troops their ordeal was only just beginning as they stepped onto the Irish shore. Accounts of the ensuing disaster, compiled afterwards in Spain, report that after a long march and a brief stand-off, the common soldiers were robbed naked by a

Protestant militia near Drogheda, and those who resisted were killed. The captain and some other noblemen were captured and held to ransom. When eventually they were redeemed by Spanish representatives in London, Don Alonzo was able to return to Castile. Any personal property that had meanwhile drifted ashore from the wreck would have been quickly scavenged or looted. So the fact that the neck and fingerboard survived at all is little short of a miracle. It's unlikely that any trace of them would have remained if they hadn't somehow sunk to the relative safety of the seabed.

It's an extraordinary find, and the frets are not its only striking feature. Preserved on the surfaces between them are ghostly patterns of abrasion. Like the wear marks on an old school violin or guitar fingerboard, they are the marks left by the movements of fingertips. They reveal that the player, whoever he was, had been fingering the strings over many years, and show where he was accustomed to placing his fingers when he was playing.

To help us understand exactly how it was played we need to look at a couple of other archaeological finds. Odd as it may seem, the *Trinidad* isn't the only vessel of its time to have sunk with a cittern on board. Another wreck, discovered in the Netherlands in 1980, proved to have not one but two of them in its hold, and we are lucky again that they were so well preserved.

The remains were found by workmen digging on what was by then dry land, in the Gordiaandreef area of Lelystad, in Flevoland. For much of the twentieth century this part of the Netherlands was still the bed of the shallow Zuider Zee, until 1967 when engineers began to reclaim the land by damming and draining part of it. It turns out that around 1620 a local ferry boat, technically a sailing barge or *beurtschip*, had been crossing that now almost forgotten stretch of water when disaster struck. The cause of the accident, and what became of the crew and passengers, is unknown, but whatever happened, the ship capsized and went down in around five metres of water. All the goods in its hold sank with it, to be quickly swallowed up by the mud and silt at the bottom. Many are now lovingly conserved and housed, alongside the boat, in a purpose-built pavilion on the Batavia Wharf at Lelystad, where they offer fascinating glimpses into daily life at the start of the seventeenth century

Both instruments were in pieces by the time they were recovered, but their forms have since been handsomely reconstructed in modern wood by the Utrecht luthiers Sebastián Núñez and Verónica Estevez. When we met in 2002 they explained that the wood-and-metal frets are so well preserved that it's possible to see precisely how the maker has spaced them. It appears that unlike those of the *Trinidad*, lost to the sea thirty years earlier, they are set to what's known as *meantone temperament*. That's to say, they play a perfect octave, divided into twelve perfectly equal semitones. A consequence of this is that the all-important fifth note isn't quite a full or 'perfect' fifth: it's very slightly flatter. To a well-tuned musical ear, the interval is by a fraction narrower than it is in the older 'Pythagorean' methods of tuning. Known as *just intonation*, those older Pythagorean fifths gave a brighter sound. But a melody played with just intonation would only sound fully 'in tune' when you were playing in the mode or key to which the frets had been tuned. Play it in almost any other key and it wouldn't sound so good. Meantone temperament did away with all that, and even allowed the player to change modes in the middle of a piece – which is to say modulate. It did mean that all the notes that you could play on an instrument were averaged and very slightly out of tune. But the difference was sufficiently subtle that in time our hearing has adjusted to it and it's come to seem in tune – technically it isn't, but it *feels* like it. Since temperaments of this sort were only described in the late sixteenth century, the Lelystad fingerboards provide archaeological proof that by around 1620 they were already in widespread everyday use.

These finds give us all manner of clues as to the way fashions were changing, not just in music theory but in the real world of seventeenth-century musicianship. Some of that musicianship involved considerable movements of people and things. There's often a temptation to suppose that things found in a particular place must always have been rooted to that location, that they belong there; and certainly the Lelystad citterns match the instruments shown in portraits of musicians painted by the old Flemish masters. But the Netherlands is not where the cittern was invented. If history places its origins anywhere in Europe it's in Renaissance Italy, where it began life as a folk instrument, or in Spain. And of course that makes perfect sense because those are the very lands where the *Trinidad* and her crew originated.

Archaeologists describe displaced items like these as *allochthonous*, meaning 'removed from their place of origin', and their displacement is going to offer us an important concept to take forward. If we wished to find archaeological evidence for the history of Scottish bagpipes, for example, the medieval cities and ruined castles of Scotland might not be the best places to search. It might be better to trace the footsteps of the Scots Brigade in 'Low Germanie' during the wars of the seventeenth century, or to explore the haunts of Scottish merchants in medieval Scandinavia. By the same token, if we were lucky enough to find part of a set of pipes near, say, Amsterdam or Zwolle, we shouldn't automatically assume them to be Dutch.

And that may be the most important lesson to take away from the lost citterns of Lelystad and Kinnagoe Bay. We think of music today as a modern global phenomenon in our modern global world, but as we continue to dig we're going to find that the roots of globalism go far, far deeper.

Chapter Eight

What's in a name?
A signed trumpet from the River Thames

London, England, 1567

It's late afternoon and members of the 'Thames Mudlarks' are beachcombing along the tidal foreshore of the River Thames in the City of London. The tide is very low, and a strip of beach has been exposed. It isn't a swimmer's beach of soft golden sand. There are some patches of sand here and there, but they alternate with stretches of grey river mud and clay, sprinkled with small stones and builders' rubble: exactly the sort of shoreline you might see at low water on the margins of any port city. But the actions of tide and weather have a curious way of exposing odds and ends of history, and this afternoon the beachcombers have come across a small but rather fascinating piece of rubbish. Covered in mud, and crushed flat like an old drinks can, it's hard to make out what it is, except that it seems to be brass, and it must once have been vaguely conical in shape. Could it be the remains of a cup or a beaker? Whatever it is, it seems to have taken some shrewd knocks, even before it was thrown away. In one place something sharp has been plunged straight through it, and someone has made good the damage by soldering an oval patch of brass over the hole. As repairs go, it's crude and inexpert. But as we've already seen, in archaeology first appearances can deceive; and like so many other musical finds, there's going to be rather more to this discovery than meets the eye.

As I examined the remains in the offices of the Museum of London a few weeks later, it became evident that it must once have been part of something rather more delicate. The first clue was a ribbon-like band of stouter brass that was found nearby. One of its edges was toothed in a decorative way, while the other was smooth and straight. A series of punched holes along the band corresponded so precisely to punch holes around the rim of the cup that they must once have been joined together. A still closer look at the cup revealed the ghostly shape of the band's toothed edge, impressed in patches of solder. By taking careful measurements and plotting them on paper, the whole structure eventually began to reveal its shape. It was the flared end of a brass instrument: the 'bell'. What we had in front of us might only be a small piece of the original trumpet – the finder had recovered neither lengths of tubing nor any kind of mouthpiece – but what there was now started to yield a surprising amount of useful information. It proved to be very old. The band in particular held signs that would reveal the very date when it was made.

Bands like this are essentially there to strengthen thin metal rims but they also offer makers opportunities for embellishment. This one was no exception. Today's trumpet-makers would call it a 'garland', and a very pretty garland this one was. Looking through a magnifying glass we could see that within the hachured decoration was an inscription: a legend in words, spelled out in fine Gothic lettering. Out of the silent past, a human voice was speaking to us, and this is what it appeared to say:

M°IL°ISPESINI^{ccccc}LXVIILEN^{ch}IENESFAR

The immediate challenge was to identify the language. Slowly some of the letters began to form themselves into a phrase, in some kind of French. It read: L'ENCHIEN ES PAR MOI – perhaps 'the device is by me' – and from here, we were able to make sense of the rest. Lois, or Louis, Pesin was the maker's name, and this was followed by the date of manufacture: IcccccLXVII, meaning 1567. But who was Louis Pesin? Where had he made the trumpet? And just how fine a trumpet had he made?

Under the microscope the corroded metal surface showed further telltale traces of the now-missing parts, making plain the type of trumpet that it had once been. It had been fashioned from a thin brass sheet, with an elegant coppersmith's seam revealed as a neat zigzag of silver solder, now black against the brown and green patina of the brass. A lozenge-shaped patch of solder marked the attachment point for a 'stay' or crosspiece which, even though now lost, showed that the trumpet had been shaped like an elongated letter S, folded back on itself. We see similar trumpets being played by angels and heralds in Late Renaissance paintings. It was eerily similar to one found on the seabed among the exploded remains of *Kronan*, the seventeenth-century Swedish warship that produced the violin we saw in Chapter 6. The *Kronan* trumpet had a similar attachment in the very same place. It would have served to prevent the S-shape from flexing, and so give the instrument a more rigid and practical structure.

At first sight, relics of this sort make a curious and, it has to be said, unfavourable impression, compared with all the beautiful trumpets in the Renaissance paintings, or the gleaming historic instruments that we see in the galleries of museums. The exposed surfaces of the London piece were discoloured through exposure to the air and river water, to the dull brown of old brass, mottled with areas of greenish corrosion and dirt. In several places there was dark grey solder left over from multiple repairs. And squarely in the centre was that one broad oval patch, sealed at the edges with still more solder. In their day, highly polished, the repairs might have seemed reasonably neat, but time and tide had exposed their shortcomings. On the other hand, they now represented something rather special: they formed in effect a narrative sequence that charted the way it had been used throughout an intense working life; and it was a narrative of a kind that we might not have noticed in a better kept, more skilfully curated instrument.

But the feature that kept catching our attention was Pesin's name. In archaeology it's seldom that we find equipment labelled like this with the name of its maker. Much of what we find remains, literally, anonymous. And this is what makes the Thames and *Kronan* trumpets particularly special. Like Pesin's trumpet, the legend on the *Kronan* garland announces the name of the person who crafted it. He calls himself Michael Nagel; and he tells us that in 1654 he was working far from Sweden's Baltic coast, in Nuremberg in Bavaria.

Michael Nagel may have been quite a name in sixteenth-century Europe – there are several of his instruments in museum collections. Pesin, however, proves more elusive. He doesn't appear in any records we have of early wind-instrument-makers, and as far as I'm aware no other examples of his work remain. Nevertheless there are some inferences to be drawn from his workmanship. He, or his firm, obviously had the ability and the ambition to create fine instruments, and he was sufficiently jealous of his reputation to put his name to them. We know too that he, or his engraver, was writing in French. So he was either working in France or somewhere where French was spoken. But does this help to pin him down? In the sixteenth century, Tudor England still used French on occasion. The north shore of the Thames was also an extremely busy waterfront, indeed one of the busiest in the world at that time, and the principal gateway between England and the Continent. Many people as well as goods passed through it. What's more, Elizabethan London was witnessing an increasing flow of Protestant refugees from Flanders and France. It's not inconceivable that Pesin was a Huguenot fleeing persecution. But amid all the wars and upheavals of the sixteenth century it was also a time of great music. It was especially a golden age of brass, both secular and religious. So while his trumpet may have ended its days in ignominious obscurity, Pesin might have crafted it for one of the glorious ensembles of the kind that now seem so redolent of those times, the age of Thomas Tallis and Andrea Gabrieli, Orlando di Lasso and Innocentio Alberti.

This contrast between the instrument builder's ambition and his product's squalid fate – squalid because the unsanitary state of the Thames shore would be hard to exaggerate in that era of

unregulated waste disposal – brings with it an important realisation. It's that when we're fortunate enough to obtain a date for an
archaeological find, we're dating not just one moment in time but
part of a whole chronological sequence. There are dates of manufacture, for sure; but there are also dates of deposition to consider,
and in between are whole time spans of use. Whether we're reading it on a written label like Pesin's garland or deriving it from
scientific analysis, the moment of manufacture is only the beginning of an object's useful life. And even its deposition in the ground
is no more than a punctuation mark in its longer archaeological
trajectory. These things had lives, with beginnings, middles and
ends.

The beginnings and the ends can sometimes be quite close
together, as they were in the case of Michael Nagel's trumpet, just
twenty-two years into its useful life when it went down with its
ship – a mere heartbeat in archaeological terms. In the case of our
Thames trumpet, we may be talking about a much wider time
frame. Finds on exposed foreshores are much harder to date than
shipwrecks: it's hard to say when something was put there. It was
retrieved by 'mudlarks', which is to say by antiquity collectors, and
came to the museum with no more context than a pencil mark on
a map. Had there been careful excavation, perhaps we'd be able to
say more. But what we can see from the repairs is that by the time
its last owner abandoned the instrument a considerable passage of
time – a lifetime of use and abuse – already separated it from its
maker.

There's a second clue too that's going to help us to steer a path
through the depths of time, and it's in the way we view people like
Louis and Michael, coming as we do from a world where history (as
it's taught in schools) has tended to value and privilege associations
with named people and places. It could be described as the prehistorian's viewpoint. To a prehistorian, accustomed to working with
materials rather than texts, knowing that our trumpet is associated
with a name carries little extra meaning. After all, who was Louis
Pesin? We simply have no idea. Indeed, we know him only from

this one product. We'll find this to be a pattern in our story. What really matters is what the product itself can tell us. Between the objects and the circumstances of their eventual deposition, we're gaining glimpses into the material realities of people's lives: the lives of real people, with real craft skills and real musicianship, even if we can't put names to them.

Finds like Pesin's trumpet also remind us of the sheer number of individual lives that they must have touched. Even before our trumpet was put to use, producing it would have involved several different skills, and probably a number of people – not just Pesin himself but a whole craft community. There would have been the metal founder and the sheet-metal-maker and supplier; there'd be the coppersmith (presumably Pesin himself) and the engraver of the decoration and inscription. There's evidence of at least one subsequent repairer, and probably several more. What's more, during its lifetime it may have been traded or exchanged several times, during the hundred years or more before it met its watery fate. And this is to say nothing of the audiences that would have thrilled to the music it played.

CHAPTER NINE

'Music the mermaids love': four silver whistles from the wreck of the Mary Rose

Hampshire, England, 1545

From his castle at Southsea, the king enjoyed a grandstand view of the Solent, the four-mile-wide stretch of sea opposite Portsmouth. Across its glittering waters lay the Isle of Wight. The sun shone and flags fluttered in the freshening breeze. It was the morning of 19 July 1545, the day of the Big Match. To the king's left massed the ships of the approaching French fleet, their backs to the open sea and their fast galleys forming a screen in front. Sailing out of the harbour to his right came the powerful ships of his own navy, hurrying to engage the enemy. They knew their king was watching.

Henry VIII had characteristically relished nearly every minute of the build-up to the confrontation of the two fleets. But for all the colourful banners and the pageantry, such a bold display of military might was bound to end in tears for one side, and in the course of that summer morning it did just that. Even before battle had been joined, disaster struck. In executing a sharp turn, the king's lead ship and his pride and joy, the seven-hundred ton carrack *Mary Rose*, toppled over and sank, taking most of her officers, crew and marines down with her. Out of a total of more than four hundred men on board, fewer than two dozen survived. And the king saw and heard it all.

We can't say for sure what caused the catastrophe. A recent rebuild may have left the *Mary Rose* top-heavy, or there might have been an unexpected change in the wind. But with her new gunports opened wide for battle, water quickly flooded in, and the nets designed to keep French boarders off her decks now sealed her crew's awful fate. The fleet commander, Vice Admiral Sir George Carew, drowned with them. Even though the contest between the two fleets that day ended in a draw, the loss of Carew and the *Mary Rose* must have marked one of the worst days of Henry's reign.

The wreck of the *Mary Rose* was discovered in 1971 and its raising in 1982 became one of the epic stories of modern maritime archaeology: the recovery of the cannons and the crew's remains, the ship breaking surface for the first time in more than four hundred years, and the nail-biting moment as part of the massive steel support frame collapsed. But you'll have guessed by now that I wouldn't be telling you this story if the ship hadn't also contained some musical treasures. It had. Even before the hull was finally floated into dry dock, conservators had been at work on two fiddles, a tenor shawm (a kind of large oboe), three 'tabor-pipes' (long flutes, played one-handed) and a drum. Together the instruments paint a lively picture of musical life aboard ship at the close of the Middle Ages. But in the wreckage lying on the sea floor the diving team had also found something even more unusual: four fine silver whistles. Strictly speaking, they may not be musical instruments; as far as we know they were never used for shipboard entertainment. They were essentially 'sound tools': the shrill sounds they made would have added to the rhythms of life onboard ship and formed an essential part of the atmosphere – the soundscape of daily existence at sea and in harbour. Together with the ship's bell, they played a central role in everyday routine, announcing everything from mealtimes to raising the anchors and setting the sails. To do this they made use of a tuneful system of recognised phrases, rather like snatches of birdsong, each of which carried a precise and unmistakable meaning. They were wordless orders, audible even to the men and boys perched high in the windswept rigging. Such whistles continue to be used in modern navies, including the British Royal Navy, where they can be heard 'piping the still' over the ship's loud-speakers, commanding attention, or 'piping the side' as visitors of rank are welcomed at the head of the gangway. Nowadays there may be fewer masts for sailors to climb and fewer sails to furl, but the calls are still sounded and the meanings they convey are still understood by the whole ship's company.

The *Mary Rose* whistles clearly resemble their modern equivalents. Chrome-plated brass is now more usual than silver, but to all intents and purposes they are identical, in appearance and construction. Imagine a small plain sphere made from thin sheet metal: at a little over a centimetre in diameter it's something like a small nutshell or a songbird's egg. In the top of the sphere there's a circular sound hole about four millimetres across, and if you blow across it at just the right angle, it makes a shrill noise like a whistling kettle. To make it easier to find the angle and ensure the strongest tone, a slender mouthpipe has been added. And that's the essence of what's now known as the boatswain's (or bosun's) call. To play it you simply hold it in the hollow of your palm, trapping the tube in the crook of your thumb and forefinger, and blow into the open end. It's surprisingly effective for its size, and curiously versatile in the sounds it can make. If you open and close your hand around the sphere while you blow, you can make the note rise and fall, and in this way a skilled boatswain can achieve the complicated tune-like phrases that, like military bugle calls, are able to convey elaborate coded instructions. Its simplicity is the key to its success: it's a hugely practical tool.

Three of the *Mary Rose* whistles were suspended from silver chains, rather like an old-fashioned pocket watch. The fourth and smallest whistle was suspended on a ribbon of gold braid. All four are fully working instruments. As a group, what we do notice about them is their contrasting sizes: they range in length from fourteen to just four centimetres. So what might these differences tell us about their use?

We may find some clues in early eyewitness descriptions. From these we learn that it wasn't just the boatswain who needed a whistle. In 1635, ninety years after the *Mary Rose* sank, Sir William Monson tells us that the sailing master used one too:

As the Master commands the tacking of the ship, the hoisting or striking [down of] the yard, the taking in or putting forth the sails: upon the winding of the Master's whistle the Boatswain takes it [up] with his, and sets the sailors with courage to do their work, every one of them knowing by their whistle what they are to do.

The captain's coxwain might also make use of one, when steering the captain's barge. From there, their use extended up the line of command to ships' captains and even as far as admirals. And at all levels they came to hold a symbolic value, as badges of rank. Henry himself took to wearing and blowing a golden one on important naval occasions, and awarded others to his lord admirals. Indeed, they were such potent marks that when the English Lord Admiral Sir Edward Howard captured the Scottish privateer *Sir Andrew Barton* off the coast of Kent in August 1511, he took his whistle as a trophy.

Yes, it seems that even pirates needed them. But how and when did they come to be used in ships in the first place? One of the earliest instances was recorded by a Swiss friar called Felix Fabri, who in around 1480 sailed from Venice in a fast galley not unlike the French ones that would threaten the *Mary Rose* over sixty years later. He gives us this description of the boatswain at his station between the rowers' benches: 'Round his neck hung a silver whistle with which he gave the signal for naval duties. Day or night, whenever the whistle was heard, the men stirred themselves and responded to the whistle with a shout.'

Now, this is all reassuring background, but there's something puzzling about the *Mary Rose* calls as physical artefacts: it's that here, at their very earliest appearance in the archaeological record, they already seem to be fully developed, instantly recognisable for what they are. Yet if we take only a short step backwards in time, there's not a trace of their kind to be seen – no hint of where they've come from. Our earliest glimpse, as I write, is a beautifully embroidered bedcover from Sicily, now in London's Victoria and Albert Museum. Made in around 1380, it shows scenes from the medieval tale of the doomed lovers Tristram and Yseult. Two panels depict rowers in galleys, of the fast and manoeuvrable kind that was to ferry Friar Fabri down the Adriatic, and in each galley there's a figure standing with the same kind of whistle in his mouth. But with these images the trail runs cold. If there are any earlier examples, I haven't been able to track them down.

What does the absence of any further records mean for the instrument's origins, and for the signalling tradition that it served? Was the call a wholly new invention of the fourteenth century, driven by the increased size and complexity of ships and their rigging? Or is there some deeper history that we're missing? For we are definitely missing something. By rights, we ought to be seeing simpler forms of the whistle among the hundreds of thousands of objects now recovered from earlier maritime and coastal excavations – Viking, Roman, Greek, Phoenician. But we're not. Archaeologists are familiar with this conundrum: they call it a 'first appearance datum'.

The expression was first coined by scientists to describe the earliest – that is to say, the oldest known – instance of a particular fossil plant or animal in sedimentary rocks. But 'appearances' are just what such datums mark: the first *evidence* of an organism. They don't provide the organism's actual time or place of origin, which must lie still further back in time. They are merely a provisional marker, within the limits of what we *currently* know: a tacit admission that our geological and archaeological records are incomplete. The question then becomes: how incomplete? How much of the puzzle is still missing?

There's another, wider point to consider here. This kind of signalling, communicating information in a musical way, isn't limited to the military sphere. We still whistle to attract someone else's attention. We sound our car horns in different ways to express different things, from a friendly greeting to a distinct rebuke. Such patterns can run very deep. And for music's prehistorians the million-dollar question is: just how deep? How long has our species been exploiting sounds in this practical way – and what might it tell us about music?

For the London playwright Thomas Heywood, writing in 1665, the boatswain's calls clearly were musical in character:

Boatswain with your whistle
Command the saylors to the upper deck
to know their quarters, and to hear their charge . . .
Oh, 'tis a music the Mermaids love!

As musicians, we may wonder whether such whistling really falls within our definition of music. Yet speaking as archaeologists, would it really make sense to exclude them? These are matters that we're going to have to explore in more detail.

PART THREE

Residues of Medieval Lives

The Fifteenth and Fourteenth Centuries

At the end of the fifteenth century, a series of European adventures has begun to shrink the world, creating for better or for worse the global planet we know today. By January 1499, Christopher Columbus is already on his third visit to the New World and Vasco da Gama is making his way around southern Africa to India. By 1522 Ferdinand Magellan will have been the first to circumnavigate the globe. But step a century back in time and Europe and its music are in quite a different place.

In Europe this period is known as the Late Middle Ages. As we begin to fill material gaps in its musical history some important discoveries lie ahead. There will be more 'first appearances' to match the Trinidad steelpans and the *Mary Rose* boatswain's whistles, prompting us to ask what they might mean for the way musical traditions begin.

Returning to life on land, archaeology will reveal what it has to say about musical life in a medieval castle, and about musical literacy in the remote countryside. We'll witness the power of trumpets as instruments of ceremony and terror, and glimpse the white-hot heat of technology in a medieval bell foundry.

If we've seen the practical difficulties and dangers faced by underwater archaeologists, we've also considered their consolation: that shipwrecks are singular events, clearly defined in time. Now we discover what happens when things get more complicated. To do so, we first delve beneath a modern city street, to explore a pattern of finds that reveal something very special: a workshop where medieval instruments were actually being made.

CHAPTER TEN

Craft and criminality: a music repair shop in fifteenth-century Oxford

England, c.1450

For something that's become a byword for permanence, the ground beneath our feet has a surprising tendency to move with the passage of time. Excavation shows that its surface marks no more than a passing moment in an age-old process, a thin veneer separating us from our buried past; and as we become better acquainted with what lies below it, we can discern the telltale signs. In some parts of the world it's slowly vanishing, literally blowing away on the wind or being washed away by rain. In others it's just as quickly building up. All that dust and outwash has to settle somewhere. So too do leaves. Vegetation grows and dies back. But Nature isn't the only force at work. We ourselves contribute enormously to the way the earth's surface changes, in the way we litter our environment and re-engineer the places where we live and work. We'll witness the impact of erosion in the chapters ahead; but first, we're going to see the processes of accumulation and accretion, and discover what they mean for music's history.

As you walk through the centre of any historic city today, the history you tend to notice is mostly above your head, and this is certainly true of the city of Oxford with its fine old university buildings built in the Gothic and neoclassical styles. Shaped from smooth, warm-toned Oxfordshire limestone, they are beautifully maintained and of course still in use. It's a splendid exhibition of architectural history, and of music history too if we know where to listen. But in a sense the reality that they present is an idealised, curated and somewhat sanitised version of the past. Beneath our feet there's a rather different narrative to be read: here we find the kind of randomness that archaeologists particularly value. It's a randomness that draws us closer to some of the harsh physicalities of the city's musical history, not as it's been documented and reported but as it was actually lived, representing the 'dark matter', so to speak, of everyday human behaviours that lay behind music-making in a medieval university.

Several excavations in the old city centre have produced musical finds, but perhaps the most fascinating discovery, so far, has been made beneath a row of houses on a street called St Aldate's. Here the finds combine with documentary records of the neighbour-hood to offer timely clues to the human complexities and real-world frailties that lurk unseen behind some of the stories we read in our history books.

As the main southern thoroughfare in and out of the city centre, St Aldate's takes its name from the nearby parish church. The site was excavated in the 1970s, after demolition works had exposed old foundations. The buildings had stood on the west side of the street, just above its junction with Speedwell Street, so that their fronts would have caught the morning sun; and in the fifteenth century, as now, they were at the foot of the gentle slope between the city's South Gate and the river. At the time of the excavations their seventeenth-century timber frames had fallen into disrepair and had recently been pulled down. It was the 1970s when, sadly, that sort of thing still happened; but it made it possible to open up the whole area to excavation, including the yards at the rear. This is what the archaeologists did. As they worked their way down through the compacted earth they uncovered a sequence of wall footings and floors that corresponded to earlier phases of building and rebuilding. Within the layers were traces of household and craft activities; but there was also something more unusual.

Among the usual rusty nails and general building debris were craft tools and waste, evidence that there had once been a workshop here. And it had been more than just any old workshop. A light scatter of bone-working debris included small bone pegs, squared at one end and perforated at the other. They looked suspiciously like the harp tuning pegs encountered at Montgomery Castle, and with them was a length of fine brass wire, twenty-four inches (60 cm) long and one sixty-fourth of an inch (0.4 mm) thick. It seemed that someone here had been repairing – and in all likelihood trading – musical instruments. For archaeologists this was a new kind of musical setting. It wasn't the sort of place where people made music for entertainment or religion. For the first time, we had the remnants of a shop that people would have visited to buy an instrument or have one repaired. And that was only the start.

The value of the debris field lay in the large number of objects and the condition they were in when they were found. Some pegs were unfinished, others had been used and then discarded. Why they'd been thrown away became clear under the microscope: their broader ends had been made square in cross section to receive a metal tuning key; but it looked as if some keys hadn't offered an accurate fit and had damaged them. They were no longer usable. Other finds added more detail. One peg showed no evidence that it had ever been used, or had even been fitted. Tuning pegs usually develop patterns of fine polish on their shafts where they've been rubbing against wood. This one showed none. Other pieces of bone, although squared in cross section, had for some reason been left unfinished. And out in the backyard there were eighty more fragments of waste from the same process.

By recording the layering of the deposits and plotting them on the site plans and elevations (vertical cross sections), the archaeologists began to work out the sequence of stages that the site had passed through in its long development, from river sediments laid down before the place was first occupied in the ninth century up to the present ground surface. Archaeologists call this layering 'stratigraphy' and the interpretive process 'structural phasing'. It's the most fundamental task of any excavation, and the resulting drawings are often works of art as well as documents of science. In the all-important elevations, the gradual build-up of earth shows as a sandwich of horizontal layers, each with its own distinctive colour and texture. As the analysis progressed, it became clear that the musical activity began within the tenth of the structural phases. Coins and sherds of pottery dated it to the late fourteenth century.

But it increased markedly in the next phase, the eleventh, in around 1400. While a layer of detritus began to accumulate on the floor of the northern building, which had a large hearth for heating, the clay floor of the unheated southern building was kept more or less clear. Some bits of worked bone were found trodden into the surface, and they included another tuning peg.

All this creates a strong impression of an organised craft activity, involving repairs to stringed instruments. Looking more closely at the pegs, at their different sizes and designs, it's possible to deduce that a variety of instruments must have been passing through the premises. And not just stringed instruments. There's also a pottery whistle, and three sheet-brass pellet bells very like the finds being traded to the Natchez in late-seventeenth-century Mississippi. It's a first intimation that the occupants may have been engaged in more activities than just repairing stringed instruments.

In around 1450 such a workshop would certainly have had a market to serve. Several Oxford instrument-makers are identified in historical documents from around this time. Some of their clients would no doubt have been ordinary householders, home instruments being as widespread then as home entertainment systems are today, and no less in need of servicing. Stringed instruments of one kind or another would have supplied a ready means of recreation, being the perfect accompaniment to singing and dancing. Wealthy merchants' families are sure to have had them. Scholars at the colleges too would have demanded them for their amusement, and religious communities for both entertainment and more solemn observances. Taverns would have hosted performers of all kinds, and there would be the 'town waits' – the local guild of official musicians, who are first mentioned in 1501 – to supply.

If we want to know what kinds of instruments were being

repaired here we have to look closer. It's a story of small details slowly developing into a bigger picture, and an example of how archaeology can begin to construct a sense of music's social history from numerous beginnings that by themselves may seem quite unpromising. From the pegs' shapes and sizes we can see that some belonged to instruments like our modern violins and mandolins. Others appear best suited to small harps. A third type would be familiar to anyone who's ever played a reproduction of a medieval psaltery or looked inside a modern piano. In fact it could even have belonged to an early string keyboard.

But what distinguishes St Aldate's from all the other places where tuning pegs have been found is not so much the kinds of instrument that they represent as the way they place musical industry for the first time in an urban landscape. What's more, the location benefits from a unique piece of supporting evidence. It's preserved in surviving written documents.

The first document is an old manuscript volume. The Osney Rental Book was the rent book of Osney (or Oseney) Abbey, one of Oxford's four main religious houses. It seems that Osney's fifteenth-century portfolio included properties in and around St Aldate's, and the book shows who the tenants were in 1453. They included at this very address one Thomas Brikar; and it isn't the only time he appears in the records. A Thomas Briker, spelled with an e, is mentioned in legal documents in 1467 as one of fourteen men arraigned on charges of counterfeiting the king's coinage. It seems they've been making money all too literally. But crucially, the arrest warrant supplies Thomas's trade: he's listed as a 'harpemaker'.

The trade title *maker* is a game-changer too. The archaeological evidence at St Aldate's has been able to take us as far as the repairing of harps and other stringed instruments, and maybe a sideline in some musical knick-knacks. But no further. With *harpemaker* it becomes clear that what we're getting from the archaeological remains is only a keyhole glimpse of a much broader and more ambitious business enterprise.

For a trade spanning some fifty years, maybe more, the number of surviving pieces may seem small. This, however, turns out to be typical of workshop residues when we find them. It's common sense when you think about it. By definition, the finished products will have left the site, while any parts and raw materials remaining there at the final closure of the business – and any combustible scraps of wood and bone – will have been scavenged. What remained at St Aldate's, therefore, is the merest residue left after the site has been cleared. Unless its occupation has been interrupted by some major disaster, such as fire or building collapse, the things we find are never going to represent the sum total, or anything near it. They are simply indications, clues. But with that thought comes a realisation: that every new musical discovery becomes much more than it first seems. It could be merely the tip, the visible manifestation of another musical iceberg.

Chapter Eleven

Echoes from the ruins: a coil of musical wire in a Scottish castle

Berwickshire, fifteenth century

Compared with the glamorous, headline-grabbing discoveries made in ancient tombs and shipwrecks, rummaging through archaeology's leftovers may at first seem to represent one of music's quieter archaeological backwaters. But some startling discoveries have been made in this way. One of them appeared on my desk, one weekday morning in 1994. It was in a small cardboard box, postmarked Edinburgh. Inside it I found a letter with an X-ray image attached, and a small polythene bag containing something fragile wrapped in tissue paper.

The letter explained that they came from recent excavations inside the ruins of a Scottish castle. The image showed a small lump of rusty concretion, about the size of a hen's egg. The object in the tissue wrapping was a loop of fine brassy wire. As a detective puzzle this was, to say the least, missing a few pieces. Yet it's in just such small and enigmatic debris that music's story often finds its beginnings.

The object in the radiograph was just one of a number of small rusty nodules that had been found. They weren't things of beauty, but the archaeologists had realised that they were seeing encrustations formed around corroded iron objects, and when they X-rayed the individual pieces they wondered if the ghostly image that appeared on one of the plates might be a little metal mouth harp. It's a folk instrument that's still played today by people who love and appreciate its quirky sound, and was popular in Scotland where it was known as a 'gewgaw' or 'trump'. Looking closely at the way the tapering prongs were set – exactly parallel, with a narrow space between – I could now confirm that that's exactly what it was. It seemed that almost all of the metallic iron had oxidised out to form the crust, but the original shape remained within it as a void. Its outline was typical of instruments of the late medieval period.

The spool of brassy wire was even more remarkable. Resting in the palm of my hand, it seemed so slight as to be almost weightless. And as I turned it over it gleamed and sparkled in the light of my desk light. The yellow metal showed no trace of corrosion. The challenge now was to see whether it was musical wire, and if it was, to say what role it might have played in the cultural life of the castle.

The name of the place is Fast Castle, and if you like your archaeological sites to be in romantic settings you could hardly hope for better. The ruins are perched on a remote sea cliff on Scotland's rugged south-east coast, where the Lammermuir Hills fall suddenly into the wild North Sea. It's a stiff walk from the nearest road. The 'Fast' in the title seems to describe the castle's unusual strength, as in 'held fast' or 'stuck fast on a reef', and it's certainly in a powerful defensive position. Even now it retains something of a swashbuckling, piratical air, so that we might be forgiven for suspecting that piracy of some kind was rarely far from the minds of its inhabitants. Its thick curtain-wall was penetrated only on the landward side, by a bridge over a deep ditch. At the cliff's foot there's a cave, and on the seaward battlements above it there are still signs that a crane was once mounted there to upload provisions from the beach far below.

To all intents and purposes the castle is prehistoric, in that literal sense of lacking historical records. But the ruins that are still standing or poking through the grass today are mostly medieval. By the fifteenth century the place belonged to a branch (or 'cadet') of one of the most powerful aristocratic families of the Anglo-Scottish border country, the Humes, or Homes. The Humes certainly knew how to live, so it wasn't entirely without creature comforts. Within the curtain-wall there were two courtyards and a substantial hall, with a kitchen and a brewhouse to provide them with meals and refreshments. All the buildings are now tumbled and overgrown, having been deliberately 'slighted' like the ruins of Montgomery Castle, but it's not hard to imagine the medieval family and their guests leading a reasonably snug existence in spite of their exposed and windswept location. Surely, music must also have had its place there, and the objects from the dig now supplied the first proof.

A pocket-sized instrument, in some ways foreshadowing the harmonica, the mouth harp is remarkable for its musical qualities and occupies a correspondingly special place in music's archaeology. In spite of its simple appearance it can make music of singular beauty, power and complexity. But in the spool of brass wire the team had found something altogether rarer, and more challenging. Found in a debris-filled quarry pit in the castle's lower courtyard, and dated to the late fifteenth century, it exhibits a number of musical clues. For a start, it's beautifully made: cold-worked through a small hole in a steel die. (You can do that with brass, as it's what's known as a ductile metal.) It's uniformly one sixty-fourth of an inch (0.4 mm) thick throughout its length and of a quality that would have allowed it to vibrate uniformly under tension, and produce a pure tone. The brass alloy too is consistent with musical use, at nineteen per cent zinc. It's true that the same could be said of many wires; but in this case its musical purpose is finally clinched by the signature way in which it's been coiled. When lengths of ordinary wire stock are found on medieval sites, which they often are, they usually appear to have been bundled loosely around someone's fingers and the final loop tied around the middle to prevent it from springing apart. It gives them a characteristic figure-eight shape. This one is no ordinary bundle. It's been spooled with care and attention. The coils are broad, near circular, and all to the same diameter. Its ends have been twisted over, to hold the loops neatly together.

Gentle, purposeful spooling of this sort is something that musicians and their suppliers do instinctively with strings. You'll see the evidence today in the supplies section of any modern music shop or online catalogue. It's done to avoid weakening the string. Whether it's made from gut or metal or even horsehair, if a string should become kinked, which is to say bent beyond its elastic limit, the kink will become a weakness and will eventually fail when it's under tension. An instrument string has to withstand a good deal of tension when it's wound up to its working pitch. On a violin, for example, a slender gut E string may be loaded to five kilograms in order to reach pitch, and this may take it quite close to its breaking strain even when it's new. So because we don't normally see careful spooling, it's tempting when we see it to interpret it as something of a specialist signature. Every trade has its tricks.

As a string player, finds of strings hold a special fascination for me. There's something particularly tactile about them, something immediate and somehow intimate. But what type of instrument should we imagine the Fast Castle wire serving? What kind of sound would it have made, and what kind of music might people have played on it? Its length is too short to fit a cittern like the ones from the wreck of the *Trinidad Valencera* and the Lelystad ferry boat, but it might well have suited some sort of fiddle. However, from what we know of music-making in the late Middle Ages, the instruments that immediately spring to mind are harps, psalteries and similar instruments with large numbers of wire strings.

We've seen evidence for a brass-strung harp at Montgomery Castle in Wales, and from at least two peat bogs in Ireland. In Edinburgh two complete brass-strung harps survive, without ever having been buried: the famous Queen Mary and Lamont harps. The bright brassy sound they make was evidently well loved by Scots musicians and their audiences. But harps were not the only portable wire-strung instruments that would have offered households a measure of refinement. There were tabletop and laptop instruments such as the psaltery, struck with little hammers or plucked with quills, which would eventually develop into string keyboard instruments such as the clavichord. Could there have been a clavichord at Fast Castle?

Most of the ones we know are later in date, but it's not impossible. A stained-glass window in St Mary's Church in Warwick shows angels playing two such instruments as early as 1447. Also in the 1440s a Paris organist called Henri Arnaut describes a similar keyboard with a span of not one but three chromatic octaves. It would have demanded a lot of strings. Of actual examples that survive in music collections, the earliest seems to be a German-made 'clavicytherium', an upright instrument from around 1490 now in the Royal College of Music in London. So I guess it depends on how luxurious a lifestyle we think the inhabitants of a stronghold like Fast Castle might have enjoyed, and how connected they could have been to musical fashion in the wider world. Looking at the desolate ruin they left behind, and its remote location, it's hard to imagine them as sophisticates. But who's to say?

In the fifteenth century the Anglo-Scottish borders, scarred by centuries of tribal conflict, were the Badlands between Tudor England and Stewart Scotland, and were descending into the lawlessness that would soon become infamous. Yet this was precisely the culture that gave us the famous border ballads: songs of raiding and reprisal, of heroes and antiheroes like Johnie Armstrong, Hobbie Noble, Kinmont Willie and Hughie the Graeme, while simultaneously preserving earlier epics like 'Chevy Chase', the story of a bloody battle fought on the English side in 1388. The lands around Fast Castle, presided over by the Humes as wardens of the Scottish East Marches, were by no means the worst of the bandit country: that title must go to the more remote and mountainous Middle and West Marches. But danger and adventure can never have seemed very far away; and as they sang and strummed and danced their winters away in the firelight of the great hall of Fast Castle, they would surely have had no shortage of things to sing and dance about.

CHAPTER TWELVE

Writing on the wall: musical graffiti in the late Middle Ages

England, c.1400

Up to this point in our story we've been able to infer the presence of a range of sounds and forms of music from the material hardware, which is to say archaeological finds of musical instruments. We've begun to consider the tunes and harmonies and rhythms of music-making, and we've imagined the lived experiences of the musicians who were making it. We've seen ways in which the instruments have been made and tuned, and how their tunings imply tonal rules or frameworks within which musicians were accustomed to set their work. But some archaeological discoveries have the capacity to take us one step further and provide us with a direct line to the actual software: to melodies themselves, in the form of written notes. Preserved on ancient surfaces of various kinds, what gives this group of finds its particular value and importance is that the musical paths they mark are going to take us back not through hundreds but eventually through *thousands* of years.

We tend to regard the early development of modern musical notations as the province of musicologists and music historians, steeped in the musical output of medieval scriptoria, the workshops where manuscripts were hand-copied for distribution in the age before printing. From today's printed scores and sheet music they've traced them back through the libraries of medieval Europe, to medieval Islam and South Asia, China and Japan. The archaeological trail begins in a far more modest way than this, among notes carved, scratched or casually scribbled on stone. It's the domain of epigraphy, the study of formal, devotional and commemorative inscriptions on buildings and other monuments, and of their altogether more informal equivalent, the humble graffito.

Compared with all the care and planning that's gone into the creation of a musical image or the writing out of a musical score, the casual nature of graffito art and writing may seem to have little to add to our knowledge. There is, however, one thing that they do much better than those higher, more formal media. They allow us to sense how far musical knowledge and musical literacy permeated people's everyday lives. It's something that's close to the heart of archaeologists and museum visitors, for whom everyday life in the wider human landscape is no less fascinating than the workings of high culture. We know that in various parts of the world there were strong traditions of musical knowledge and education, and within these traditions were people skilled in both writing and reading 'music'; but how musically literate were people out in provincial towns and remote villages, beyond the narrow confines of cities and religious institutions? As it turns out, it's a question that archaeology can sometimes answer, and this in chapter we're going to look at some instances from medieval England.

Medieval graffiti offer a unique perspective on Europe's cultural past. In them we see human expression in the raw: casual, personal and engagingly spur-of-the-moment. The messages can be quite harsh, even brutal; they include blood-curdling curses and wicked, mocking caricatures. But they can also be romantic, sentimental and gently humorous, even beautiful. And sometimes they reference music.

One knife-point graffito in the parish church at Howell in Lincolnshire shows a human figure surrounded by at least four medieval harps, each with around fifteen strings. The harps have been lightly sketched, possibly by different people at different times, but are instantly recognisable. If only there was a clue as to *why*. Another drawing, this time scratched in a Suffolk church, shows a man with a funny face. He's wearing a round hat and protruding from his lips is a fine musical pipe with four finger holes.

Again, it's not known who he's meant to be, or why he's been cari-
catured. Mostly these graffiti appear to be the work of an instant or
two, sliced lightly into chalk or soft limestone with a sharp pocket
knife. It's art of the fleeting moment. Presumably it's also, as now,
the work of misspent youth. Idle choristers are the usual suspects.
Of their written words, most take the form of simple names or ini-
tials, but among them there are sometimes passages of text – and
occasionally they include notes and lines of music.

On a smooth limestone column in Norwich Cathedral, two four-
line staves have been scratched, and populated with about twenty
square notes with tails. The manner of the notation dates from the
second half of the sixteenth century. The melody is incomplete:
maybe the artist was interrupted. But there's enough to allow us to
try to reconstruct at least part of it.

Others aren't even melodies, but simply the means of delivering
a different kind of message: a message with a hidden meaning.
Square notes with tails form parts of one cryptic graffito scratched
on the wall of another parish church, St Mary's at Lidgate in north
Suffolk. The encryption, such as it is, uses what's known as a rebus:
a trick employing symbols (numbers or objects, potentially even
emojis) whose names sound the same as the word they replace. In
this case, parts of the clue are expressed in musical notation. It
begins with the word 'well', followed by a short three-line stave.
On the stave is a C clef and three square notes with tails. Their
modern letter names C, A, B and E form a pleasant little phrase, of
the kind that J. S. Bach would later be fond of working into his
fugues. It could be a fragment of a tune. But in this case its appearance is trying to throw us off the scent.

When they are converted into their equivalent values in medieval 'tonic sol-fa' (about which more later) the notes read *fa, re, mi*
and *la*. They are followed by the seemingly inconsequential syllable
'dy', then a die (one of a pair of gaming dice) with a face value of
four dots, and finally another enigmatic syllable, 'yne'. It's the die
that finally gives the riddler's game away. French was still sometimes used in England in the fourteenth century, and the old French

word for the four-face of a die was *cater*, as in modern French *quatre*, 'four'. Thus the intended message reveals itself as *well* + *fa re mi la* + *dy* + *cater* + *yne* – 'Well fare my lady Catherine.'

For once, we think we know who the graffito artist was. An adjacent inscription in the same handwriting supplies the signature of a local youth who would later grow up to be a high-flyer. He's John Lydgate, the medieval poet. Born in around 1370, he left the village to become a student at Oxford and in due course a Benedictine monk of St Edmund's Abbey in the nearby town of Bury (now Bury St Edmunds). But from Oxford his literary skills had carried him further afield. He became a follower and close family friend of the great Middle English poet Geoffrey Chaucer, travelling widely, as Chaucer himself did. Chivalric epic became his chosen genre, with topics that ranged from the Trojan Wars to the lives of Anglo-Saxon and late Roman-British martyrs; and when he died in about 1450, probably at Bury, he left behind a vast body of poetry. By his own later admission he'd misspent much of his village youth, and his schooldays had been largely wasted. But perhaps they hadn't been as wasted as he liked to boast.

Of course, what he scratched on the church wall may be no more than an admirer's greeting, or the opening words of a love poem. But to an archaeologist that's not really the interesting bit. What it reveals is that even in this remote village in rural England there could be at least one young person who somehow knew how to write and read music. To be able to do so would have been part of his education. He'd have been taught it by someone, and quite likely his classmates would have been taught it too.

Given the extraordinary wealth and beauty of extant medieval music manuscripts and their embellishments, small throwaway scraps like these may seem an obscure, even perverse, way to begin exploring the deep history of musical literacy. Their staves and notated melodies, such as they are, give us tantalisingly little to perform or to listen to. But in fact they are the first steps on a particularly charming archaeological trail.

CHAPTER THIRTEEN

Fanfares and foghorns: a brass trumpet from the River Thames

England, c.1400

For sheer drama, the exquisite gilded miniatures of the medieval manuscript known as the Welles Apocalypse surely match anything in the long history of Western painting, indeed the paintings of the world. Created in the early fourteenth century by a man called Peter d'Abernon, also known as Peter of Peckham, they include one especially memorable musical scene. Against a deep blue tiled backdrop stands a phalanx of seven slender figures clothed in long white gowns. They are obviously supernatural beings, or at least not the kind of people you would expect to meet in your medieval neighbourhood. They are unusually tall, for one thing, and they have feathered wings. And if this wasn't already enough to mark them out as angels, Peter has placed a circular disc – a nimbus, or halo – behind each head, and picked it out in brilliant gold foil. It's a gorgeous tableau, even by medieval standards. The six angels on our left support long, straight trumpets, also of glittering gold, with flared ends resting on the floor and narrow mouthpipes reaching up almost to their shoulders. But on their left, our right, their leader blows a seventh trumpet, held horizontally so that its sounds appear to blast out across the adjacent text. They seem to be drawn with startling attention to detail; but how realistic are they as portrayals of real instruments? This chapter is going to explore the degree to which images can be relied upon as evidence, in the face of the hard facts that archaeological discoveries provide.

There was a time not so long ago when, for want of more tangible proofs, historians used to mine pictures of this sort for details of ancient music technologies and ways of playing. Except where designs appeared sketchy, or showed clear signs of confusion, they had to be taken on trust, on the basis that, since they were of their time, they must be reasonably authentic, even accurate. Today we know that things are rarely that simple. Composition is everything in ancient art. In our modern technological world we habitually use our cameras and mobile devices to snap people, places and events that seem important to us. The results we get are technically realistic, and generally they carry no hidden meanings. This is not the case in painting. For traditional artists, the creative process has always been more complex, intricate and involved. Photorealism is not their aim, though they might draw from experience and even from life. Beauty too is to some extent by the by. The aim is to encapsulate a mood, an idea or a moment in a story. Imbued with symbolic meanings, a medieval work of art was typically created to convey or reinforce a message; so before we can begin to make use of any of the technical details it shows, we need first to unpick what art historians call its iconography: references that tell us what's really going on. We need somehow to guess the story and decide how far hidden meanings might have distorted some of the aspects that interest us.

To anyone familiar with scripture, as even the lowliest European peasants were in the Middle Ages, the sense of this particular scene would be self-evident. But for anyone who could read, it was spelled out by the words that accompany it. Written in medieval French, they read *E lui set aungeles ki aveient set busines se apparaillerent pur businer* – 'And before him were seven angels who had seven busines [and were] preparing themselves to play'. What we're looking at is an illustration of one of the apocalyptic visions of St John the Divine, preserved in the Book of Revelation. The King James translation of 1611 provides the context:

And I saw the seven angels which stood before God, and to them were given seven trumpets . . .

And the seven angels which had the seven trumpets prepared themselves to sound.

The first angel sounded, and there followed hail and fire mingled with blood, and they were cast upon the earth, and the third part of trees was burnt up and all green grass was burnt up.

So these musicians are not just musicians but part of the angelic host, and their trumpets are their principal weapons in what to a medieval mind must have been one of the most terrifying portrayals of divine power in the whole of the Bible. However, this doesn't mean that the artist hasn't taken inspiration from real instruments. Like bells and drums, the clamour of real trumpets had long formed the soundtrack to splendid and glorious events, religious and military and civic. To medieval people they were the ultimate acoustic projection of secular power and so (suitably presented) were appropriate to portrayals of divine wrath and revelation.

That strange word *busine* wasn't reserved solely for heavenly instruments. It's a regular medieval French word for this kind of trumpet. Trumpeters and their instruments are often referred to in official records. An English royal household document from around 1303 lists a grant equivalent to several hundred pounds in today's money, being disbursed to a certain 'Janin de Catalonia'. It's to buy him a new brass trumpet, and a year later he's awarded a silver one.

What emerges from records like Janin's, and from occasional images of real ceremonies, is the trumpet's dual function as, on the one hand, a thoroughly musical, melodic instrument, capable of a brilliant fanfare, and on the other, a military and ceremonial signalling device. In portrayals of ceremonies, celebrations and feasting, they are blown in pairs or ensembles. The players are typically costumed, their trumpets decked with flags, banners and pennants. One image from around 1500 shows four trumpeters perched high on balconies above the coronation of the French king Louis XII, each trumpet with its banner attached and the players' cheeks puffed out. But in another scene the same kind of instrument can also be seen in the hands of a solitary trumpeter, standing on the sterncastle of a ship at sea, making signals to other vessels in the fleet.

The imagined sounds of this naval kind of trumpeting suddenly became very real in the spring of 1984, when excavators made an astonishing discovery at Billingsgate in the City of London. Downstream from the original Old London Bridge, Billingsgate is now in the heart of London's financial district, the so-called Square Mile; but in the Middle Ages this part of the river was where much of the city's maritime trade and exchange took place. The shore was lined with wharves, and as the centuries went by they extended further and further out into the tideway, the ground made up with refuse and spent ballast from ships. But beneath all that backfill the old tidal shore remained, and now out of its waterlogged mud the team pulled four sections of a complete brass trumpet. It was in almost perfect condition.

How such a useful and expensive object could have come to be in such a place was a mystery. It seemed to be in working order. Maybe it was lost overboard from some river craft in an accident. Maybe it happened at night and no one noticed until it was too late. Maybe the crew were drunk and it was deliberately thrown into the river, in a moment of high spirits or mischief. We'll never know. At any rate, they didn't retrieve it. The four sections had evidently been bound or bagged together in some way; and there, in the fetid tidal mud, they were joined by all kinds of other detritus – including old shoes and a pair of loaded dice – to become part of the dismal litter, which is to say the magnificent archaeology, of London's dubious past.

The bundle consisted of four lengths of straight brass tubing, between forty-three and fifty centimetres long. One of them was the trumpet's conical 'bell'; another included a simple conical mouthpiece with a turned-over rim. There were small spherical knops on two of the tubes, and the traces of one on a third, more or less exactly in the places shown in the Welles Apocalypse. The bell lacked an elaborate 'garland' of the sort seen earlier carrying the names of the sixteenth-century trumpet-makers Louis Pesin and Michael Nagel; instead it's been reinforced with a plain strip of brass, attached with silver solder. But by some miracle, except for a couple of dents the whole instrument has somehow kept its original shape.

Images of music-making and the physical character of musical finds often disagree, but they can also complement one another. In this particular case the trumpet corroborates much of the image in its general aspects: in its overall structure and its approximate dimensions and proportions. But it does much more than that, so much more that in the final analysis it far outstrips the image for quantity and quality of detail. One of the most profound differences is in the way that, being material, we can interrogate it scientifically to expose its complex life story.

Much of that story is revealed in its surface details. When it first came to the conservation laboratory at the Museum of London, wet and shiny, the freshness of some surfaces was breathtaking. Preserved at one end of each of the straight tubes are traces of bruising and scratching where players have repeatedly push-fitted it into the next one. The lengths of the marks show exactly how snugly they fitted together and therefore how long the whole trumpet would have been. So far it closely matches the Apocalypse scene. But there's something significant about two of the sections: they seem to be made from metal of a slightly different colour, and to have been formed in a different way. The bell and the longest tube are brass, with seams of a hard silver solder, but the others are merely latten – a softer alloy – and joined with ordinary lead solder.

As we began to gauge the musical character of the instrument and its history, X-ray imaging provided a crucial piece of the puzzle. In the radiographs small blotches and streaks of darker metal showed up as pale patches (being less transparent to X-rays) and turned out to be soldered repairs to small punctures. It seems that like Louis Pesin's trumpet, the instrument has been repeatedly damaged and repaired. Indeed we can now see that the two latten sections are complete replacements, and this immediately raises a question. What exactly could they have replaced?

The question introduces a very particular musical complication, because one of the replacement parts includes that all-important element, the mouthpiece. In a fine musical instrument we'd expect the mouthpiece to be shaped inside like a little cup, with a narrow throat leading into the first section of tube. The cup and throat allow the player to articulate the notes precisely. This one has been formed simply by expanding the tube into a cone. There is no throat, as such. It's an unexpectedly coarse way of doing it. Could it be that the instrument has undergone a change of character, and purpose, mid-career: beginning its life as a musician's instrument, and ending it as a mere foghorn? Looking at the two original parts it does seem to have left its maker's workshop as a much more elaborate and sophisticated piece of kit.

Behind the bare bones of narratives of this sort, are hints of changing utility, of changing fashions and ultimately obsolescence. It's a salutary reminder that objects, like their owners, have changing fortunes. And of course, finite lives.

CHAPTER FOURTEEN

Pits of fire: bell-casting in medieval Transylvania

Sibiu, Romania, fourteenth century

In the summer of 1909, just a few years before the outbreak of the First World War, archaeologists were exploring the centre of the old Saxon city of Hermannstadt, now Sibiu, in southern Transylvania, when they found something that hadn't been seen before. They were working in the inner courtyard of the imposing Old Town Hall, constructed in the late fifteenth century over the remains of earlier buildings and yards, and there they came across a circular patch of disturbed earth, about three metres across. It had plainly been a pit of some sort, but why was it there? The practice in cases like this is to carefully remove the fill, making note of any layering of the soil and any objects and materials found within it, until eventually the bottom is reached and the depth and shape of the whole structure can be seen. This hole proved to be a deep one with sloping sides and a trampled floor some two and three-quarter metres below today's ground level. But there the remains of two hearths appeared. Among the surrounding debris were some small pieces of brassy-looking waste and a scatter of metal slag. It seems that someone had been using the pit to melt and pour hot metal.

What had they been making in such a deep hole? The first clue was in the location: it was right next to the old parish church. The second came more recently, when X-ray fluorescence and neutron activation analysis revealed the metal to be bronze, but a particularly hard bronze, known as bell-metal. As the name indicates, it's principally used for casting bells. The hardness of the metal makes a difference to the way a bell sounds: a bell cast from softer metal will sound less bright. But sound isn't everything. It also needs to withstand repeated sharp blows from the iron clapper when it's being rung, and if the alloy is too hard and brittle it's likely to crack. The coincidence of metal and location now made clear the purpose of the pit. Someone had dug it in order to cast a large, heavy bell, to be hung in the belfry high up in the nearby tower.

While it may appear counter-intuitive to dig a hole in the ground before casting a large bell, it was common practice in the Middle Ages. Surprising as it may seem in an age long before modern health and safety standards, one of the prime reasons may have been to keep people out of harm's way. Once the hole was finished, a clay mould was assembled on its floor, and when the clay had fully dried, the surrounding space was packed with earth or sand, right up to ground level, leaving only tubes through which the molten metal could be poured and hot gases could escape. Molten metal and steam are always hazardous and would have been best shielded, especially if the foundryman had an audience, which was more likely than not. People would probably have been queueing up to see any major casting. But it also brought with it a number of technical benefits.

Today bells are still sometimes cast in the same way, in spite of vastly improved casting technique and new ways of controlling the temperatures of both mould and metal. In the mountains of central Italy there's a foundry I know that still uses pits. It belongs to the Marinelli family, who have been making bells in the hill town of Agnone since the fourteenth century. The holes are backfilled when they aren't in use, mere circles of dark earth on the foundry floor, and you might walk straight over them without noticing they are there. Next to each pit is a furnace that can be fired with wood, electricity or gas, and there's a system of gutters through which the liquid metal can be poured. When I paid a visit on a dull rainy day in January last year, the workmen were crouching in one emptied pit, under floodlights, putting the finishing touches to a very large clay mould. Everything was dim outside, but the lights filled the pit and lit up the clay mould like a piece of prehistoric sculpture. There was a tension in the air and the thrill of impending danger. They told me that the pit meant that if anything should go badly wrong no one would get hurt. Its principal benefit, though, was that it would slow the cooling process and ensure a better casting.

Today the finished bell is usually winched out of the pit and, after fine-tuning, it's lifted onto the back of a truck for delivery to the customer. In the Middle Ages of course things were different. Transportation was risky, so instead of running a single, permanent foundry, foundrymen would cast the larger bells at point of use, as they'd done at Sibiu, and winch them directly into the belfry where they were to make their music. Several pits of this sort have been found during excavations in England, all of them near or even inside churches. My favourite was unearthed in 1974 in the small riverside town of Wallingford in Oxfordshire. It was roughly three and a half metres across, and like the Sibiu pit, its sides sloped down to a flat circular floor, more than three metres below today's ground surface. They were blackened by fire, and at the very bottom, in the first layer of soil to be backfilled after the pit had served its purpose, there were traces of wood ash. Near them were small pieces of coppery alloy. Once again the location told the tale. It was within a few metres of the site of the parish church. Sadly, no trace of the building can now be seen above ground: it fell into ruin and its building materials were recycled long ago, together with its bells. But documents from the time of King Henry III suggest that the church must have been built during or just before the thirteenth century. In 2010 another pit was uncovered in the small village of Easton in Cambridgeshire, very close to where I'm writing now. This time it was discovered *inside* a thirteenth-century stone belfry tower. From there the finished bell could have been winched straight into place.

These days, a bell ringing in a church tower can seem to be just another feature of the historic landscape, but these pits remind us that in their day they were so much more. They announced events in the life of the church and the community; they alerted people to dangers; and the measure of their importance is in the massive sacrifice of labour and materials involved in their making. Just digging the pit would have been a massive undertaking. Anyone who's ever planted a small rose bush with a spade can guess how much time and energy must have gone into creating a hole of that size. And digging was only the start. Add to it the task of gathering and preparing the right kind of clay for the mould, and the skill and patience needed to form it. Now think of the difficulty of sourcing the metals in the correct proportions, and the prodigious quantities of fuel needed to heat them to the pouring point of bell-metal at over 1,100 degrees Celsius, and you get some idea of the scale of the enterprise. Then there's the expense. Today the four hundred kilos of scrap copper and over a hundred kilos of tin or scrap pewter needed to make a tenor bell would cost around £3,500. Now imagine the mould, firing up the furnace and judging exactly when and how quickly to pour in the molten metal. All this would have demanded extraordinary commitment from the local community, as well as from the craftspeople doing the work.

Of course, when we find an old bell pit today the bell itself has long gone. As we saw in Thomas Brikar's shop in Oxford, absence of finished product is a perfectly normal feature of workplace debris. Yet there's still something eerie about a pit in this state: emptied of earth, and now cold and silent after the moments of high drama that it must have witnessed: it's as if we're looking into an empty slipway or dry dock where we know that a great ship like the *Titanic* was once built and fitted out, never to return. But there may still be signs to see if we know what to look for.

PART FOUR

Divided World

The Fourteenth to the Twelfth Century

As we descend ever deeper into the medieval world, there's going to be no less diversity to see, or to hear, in musical technologies and traditions of music-making. From the confines of our global village, the world inevitably seems to become more diverse, more disconnected with each century we retrace, and the journeys that separate cultures from one another become more arduous. In the fourteenth century the Old World is more profoundly isolated from the New than it was even in the middle of the fifteenth. But it's still one planet; all humans still share the same ultimate origins; and in spite of geographical separations, this ultimate kinship is going to reveal itself in some of the curious instruments that they made and played.

Along the way we'll unpack the curious case of the mouth harp, and how its tuning – like that of the tree-bark flute – is defined not by human cultural preferences but by universal laws of physics. We'll see how finds of iron gongs from Great Zimbabwe have recently been joined by a small key of tempered steel from a thumb-piano, or *mbira*, and discover what it means for the future of music's archaeology south of the Sahara. In Ireland we're going to examine the remains of harps that illustrate how peat bogs and swamp sediments can preserve objects in near perfect condition. And in Germany another case of 'vertical archaeology' – the archaeology of the built environment – will offer an impressive instance of household objects being reused to improve a building's resonance.

But first we need to travel to Precolumbian Mexico to investigate the phenomenon of the fired clay 'flower flute' of the Aztecs, an instrument with ominous connotations but one that illustrates more than just an authentic Native American musical experience. In it we can begin to discern some of the musical threads that connect all modern humans.

CHAPTER FIFTEEN

Flower flute: music and human sacrifice in the Valley of Mexico

Central Mexico, c.1350

There are many wonderful things to be enjoyed in museums and galleries around the world, objects of great beauty and triumphs of human ingenuity. But among them are also reminders that the past wasn't always a nice place. Some ancient objects hold memories of terrible times, and it seems that even musical collections can bear witness in this way. Music hasn't always been a leisure pursuit – a joyful, soothing, relaxing activity. It's provided the background to some dark and disturbing events. Sometimes it's even played a part in how they unfolded. And few musical events come darker or more disturbing than the rituals that have given us the flower flutes of Mexico.

There's nothing particularly sinister in the way they look under glass in a modern, well-lit museum. Neither do they sound in any way menacing when exact replicas of them are made and played. They are fine, splendidly preserved instruments; and as life is breathed back into their forms the tones that ring out can be bright and cheerful. It isn't the flutes that are the problem: it's the company they kept.

One fine example is on display in the music department of the Metropolitan Museum in New York. It's twenty-seven centimetres long, shaped from clay and fired in a kiln. It's been moulded in one piece, with a sleek, beak-like mouth tube to blow into; it has an oblong sound hole about halfway along its length, then a row of five neat finger holes, and at the other end it expands into a short, decorated cone. It looks like a slightly eccentric version of a modern school recorder. It's been beautifully finished too. While the clay was still damp and leathery, the surface was rubbed with a polishing tool, perhaps a round pebble, to give it an attractive gloss; and it's had a series of broad stripes painted onto it in thinly diluted clay of a different colour. During the firing the stripes have turned a fine dark red-ochre, contrasting pleasantly with the beige-pink background.

Two more flutes of a broadly similar sort can be seen in the Museum of Archaeology and Anthropology in Cambridge, and there are twelve more (and a lot of fragments) in the Ethnological Museum in Berlin. While there are differences in fabric and in the number of finger holes – some have just four – what they all have in common is the moulded decoration of their cones. If you look carefully you can see that each is made up of four quadrants, like the petals of a flower. It's this resemblance to a flower that gives the flutes their name.

You wouldn't guess that such pleasing little objects could hide a dark secret. The only clue is in another common detail: they've each been snapped violently in two and glued back together again. The glues are modern, the work of recent restoration, but the breaks are ancient – and it seems that they were all broken quite deliberately. It was no accident. The two parts were then placed in the earth together, and this too was intentional. They've been deposited with surprising delicacy, and it's clear from their numbers that it happened many times, over many years. What can it mean? To an archaeologist repetition is evidence of a cultural trait, a tradition, a ritual. But what sort of tradition could account for it? We're now on the shores of Lake Texcoco, in the Valley of Mexico as it was in the days before the arrival of Spanish drainage engineers; and, to put it mildly, things are about to get a little weird.

Part of the challenge that the flower flutes set us today is to do with their provenance, or rather the sketchiness of it. Because of the way they've been acquired by museums, we have no precise record of where or how most of them were discovered. We know that they were found somewhere in Mexico, but beyond that we have little detail. This is a pity, because it could have added so much to their story. But every cloud has its silver lining, and this one comes in the form of two European eyewitness accounts. The Franciscan friar Bernardino de Sahagún, who travelled to Mexico in 1529, has left us an explanation of their floral imagery that restores at least some of their original cultural meaning. From his *Historia general de las cosas de la Nueva España* or *General History of the Things of New Spain*, we learn that in Nahuatl, the Aztec language, the word for 'flute' is *tlapitzalli*, which means 'blown instrument'; sometimes it's also described as *tlapitzaya xochimecatl*, 'blown instrument bound with flowers'. Another fluent Nahuatl speaker, the Dominican friar Diego Durán, describes the shrill sound of its music in his *Historia de las Indias de Nueva España e Islas de Tierra Firme* or *History of the Indies of New Spain*, completed in around 1580. Fray Diego was no tourist from the refined cities of early-sixteenth-century Spain: he'd lived in Mexico since childhood, and like Fray Bernardino, he'd become steeped in its language and customs. So when he describes something as 'shrill' we have to assume that he knows what he's talking about.

And yet in the laboratory their shrillness isn't immediately obvious. They prove equally adapted to expressing gentler, sweeter and more melodious sentiments. In fact, with their multiple finger holes they can do pretty much all of the things that other flutes can do anywhere else in the world: whether it's performing elaborate and extended melodies or exchanging remote signals; whether it's imitating the calls of wild animals or creating new sound effects. Our only disappointment is that their exact tunings can no longer be determined: they allow you to play scales, but even a small fluctuation in the flow of your breath will significantly raise or lower the pitch of the notes, so they have no set values. On the other hand, from a player's point of view they offer generous scope for adjustment, to meet different tonal needs in musical improvisation or mimicry. Perhaps the Aztecs and other Nahua people didn't need potters to define and fix their scales for them; maybe flexibility was exactly what they wanted. If they'd wanted fixed scales the instruments could surely have been configured that way.

We may not know the tunes the Aztecs played, although some people suppose that they lie hidden within today's repertoire of Mexican traditional music; but we do know some of the things the flower flute came to be used for in Bernardino Sahagún's day. We can therefore begin to build up a sense of its special cultural and religious importance. I'm afraid the picture he paints is not for the squeamish, so if you don't want to know the gruesome facts, you might like to skip the next couple of paragraphs.

Sahagún illustrates his descriptions with brightly coloured miniatures, painted for him by indigenous artists. One sequence relates to a particular ceremony, possibly an annual event. The first few images seem inoffensive enough. One shows a man standing, wearing sandals with red ribbons, a grey-and-white loincloth, and what appears to be a net of knotted ropes like a cape around his neck and shoulders. In his left hand he's carrying something that looks like a lit cigar, with a wisp of smoke emerging from the outer end, and a large lily flower. With his right he's playing a flute with a conical bell. So far so good.

But the next sequence comes as a surprise. Here, on the top of a temple mound, we see the same man, surrounded by priests, who are opening up his body with a razor-sharp stone blade and preparing to cut out his beating heart. Scattered on the bloodstained temple steps below him, like so much litter, are four broken flutes.

Sahagún tells us that the sacrificial victim has been on a year-long spree of feasting, drinking and dancing. During this time he's become the musical manifestation on earth of the jaguar god of night, Tezcatlipoca. But now it's spring, and his time is up. He's been ferried across Lake Texcoco by canoe and escorted under guard to a temple called Tlapitzahuayan on the eastern shore. As he climbs the steps to meet his fate, he carefully snaps his flutes and, according to ancient custom, drops the pieces. It's all part of the ritual. Then, finally, on the top of the mound in the broad light of day, the priests slaughter him.

This ceremony, says the friar, is performed every April without fail, and it now seems probable that similar rituals were performed at other, less important temples to honour the same jaguar-god. It means that numerous young men were likely killed in this way every year, across the region. Certainly, flutes were broken and deposited in a similarly ritualised way. It's hard to put a reliable estimate on the scale of the phenomenon, but even if there were only fifty such sanctuaries within the wider territory of modern Mexico, each performing the sacrifice annually over, say, two or three centuries, a very substantial number of flower flutes must still be out there, somewhere. Pottery can become broken into small fragments, even shattered, but generally speaking, it's one of the toughest materials known to archaeology and pieces tend to survive.

It's easy to become absorbed by cultural details of this sort when they have such a fascinating story to tell. But marvellous and terrifying as they are, the instruments also contribute to a much bigger picture and to a still greater mystery. It stems from their curious resemblance to ancient instruments found in Europe and Asia: flutes and pipes with finger holes. Today we tend to take such things a little for granted, and to imagine the concept that lies behind them to be self-evident: an obvious way to generate more than one or two notes from a single tube. But as we search for the origins of musical ideas, it's worth considering what an ingenious device the finger hole really is. Just think about it for a moment. It means you don't need to make multiple pipes, like the pipes of an organ or traditional panpipes, and you don't need to bind them together. It's several tubes in one. It's both labour-saving and space-saving. To conceive it from scratch must have needed a particular way of thinking, so it seems somehow significant that people in the New World and the Old should each have thought of it. Received wisdom tells us that the two traditions ought not to be related. The Bering Land Bridge between Asia and Alaska, which Stone Age migrants had walked across to populate the Americas, was interrupted by rising sea levels around twelve thousand years ago, and became too tough a route to support regular traffic of goods and ideas. The balance of opinion is that the wild Atlantic Ocean presented an even stronger barrier to East–West travel, at least until medieval shipwrights created vessels strong enough to survive the dangerous voyage. All of this poses the obvious question: could Native Americans have inherited the principle from a common ancestor, back in the remote depths of prehistory? Or did they invent or discover it for themselves, at some time in their remote past, quite independently of the rest of humanity?

In fact, it's part of a familiar archaeological puzzle. Like biological species, creative minds can sometimes come up with surprisingly similar solutions to problems when exposed to the same sets of circumstances, and they can evolve in parallel. One of the striking features of the Americas is the way that, in spite of their insulation from Eurasiatic influences, Precolumbian technologies have mirrored certain Eurasiatic technologies that developed long after the Americas were first populated: the development of crops and animal husbandry; irrigation, stone architecture and urbanisation; canoes, ceramics and textiles; complex religion, writing and, finally, even books. The Aztecs were producing books and keeping libraries long before their encounter with the Spanish. So why not flutes? Was it something in our shared DNA?

CHAPTER SIXTEEN

Fiddles for gewgaws: a 'mouth harp' from medieval Trondheim

Norway, c.1300, and introducing Fredericksburg, Virginia

Of all the instruments of music humans have ever devised, nothing quite matches a good mouth harp for cheerful entertainment. Otherwise known as a Jew's harp or jaws harp and by a hundred other folk names in different languages, its little metal frame and twanging spring are up there with the fiddle and the harmonica, the penny whistle and the concertina, as the perfect antidote to melancholy. It's very small, not much bigger than a door key. It's also surprisingly robust. You can carry it with you almost anywhere (though it's been known to raise a few eyebrows at airport security). Its lively, bouncy rhythms make it the natural accompaniment to dance, and along the way it's capable of all manner of jolly and comedic effects. It's capable of expressing a range of emotions too. There's a seductive quality about its gentler sounds, especially the soft sweet overtones that give it its melodic range. Mouth harps – *Mundharfen* in German – were at one time notorious for their (alleged) persuasive power when used by young men to serenade eligible young women and girls. In Vienna they were regarded as such a nuisance that the city fathers banned them, or at least the sweetest-sounding silver ones. But what makes mouth harps additionally fascinating for our purpose is that they are tough enough to survive being buried in the ground. And this means they turn up surprisingly often during excavations.

In the maker's smithy the harp's frame begins life as a single rod of iron or brass, about the length of a pencil and around half the thickness. It's hammered and filed to a square cross section, then bent round into a rigid oval loop with two parallel extensions, or 'jaws', so that it looks like a two-pronged fork. And finally a long slender leaf spring of thin tempered steel is fixed between the jaws. It's tapered towards one end, while the other, broader end is hammered firmly into a notch in the centre of the loop, leaving it free to vibrate like the springboard on the edge of a swimming pool. It's related to the harmonica reeds we've seen at battlefield sites in the United States, except that here it isn't air flow or air pressure that makes it vibrate, but you the player, twanging the turned-over end with the tip of your forefinger or your thumb. Once you've mastered the technique, it's a delight to play, especially if the instrument has a light, responsive spring, fitted to the most exact tolerances.

The way the mouth harp generates such great music is another example of musical genius. By itself, held loosely in the fingers of your left hand, the sound it makes when you strum it is faint and quickly dies; it has no power and even less resonance. But pressed against your front teeth and sealed by your lips it's an instrument transformed. It rings. It becomes almost your second voice. If you close the very back of your mouth with the back of your tongue, as if to say 'ung', a twang on the spring will set up a fine resonance inside the hollow of your mouth. But something else happens too. In addition to the steady note from the spring itself, which doesn't ever alter, you can also hear a quite separate, higher-pitched note. This is an overtone, a 'flageolet tone' or harmonic. And if at the same time you raise and lower the front of your tongue, as if to say 'eee' and 'aah', you'll hear this upper note change. But unlike your singing and speaking voice, it isn't infinitely variable. As you experiment, you'll discover that it's trying to play one particular musical scale.

It's what's called a gapped scale, made up of the notes of the 'harmonic series' and it works in the same way as the tree-bark flute, and with the same result – except that this time it's your own airways that are the pipe. You've become one with the instrument: it's more like singing than playing. By itself the harp is a mere spring in a frame. It just supplies the vibration. It's a single-tone generator. The part that gives it its musical power is your own body – and your sense of pitch and rhythm.

It took many years and a good deal of effort by many people to tease out the instrument's archaeological story. The first time I saw an ancient one for myself was in 1975. It was from a village called Meols (pronounced 'Mells') near Hoylake on the Wirral peninsula. It has a neat little brass frame, corroded to a greenish-grey colour, with long jaws and a small loop where the spring was once attached. There was even a trace of rust-brown stain in the central notch. There was no indication of how old it might be. However, bit by bit, finds from other excavations were beginning to put dates to the instrument's development.

In the 1970s and 80s, Britain and Scandinavia were fast becoming archaeological hot spots. We've already met one mouth harp from a sixteenth-century layer at Fast Castle, the dramatic clifftop stronghold in the Anglo-Scottish borders. It had been preserved as an X-ray shadow inside an otherwise shapeless lump of rust. The iron frame had a loop that was somewhere between the larger oval loops of nineteenth-century Austrian instruments and the small loop of the Meols find. So, did this mean that smaller loops indicate an earlier date? It was already beginning to look that way.

Another telling discovery was made in 2020 during excavations at Fredericksburg, Virginia. It was from the site of a late-eighteenth-century house, and at first it appeared to be just one of more than fifteen hundred iron concretions that had to be X-rayed. But the images revealed a ghostly outline hidden inside, and again, someone with sharp eyes recognised the telltale shape. It's the kind with the larger loop of nineteenth-century instruments. The all-important spring is long gone, of course, as it is in the overwhelming majority of cases.

However, there are some happy exceptions. One was unearthed in 1972 by archaeologists working in the Norwegian city of Trondheim. The site was only a block away from the modern public library where we've already encountered a child's clay tobacco-pipe flute. Deep underground were the remains of wooden huts and timber trackways that once ran close to the medieval riverbank. The earth containing the mouth harp had been deposited there some time between the eleventh century and the late fourteenth. About nine millimetres of its spring remained. Another was found in a medieval layer in the cathedral city of Lincoln, with about a centimetre and a half remaining; encrusted with corrosion of course, but otherwise intact. Both instruments seem likely to have failed as a result of metal fatigue, because the break is exactly where modern mouth-harp springs tend to break.

I lost a spring myself one evening while I was playing to a live audience, and it snapped in exactly the same place. It was a pity because it had been a lovely little instrument with the sweetest tone, given to me by an old friend who'd had it made by a Norwegian maker in the mountains of Valdres. I was playing a brisk jig when I noticed that the pitch of the fundamental note was beginning to slip, like a bagpipe springing a leak. It was a puzzling sensation, until suddenly there was a clattering sound and in the ensuing silence I felt the spring loose and cold on my tongue. I guess that it's failures of just this sort that we have to thank for so many instruments ending up as archaeological finds. Replacing a broken spring must have been a specialist job, so in most circumstances it would have been easier (and probably cheaper) to throw it away and buy a new one. It's certainly true today, though I still hope to get mine restored some day. The next time I'm passing through Valdres, perhaps.

If piecing together a timeline for mouth harps was difficult, their deeper backstory proved even harder to fathom. We could now confidently place it in Europe in the early Middle Ages. But where exactly had they come from? And how long ago? The mystery had something about it of the boatswain's whistles that we saw in an earlier chapter. Back in the 1940s, examples had been found in or close to early Anglo-Saxon cemeteries in Surrey and Kent, and were believed by association to be nearly fifteen hundred years old.

Other finds suggested Roman and even pre-Roman dates. The trouble was that on closer inspection they all proved difficult to substantiate. It wasn't that a Saxon or Roman date was intrinsically impossible, or even unlikely, it's just that the facts didn't quite add up. Simply being found *near* an Anglo-Saxon grave doesn't make something Anglo-Saxon. Other finds were demonstrably ancient, but then turned out not to be mouth harps at all. One iron frame was found under the floor of a Roman house in Somerset – a perfect proof of its age – but was in fact merely the looped handle of a door key. Since then, all further finds excavated have remained steadfastly medieval, or later.

It's a fascinating riddle. Once again, an instrument, and a whole musical tradition, seems to be making its first archaeological appearance when it's already complete and fully formed. Absolutely nothing in the shape or manufacture of the oldest finds suggests the trial-and-error process that would show it to be newly invented – that sense of experiment evident in the earliest Caribbean steelpans, for instance, or the early years of sound recording. Might the source have been elsewhere, or in another material that was less robust and so hasn't survived?

It's a guess that's recently proved correct. The material in question is indeed a softer one – animal bone – but the date and place have come as quite a shock. Recent discoveries in burials in northern China and Inner Mongolia have shown that fully functioning instruments made from bone were being played there long before the thirteenth century. They were in use at least as early as the Neolithic period, around four *thousand* years ago. One site alone has produced twenty of them. The frame is typically a long thin strip of bone, with a slot down the middle to contain the delicate bone spring, carved all-in-one. The instrument corresponds, it's thought, to an instrument named *huang* from the second century BC, in the ancient Chinese encyclopedia of inventions known as the 'Book of Origins' or *Shiben* 世本.

What cultural connections would link Neolithic China with the European Middle Ages? It seems we must still be missing a great many pieces of the puzzle. Because even four thousand years ago, their designs seem no closer to anything that we would recognise as a primitive, experimental state.

But for students of European mouth harps, and for world music more broadly, perhaps the most thought-provoking aspect of the Chinese discoveries rests with the instrument's two most distinctive musical features: the scale of notes that it invariably defines, and the presence beneath those notes of a constant held note, to which all the other notes are tied by mathematical proportion. Known as a drone or 'pedal', in this case it doesn't just define the framework of the scale within which we can play. It imposes it. And what's especially remarkable is that it does it in a manner that's both universal and inevitable: true for all time and regardless of material or medium. It's those 'flageolet tones' again, of the harmonic series. What might our ancient ancestors' exposure to their strange ethereal tones have meant for their developing sense of musical pitch? What might their exposure to drones mean for the way we now imbue melody with a sense of 'centre' and 'home' – which is to say our sense of key? These musical questions have archaeological implications, so we're going to be returning to them again, in their proper place.

Chapter Seventeen

South of the Sahara: musical finds from Great Zimbabwe

Zimbabwe, c.1500 or earlier

Every once in a while we hear a piece of archaeological news which hints that some day we may have to change the way we think about the ancient world. With a steady turnover of new musical discoveries hitting the headlines each year, every new find adds a little more detail to our sound-picture of the past. But now and then something extraordinary comes along, something that really makes researchers sit up. I came across one just the other day. It was from southern Africa, a part of the world that in recent years has given us many fascinating new insights into our origins. But this wasn't another prehistoric cave or the remains of a new kind of early human. It was a small metal object, recovered from a layer of domestic waste during ground works for a visitor car park. It's not especially old. It's late medieval at best. But if it's what archaeologists think it is, its identification could signal an end to a problem that's been hampering all attempts to imagine a truly archaeological future for Africa's musical past, and the deep origins of its musical traditions. It seems to be one, just one, of the iron keys from a *mbira*, a traditional Shona thumb-piano.

At first glance a thumb-piano has no obvious connection with our prehistoric origins, and a single key has even less. This one is small, and rusty, and is clearly not prehistoric: it could be from the sixteenth or even the seventeenth century. But it may just mark the beginning of a new chapter in music's archaeology south of the Sahara.

It was found at one of the most magnificent archaeological sites in equatorial and southern Africa: the medieval stone-built city of Great Zimbabwe, in Masvingo Province. Just over two thousand kilometres south of the equator, and nearly a thousand metres above sea level, the Highveld is a landscape of grasslands and rocky hills dotted in their natural state with zebrawood and baobab trees. It tends to be dry and hot, except between December and February when it rains. To the north of the site a hilltop complex known as the Hill Ruins marks the earliest settlement in the area, and consists of drystone enclosures. They make an impressive display of Shona prosperity and power, and were obviously meant to. The walls of one enclosure were decorated with six fine soapstone figures of birds of prey, which are modern Zimbabwe's national symbol. Now a UNESCO World Heritage Site, discoveries in and around its ruins have shown that building began during the eleventh century – the time of the Postclassic period in Mesoamerica, the Song Dynasty in China and the start of the European Middle Ages. Excavations have unearthed many fascinating objects, from gold beads and soapstone carvings to agricultural tools. There are quantities of broken pottery and residues from metal smelting and working, using copper, gold, iron and bronze. Finds of sorghum and millet seeds, as well as bones from beef cattle, tell us what people were eating; and we know some of the luxury goods they were importing, including ceramics from Persia and even Ming porcelain from China. Among the indigenous finds were the first tangible signs of music.

There were three elaborate bell-like objects, made of sheet iron and heavily corroded. They resembled traditional African percussion instruments that ethnomusicologists call 'gongs', which is to say bells without clappers, designed to be struck by the hand or with a stick or a nail. Looking at them today is to be confronted with another musical puzzle. But it's a puzzle that will hold further pointers to music's ultimate origins.

It's difficult to know exactly when and where they've been made. They could be the products of a local craft tradition, but they could equally have come from further afield. Anthropologists have argued that they originated somewhere to the west, in the upper catchment of the Congo River system, and were traded to Zimbabwe overland. Nevertheless we know that metals were being worked at the site, and it's hard not to wonder whether the theory might owe something to the story of their discovery.

It's a story that makes lamentable reading. The finder of those first three gongs was a man called James Bent. Bent was an antiquarian rather than a scientist, and it seems his notion of archaeology went little further than digging for gold. Indeed, in 1891, supported by Cecil Rhodes's British South Africa Company, gold was what he was mainly tasked with finding. For his own part he was a collector of things, but even though his interests were broadly historical, it was far from the impartial history that we expect nowadays: it was history with a strongly ideological dimension, and the ideology was colonial. The Europeans were keen to justify their rule by finding proof, as they saw it, that the native cultures of the African interior were (and had always been) intrinsically inferior: incapable of proper political and economic organisation and therefore unable to develop their lands for themselves. It was to be one of archaeology's darkest hours, and it's also an object lesson in how field research and study should never be done. Bent's successor as excavator, Richard Hall, was far worse, intellectually and politically. Under his curatorship of the site, a major excavation in 1902 involved the systematic removal of every piece of evidence that might credit the Shona with its creation, with the description of the removed layers as 'the filth and decadence of Kaffir occupation'. It's small comfort to know that Bent failed to find the vast deposits of gold he was looking for, or that Hall was sacked when his methods came to the attention of his archaeological peers. Yet for all Hall's faults, among the many cultural artefacts that were saved, and that fortunately still survive, are six more pairs of double gongs.

How can we make best sense of all these instruments? Are they just gongs, for signalling, or might there be something more musical to them? If their coatings of rust are set aside, it's possible to see that they've been made with considerable skill and ingenuity. Formed from thin iron sheet, they are essentially hollow vessels, and there are two distinct forms. One is a single gong about the shape and size of a deflated rugby ball. It has a single slit that runs from end to end, and ornate iron loops for hanging. Shaped on an anvil or a last, it's been constructed in two halves, like the small European jingle bells from La Salle's trading ship *La Belle*, and hammer-welded together. The paired gongs are configured somewhat differently, but evidently created in the same tradition of panel-beating and smithing. They each have two open bell-like resonators in the shape of champagne flutes, mounted side by side and connected across the top by a rigid U-shaped handle. The result looks like an upturned double egg cup. Each cup, so to speak, is made from two flat oblong metal panels, rounded at one end, shaped to form the hollow halves of a cylinder. Standing on a flat surface with the loop uppermost, the whole structure is about thirty centimetres tall. It certainly looks as if it's meant for making sounds, and it would undoubtedly have resonated when struck with a stick or even tapped with a fingernail. And this is where we start to glimpse its true colours, as a fully musical instrument.

Back in its day, burnished to a high gloss as iron things often were, each gong would have flashed and glinted in the sun like a set of modern Caribbean steelpans, and like the pans it would have been well adapted to elaborate and delicate musical expression. The earliest steelpans show how industrial raw materials and an apparently simple music technology can achieve complex and sophisticated musical results, and the gongs seem equally capable of generating more musical pitches than we might expect. Think of a dreamy love song played by a steelpan ensemble, or the distant music of a flock of iron-belled sheep grazing peacefully on a Greek hillside, and you get the idea. Think of the subtle, sweet sounds of a gamelan orchestra ringing out on a warm starry night in Bali. There's nothing intrinsically 'heavy metal' about heavy metal.

The science of acoustics tells us that even one single gong must have been able to generate more than one texture of sound, depending on where it was struck and with what. Equally fascinating, it reveals that with their bilateral symmetry and leaf-shaped cross sections, each gong of each conjoined pair would have been capable of sounding at least two musical tones quite distinct in their musical pitch. This naturally means at least four notes. So what we're looking at is no simple instrument of percussion: the evidence hints at tunefulness and melody. In short, we're seeing the material footprint of the complex rhythmic, textural and melodic patterns of traditional African music.

It's an observation that's amply supported by eyewitness reports. The American journalist Henry Morton Stanley heard gongs being played at a place called Urangi on the Congo River in February 1877, writing:

> The great chief of Urangi made his presence known by *sounding* his double iron gong. The gong consisted of two large iron bell-shaped instruments, connected above by an iron handle, which, when beaten with a short stick with a ball of india-rubber at the end, *produce very agreeable musical sounds*.

Another Western traveller in the Congo, the Bohemian explorer Emil Holub, writing four years later, describes the chief of the Barotse's household musicians. Their instruments, he says, include small iron bells and 'a double gong without a clapper'. The gongs might well have been used to perform some practical duties, but in the Congo in the nineteenth century at least, their cultural milieu was evidently musicanship as we know it.

But it's the recent discovery of the *mbira* key in the car park at Great Zimbabwe that now brings melodic music fully centre stage. The find was made by the sharp-eyed archaeologist Shadreck Chirikure. If you haven't come across a modern *mbira*, imagine a carved wooden plaque about fifteen centimetres square, with three edges upraised like the edges of a tray. Fixed along the rear edge is a metal rod or bar, maybe three millimetres in diameter, and trapped under it are the ends of the keys: a set of slender leaf springs. They are made of forged iron or steel, like flattened nails, and most importantly they are of different lengths. Clamped by their thicker ends with their flattened ends pointing towards you, they resemble the reeds of a harmonica, or the spring of a mouth harp.

If you place your fingertips under the wooden plaque, as you might when using some hand-held device, you can pluck the free ends with your thumbs. The sound it produces is as soft and as pleasing as you want to make it. But the real music is in the range of pitches that the different lengths of key allow. If the power of melody was implicit in the designs of the excavated gongs, it's obvious in the thumb-piano: it's above all else a melodic instrument. Its springs are arranged like keys on a keyboard, precisely to enable tunes to be played. And because each spring can be individually adjusted, the instrument can be tuned, and retuned, according to need.

In a continent where small musical fragments like this have seldom been found and recorded, or recognised as musical, our sense of music's remote past has until now been limited to what we've felt we could reasonably infer from music as it's made today and in the recently remembered past. The *mbira* key might change everything. It suggests that whole new archaeologies of music may be out there and ready to be written, waiting only for someone with energy and time to start searching. Professor Chirikure may have found only one small spring, but like so many unexpected musical finds before it, it could usher in a whole new set of opportunities – and challenges – for future investigation.

Sounds of springtime. Sliding the final piece into a fresh willow bark flute. (Prologue)

All quiet. Steel reed-plate from a mouth organ, lost by a soldier of the American Civil War. (Chapter 1)

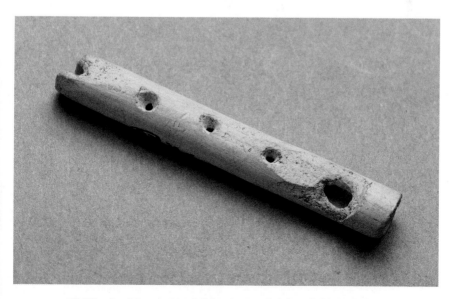

Child's play. Norwegian children's toy whistle refashioned from an old clay tobacco-pipe. (Chapter 3)

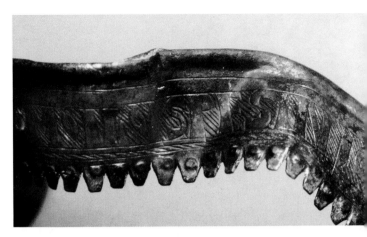

Intimations of mortality. Garland from the bell of a ruined trumpet, giving the name of the maker and the date: 'Lois Pesin', 1567. (Chapter 8)

Fingerboard from a violin lost in the explosion that sank *Kronan* in 1676. (Chapter 6)

'Music the mermaids love'. Boatswain in a galley directing the rowers with his whistle. Sicilian quilt *c*.1380. (Chapter 9)

The Last Trump. Angels with straight trumpets from the Welles Apocalypse. (Chapter 13)

Sounds of gaiety and fun. Mouth harp from a medieval English city. (Chapter 16)

Now you hear me. Medieval singers' gallery deep within the west front of Lichfield Cathedral. (Chapter 20)

Playing in the cracks. Bone flutes found among craft residues in 11th-century Schleswig.
(Chapter 21)

Alien landscape. Electron micrograph of finger wear on a medieval flute. (Chapter 21)

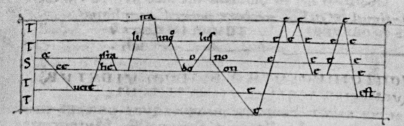

BICVONQVE ERGO IN QVOLIBET melo huius
modi reppereris inceruallū quale hic inter silla
bas.ec.œ.ce.vel.ra.be.vel.do.o.vel.no.on.semiconiū
esse non dubites. Vbi uero caltē discrepancies uoces.
ut.li.ica.vel.ca.in.vel.lus.no.vel.ce.ue.vel ultimā
non.œ primā est.t ipsā primā est.œ ei ultimam.
tonus sine dubio erit.Ja ū inter.re.œ is.œ he.
œ.li.œ quo.œ do.semiconii atq; coni est inter
uallū.Cecera pqualtē œ in directū dicunt.ut ue
re.œ ista.œ inquo.

Hitting the right note. Musical experiment in an 11th-century manuscript,
showing the strings of a lyre becoming a musical stave. (Chapter 22)

Liquid notes. Whistling bird on a Peruvian terracotta
flask, 8th century. (Chapter 24)

A little bird told me. A piece of musical street art in 21st-century Italy. (Chapter 25)

Tongue twister. King David composing the Psalms in an 8th-century English miniature. (Chapter 25)

Shape in the sand. The ghost lyre
of Prittlewell, England, c.AD 600.
(Chapter 26)

The man in Grave 58. Bones, furniture
and a complete lyre *in situ*, Trossingen,
Germany, AD 580. (Chapter 28)

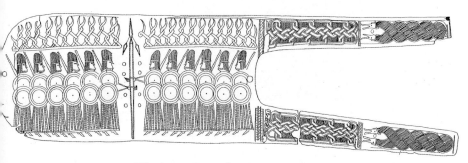

Warriors or Disciples? Images etched
on a waterlogged lyre sound board, Germany, AD 580. (Chapter 28)

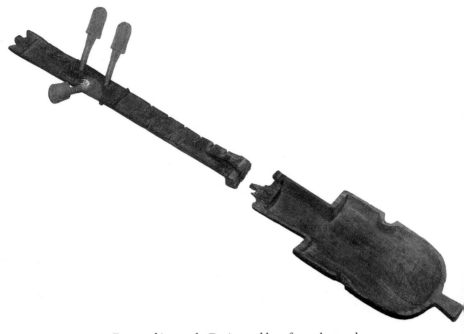

Frets and intervals. Desiccated lute from the tomb
of a Byzantine woman, Egypt, 6th century. The frets
on the neck of this instrument embody the tunings
of the scales it played. (Chapter 29)

Roman ambition. Rotating bronze sleeve of a *tibia*
from the River Thames in London, probably
3rd century. (Chapter 32)

CHAPTER EIGHTEEN

Preserved in peat: a medieval harp from an Irish bog

County Antrim, thirteenth to twelfth century

Of all the weird and wonderful places where chance and circumstance have conspired to preserve evidence of music's distant past, few are more atmospheric – and few have been more productive – than ancient wetlands. As we've seen already, the silted-up margins of river estuaries are especially good at preserving things like brass trumpets and whistles, accidentally lost from boats. We know how well the black, sulphur-smelling silts on the sea bed preserve wooden instruments and their fragile fittings, lost when sailing ships fell victim to storms or were sunk in battle. Now we're going to discover that an abundance of fresh water can also preserve music's archaeological story, and we're going to return to one of my favourite instruments: the harp. We've met remains of harps on the seabed near Brighton and in a ruined castle in Wales. We've seen a place where they were made and repaired in medieval Oxford. In this chapter we're going to venture into the mysterious world of swamps.

Today the world's surviving wetlands are very much in the news, as we begin to appreciate their function as 'carbon sinks', sequestering carbon out of the atmosphere and locking it up in layer upon layer of dead plant material. In the past, however, the decayed organic material they contain – peat or turf – proved valuable as fuel and fertiliser, and so swamps were often drained and the peat extracted on an increasingly industrial scale. Latterly, archaeologists have come to realise that their accumulated layers of dead vegetation preserve the story of our changing world through hundreds, even thousands of years: changes recorded by the presence of so-called biological markers, blown in, or washed in, from the surrounding countryside. Among them are the embedded remains of beetles, seeds and pollen grains, showing how and when their surrounding landscapes have changed.

When ancient people were drawn to marshes or the edges of swampy lakes it was primarily for the resources they offered. Water birds and deer took refuge there, and the waters teemed with fish. Reeds provided thatching for roofs, willow for wickerwork screens, peat for fire to drive out the winter cold. But the deer weren't the only ones to see those wetlands as a potential refuge. The large swamps in particular also provided safety for people, from persecution or pursuit. And if wild wetlands came to occupy a unique place in human experience, inevitably they also became a screen onto which to project the myths and legends people told in verse and song.

To the tenth-century composer of the Old English poem *Beowulf* they were the domain of serpents and ogres:

> *Wæs si grimma gæst   Grendel haten*
> There was a grim demon,   Grendel / he was named,
>
> *mære mearc-stapa   se þe moras heold*
> notorious outlaw,   who the marshes / owned /
>
> *fen ond fæsten;   fifel-cynnes eard*
> fen and fastness;   in the monsters' homeland
>
> *won-sæli wer   weardode hwile,*
> [this] woebegone being   had dwelt long,
>
> *siþðan him Scyppend   forscrifen hæfde . . .*
> since / him / our Creator   had condemned . . .

And later:

> *Ða com of more   under mist-hleoþum*
> Then came from the swamp,   under cover of mist,

> *Grendel gongan,   Godes yrre bær*
> Grendel, stalking.   God's wrath he bore.

Swamps are dangerous enough at the best of times: stray into one, in its natural state, and you can quickly get lost in the tangle of tall reeds and undergrowth. Whether it's the Cambridgeshire Fens or the swamps of East Texas, take just one careless step and you might find yourself in serious trouble. I remember one such place from my own childhood in the north of England. We found it a magical place by day but we didn't like to linger there after dusk. There were deep, dark pools and creeks into which you could easily come to grief. In the olden days, there might have been dangers of a human kind too. Like heaths and forests, desert wastes and the open sea, swamps lay outside the norms of everyday life, lending themselves to activities of questionable propriety, making them still more apt to children's nightmares. Yet in spite of this, ancient people still found ways of living in or beside them, and they made music there too.

All over the world people chose to build their houses, sometimes whole villages, on small islands or balanced on wooden stilts and piled platforms. Some still do. And when the water became so silted up that their boats could no longer navigate it, or the pools became choked with reeds, they laid down wooden planks and hurdles as walkways to find their way across them. Even so, danger was never far away, and this may perhaps explain what happened next. Quite soon they began to sacrifice some of their more valued possessions to the deep water. And that has proved a good thing for music's archaeology.

Exactly why and how people set about making such gestures is still a matter of debate. No doubt their motives varied. But among the things they deposited in this way were musical instruments. In later chapters we'll see some astonishing bog-finds from the Bronze and Iron Ages, deposited between two thousand and four thousand years ago. But our story begins with three harps discovered in peat bogs in Ireland. One of them we've already seen in Chapter 5.

Found at the beginning of the nineteenth century, it's dated 'Anno Domini 1621' and inscribed with the name of Sir John fitz Edmund Fitzgerald, of Cloyne on the south coast of Ireland. The neck is intricately carved with animal figures, and at the end nearest the player's ear it's been shaped as though it's emerging from a wolf's gaping jaws. A second and slightly older harp was reportedly found in the early 1840s, when a landowner had his workmen dig a channel to drain a shallow lake near Ballinderry, in County Westmeath. As the lake water drained away, as if by magic a submerged mound revealed itself. All around and across it were vast quantities of discarded animal bones interspersed with abandoned items of personal equipment and clothing – bone combs and metal tweezers, dress accessories and adornments. And with them were the remains of this second harp.

None of its wooden parts have survived, only the brass fittings. But someone had the bright idea of mounting them on a reconstructed wooden frame, and this model and the original mounts are still preserved in the National Museum in Dublin. A reinforcement from the side of the neck, following the curved line of the tuning pins, contains no fewer than thirty-five peg holes. A metal reinforcement of this sort strongly implies metal pegs, since its edges would have cut into bone or wood, and this in turn suggests the use of metal strings. All of which just goes to show what a fine and expensive piece of equipment it must have been. And this poses a number of questions, not least how, once again, such an instrument, or pieces of an instrument, could have come to be lost in a bog. Did someone simply throw it into the water, like so much rubbish? Or was it consciously deposited there? If it was, why were none of the other parts found?

The third piece in this strange jigsaw puzzle emerged from yet another bog, about fifty years later; and paradoxically it proves to be the oldest of the three. With each find we're stepping backwards in time. The name of the place is Carncoagh, in County Antrim, and again, it's a part of the harp's wooden superstructure: its neck or 'string arm'. But this time it's been a smaller instrument without metal fittings. Made from a single beam of wood, it's just thirty-three centimetres long and about twenty-five millimetres thick, with a shallow curve. At one end there's evidence of a socket, a mortice, put there to receive the top of the forepillar, and at the other it curves round to form a tenon that would have fitted into a socket in the top of the sound box. Drilled through the mid-line of the beam is a row of holes for tuning pegs. There are just thirteen of them, and their diameters closely match those of the medieval bone pegs encountered at Oxford. It's from a much simpler and probably earlier type of instrument. But how early exactly? It's a mystery that takes a little unravelling.

Initially there was some doubt as to where exactly it was found, but now we know. Since 1882 peat-cutters had been at work in the bogs belonging to two adjacent communities, Carncoagh and Lisnacroghera, near Broughshane in the north-east of Ireland. A lake, part of the Clough or Clogh Water, had been partially drained, giving access to the peat deposits around its margins; and buried in the peat the cutters started finding large timber posts as well as ancient iron tools and weapons. One eyewitness, the Irish antiquarian W. J. Knowles, reported in 1897 that the bog of Lisnacroghera 'appears to be exhausted of its treasures now, but in neighbouring tenements of bog an occasional "find" turns up. Two objects were found during the past year, one of which I believe is a portion of a harp.' He evidently meant Carncoagh, and fortunately he also made and published a good line drawing of the instrument, with a scale in inches.

Its shape is almost exactly the same as the harps we see in early medieval pictures, particularly those of the eleventh to thirteenth centuries. A carved ivory casket of about 1200 from the Rhineland, for example, now in the British Museum, a harp with just this shape of neck in a scene from the medieval romance of Tristram and Yseult. Another can be seen in the beautiful early-thirteenth-century Iona Psalter, in the National Library of Scotland, where it's being played by the Old Testament King David. Both the casket and the psalter show a small instrument, maybe seventy-five centimetres tall.

We can imagine the Carncoagh harp's cheerful tone, strung with animal gut or horsehair. None of its tuning pegs survives, and there's been no sign of the forepillar or the hollow sound box. Our eyewitness explains: 'I have requested the owner of the tenement of bog to be on the look-out next season for the remaining portions.' But it seems he drew a blank. The absence of the hollow sound box is hardly surprising: its thin wood would have made it the least robust of the three parts; but the absence of the forepillar is more telling. Like the neck, it would have been solid, so just as capable of surviving. Could it be that only the neck was deposited? Might we be looking at an instrument that's been ritually dismantled and only part of it buried in the bog? It's a question that's going to crop up time and again, but here it's complicated by one further, rather unfortunate fact: even the neck is now missing. This is why the drawing is such an important record. The object is no longer mentioned in the detailed catalogue of the finder's collection, when it was auctioned off at Sotheby's in November 1924.

Could it be that by that time it was too damaged to seem worth including? Knowles had previously admitted as much. 'It has shrunk very greatly in size since it came into my possession, which was immediately after being found. I kept it for a considerable time in a solution of alum and water, during which time it remained in its original shape and size. I had a drawing made of it in that state.' But that's all he says about it.

The discovery raises many unresolved questions. It looks forward to some of the discoveries that lie ahead, in the deeper, darker recesses of history, but of its period it's still unique. There's simply been nothing to match it. An ornate neck and pillar of solid ivory in the Louvre belong to a more delicate type of harp and probably to a much more courtly setting. A Gothic harp preserved among the wooden sculptures in Freiberg Cathedral, in the east of Germany, has a different shape and in any case it's no older than the late sixteenth century. What wouldn't we give to be able to go back and explore Carncoagh again, with modern excavation techniques! Sadly, nothing of the bog remains today. It's green pasture. And yet there may be other remains of swamps still out there, somewhere. There are certainly crannogs. And who knows what we may find if we're lucky – and if we're ready with a rescue plan when the moment arrives.

Chapter Nineteen

Walls have ears: resonating pots from St Walburga's Church, Meschede

Germany, thirteenth to tenth century

It's West Germany in 1948 and in Meschede, a small German town on the River Ruhr, building inspectors are assessing bomb damage to a medieval church when they come across something very strange. Buried in the stonework is a hollow space with a round opening hardly bigger than the palm of your hand. A closer look reveals that it's the mouth of a pot that's been inset into the masonry; they soon discover another nearby, and another, and another. The pots are virtually identical, and the wall appears to contain a whole pattern of them. Altogether more than a hundred are found: some up in the western loft, others in vaults beneath the floor. What purpose could they possible serve? Who might have put them there? Strange as it may seem, they turn out to be parts of the building's medieval sound system.

A *sound system* in the plague-ridden Middle Ages? It seems hard to believe. Yet the archaeological details speak for themselves. It's not the only example that's been found, and together with historical records they tell quite a story.

Dating back to around 900, the church of Meschede is what's known as a *Stiftskirche* or 'collegiate church', and it's dedicated to an Anglo-Saxon noblewoman named Walburh, or Walburga in modern German. Walburh came from Crediton in Devon, leaving her home in about 740 to join her uncle Wynfrith in Germany, where he was busy converting the Frisians and Old Saxons to

Christianity. Better known today as St Boniface, Wynfrith had been made the first bishop of Mainz, near modern Frankfurt. But it proved to be a brief appointment. The still-pagan Frisians seem to have taken exception to something he said, and in June 754 they massacred him and his companions as they preached at a place near Dokkum in today's Netherlands. Walburh was lucky to be elsewhere at the time and went on to become one of the leading Christian missionaries. After her (natural) death in 779 she attracted a cult following and was soon made a saint, becoming St Walburga or Walpurgi. All over Europe, churches were built and dedicated to her, including the church in Meschede.

These days the name Walpurgi conjures up mental images of ghouls, ghosts and witches, and the antics of revellers on Walpurgisnacht, the eve of her annual feast day on 1 May. How St Walburga (or at least her memory) came to be so enmeshed with magic and the occult probably has no bearing on the ingenious devices hidden in the walls of her church at Meschede. But they do seem to have involved something of a magic trick. The question is: by whom, and to what end?

The pots themselves are unremarkable. They're kitchenware – high-quality kitchenware certainly, but kitchenware nonetheless. They may not have been made specially, but they have clearly been chosen. All of them are storage jars or jugs, mostly from kilns in the Rhineland around Cologne, and in the northern part of Hesse. Each has been packed into its own pot-sized niche in the masonry, and laid on its side so that its mouth would open into the body of the church – that is, until they were plastered over during subsequent renovations. Now removed from the church by its post-war restorers, six unbroken specimens can be seen in the Neues Museum in Berlin, helpfully mounted in a wall of clear acrylic glass.

At first glance we might take them for nest boxes of the kind used in dovecotes – literally pigeonholes. But nesting boxes for birds would hardly have been appropriate inside a church. A buildings specialist might see them as weight-saving devices, relieving pressure on the foundations, but they really aren't big or numerous enough to have served that structural purpose. As storage spaces for valuables they seem equally ill-adapted and ill-placed. However, there's growing evidence that they represent acoustical engineering – and not just some local experiment but part of an established and widespread tradition. Key to their function is their globular internal shape.

When the air inside such a vessel is excited by vibrations entering its mouth from an outside source, such as voices, it will resonate, playing back part of the sound and therefore prolonging it. This is called 'Helmholtz resonance', after the nineteenth-century German physicist Hermann Helmholtz. It's a universal property of enclosed spaces, large or small – it's the owl-like hooting sound that we get when we blow across the top of an empty bottle. Each pot, or bottle, will play back one fundamental note, known as its 'resonant frequency', and the pitch of its note, high or low, will depend on just two things: how much air the pot encloses, and the size of the opening; the material of the pot has no detectable effect. A larger pot or a narrower mouth will result in a lower pitch while a smaller one or one with a wider mouth will sound higher. In this way, by choosing pots carefully we can turn them into tuned sets, resonating to a number of different musical pitches. We can also retune them by pouring in a material such as mortar, just as we'd pour water into a bottle.

It turns out that the pots found in Meschede were just the tip of another iceberg, and we have the archaeologist Aline Kottmann to thank for revealing just how vast a berg it is. In a heroic search lasting many years, she's located over two hundred and fifty separate examples from Germany alone – and by that I mean two hundred and fifty *churches* where pots have been found or can be detected. It's quite breathtaking. My own introduction to the phenomenon came in a more modest way in the late 1980s, when a friend in Oxford gave me a box file of notes and articles that he'd gathered over the years. They included a piece published in 1915 by a Cambridge antiquarian who'd made a study of two medieval churches in Norwich: St Peter Mancroft and St Peter per Mountergate.

Inside them he'd found precisely the same thing. The pots had been mounted horizontally, their mouths left open to the air. Again they were nothing special, just normal household vessels, made locally. What *was* special about them wasn't *what* they were but *where* they were. They'd previously escaped notice because, like some of the German pots, they were hidden under the floor – and it's there that their location establishes their relationship to music beyond doubt.

It's become apparent that when St Peter Mancroft was being built, a special pit was dug, and the pots were mortared into holes in the sides. About a hundred and twenty centimetres deep, with no means of access and no light, the pit was directly beneath the choir stalls and covered by the wooden floor that the choristers stood on. What's more, cut into the shallow wooden skirting which runs along the front edge of the floor, where it drops down onto the tiled floor of the centre aisle, are several small quatrefoil holes that look suspiciously like the sound holes of a stringed instrument. Together these are what a detective might call a 'meaningful chain of evidence', and the connecting link is music.

Discoveries like these mark another important stage on our musical journey back through time. It's already been established that not all ancient musical objects are easy to identify, and not every object that resembles a musical instrument or sound tool is necessarily musical. Looking at the objects themselves only takes us so far. To probe their real meanings we have to go beyond their forms to see what their contexts are telling us. And this is where the Middle Ages have another musical trick up their sleeve: they can sometimes, just sometimes, provide witness statements in the form of historic documents.

Documents are one of the rewarding aspects of running prehistoric questions past medieval experience – it's almost like having a Video Assistant Referee at a football match. In the final contest between Scepticism and the Resonating Pot, the video referee turns out to be a fifteenth-century chronicler of the Celestine convent of Metz in northern France. Under his entry for August 1432 he writes:

On the Vigil of the Assumption, after Brother Odo had returned from the general meeting of the Chapter, it was decreed that pots should be made for the choir of this church. He reported that he had seen them in another church and thought that they made the chanting resonate more strongly. They were all put up in one day by employing as many craftsmen as necessary.

Archaeologists are rarely so lucky as to have their ideas confirmed so perfectly. In these brief sentences the medieval chronicler not only validates the theory that the pots were meant to resound but also reveals something of the reasoning behind their installation, and how the idea was spreading. Clearly, the pots of the Celestines of Metz were not just some local initiative.

All things come to an end, and it seems that by the Late Middle Ages fewer and fewer systems were being installed. Perhaps their death knell sounded with the Protestant Reformation, when hymns and spoken sermons replaced sung Masses and the other offices of Roman Catholic tradition. The pots fell out of use and those that were in plain sight were sooner or later plastered over. But as one tradition ended another acoustic technology was already in the ascendancy, meeting the changing requirements: the sounding board. This was a wooden panel suspended like a little roof above the pulpit where the preacher stood to address the congregation. It was mounted in such a way as to reflect his voice and project it directly forwards and downwards, enhancing the clarity of his speech. Many are still in place today, often resembling an elaborately ornamented canopy; but tradition confirms their primary acoustical purpose. In fact, both technologies – the pots and the sounding boards – had been foreshadowed, and quite probably inspired, by the architectural writings of the Roman military engineer Vitruvius in the first century BC. But that's a story for another day.

What stands out from this story are the extraordinary lengths to which medieval people were prepared to go, and the investments of wealth, skill and energy that they were prepared to make, solely to maximise a musical effect. It seems that in Europe's Middle Ages great value was attached to sound and music, as it is now. And this in turn suggests that, as we venture further back in time, we shouldn't be too surprised to find music technologies of one kind or another playing as important a part in the lives of our still more ancient ancestors.

PART FIVE

Early Medieval Minds

The Twelfth to the Eighth Century

The early medieval period witnesses the rise of great civilisations and empires across the globe: from the Moche in Peru to Islam's Golden Age, from the Tang and Song Dynasties in China to Aztec Mexico, from the Eastern Roman Empire to Europe's renascent West. It's also a time of great diversity and ambition in music and poetry.

Beneath the ancient port of Schleswig, in northern Germany, we'll find bone flutes that were carefully tuned, proving that people had very particular musical scales in mind. In an Old Saxon manuscript we'll find signs that challenge the received wisdom that early Germanic poetry was simply spoken or declaimed; and we'll even entertain the thought that its musical performance could have been accompanied by dance. We'll see the power of shared memory in preserving sung traditions through the vastness of our unwritten past, and in eastern England a new type of double-pipe will reveal a musical tradition, hitherto unsuspected, that stretches at least as far as the plains of distant Hungary. And calling to mind our perennial love of bird song, a delightful little whistling bird on a pottery vessel of the Moche period in Peru will prompt us to rethink what music really meant to people in the past.

But first we take a step back from the implements and instruments of music, to look again at buildings associated with music-making. We'll discover some ingenious ways in which ancient people manipulated the sounds of their environments.

We've all been to places where we've noticed an unusual clarity when speaking or shouting, or a curious sense of separation from the outside world; we may have noticed an exceptionally strong resonance, or a strange whispering or fluttering echo when clapping or stamping our feet. But does it mean that such places were deliberately engineered? The search for clues starts with a rarely visited space inside a medieval Gothic cathedral, a space that preserves in its strange design ghostly memories of long-dead singers and power of the music they sang.

CHAPTER TWENTY

Music and illusion: concealing performers in two medieval cathedrals

Lichfield and Wells, *c.*1200

One evening, some years ago, I was sitting in front of the television, watching a history documentary. The subject was the Allied daylight bombing of Germany in 1943, and I vividly recall a particular sequence of original colour film. It showed a large formation of American B-17 bombers approaching their target, probably in the Ruhr Valley. Filmed from inside one of the aircraft, it revealed a scene of unfolding mayhem. Before the camera's unblinking eye, puffs of black anti-aircraft fire were bursting all around. Against a clear blue sky, one of the nearby bombers burst into flames. Another disintegrated in a violent explosion. Others, with vital parts shot away, fell cartwheeling down from higher formations like so many leaves in a storm. But through all the drama the main formation pressed on, white-lining the sky with their endless, measured vapour trails. To accompany the footage, a lesser editor might have chosen some dramatic orchestral piece by Wagner or Verdi, to establish and emphasise a sense of heroism. Instead what we heard was entirely unexpected: it was the slow, lyrical sound of Glenn Miller's 'Moonlight Serenade'.

It was an inspired stroke. The incongruity completely transformed our perception of what we were seeing. We were no longer being invited to participate in a triumph of arms: we were onlookers surveying an unfolding tragedy. And as the horrors of life and death played out all around, the scene became something far more human, far more complex and infinitely more disturbing.

Music has the power not only to emphasise and reinforce what we see and feel but also to profoundly alter and subvert the meanings we attach to the things we witness. But its exploitation is nothing new. Archaeological evidence suggests that it's been going on for quite some time.

At Meschede, one of the German towns devastated by bombing in the Second World War, we've seen how the sonority of a medieval church had been altered by inserting resonant clay pots into its walls. This kind of installation couldn't have come cheap. But at Lichfield, in the Midlands, there's evidence of an even greater investment, in a mystery structure buried deep in the original fabric of another medieval church. And this time it's not there to enhance an acoustic: it's to enable music to alter public perceptions.

The church is St Chad's, the ancient cathedral church of the bishops of Lichfield, and hidden inside the otherwise solid masonry of its vast Gothic front, above the great west door, is a rarely used passageway. It was created by the original builders during the cathedral's construction around eight hundred years ago; and it seems to have been designed expressly to manipulate the way a series of devotional images mounted on the church's facade would have been perceived by onlookers. The designer's ambition was nothing less than to fire their imaginations – and to do it with music.

In their day, the broad west fronts of major churches like Lichfield were their public display screens. Like the facade of a theatre or a cinema, they towered above the main ceremonial entrance. And like theatre facades they were embellished with symbols and images that represented what went on inside. Just above the doors of St Chad's the mysterious hidden passage runs straight through the whole breadth of the otherwise solid masonry, from left to right. It's quite invisible to anyone outside. The only access is at each end, through a special door that opens off a stone spiral staircase.

When I visited the cathedral one rainy October day in 2012, I found the passage to be just wide and tall enough to stand up in without scuffing the walls or grazing the top of my head. Inside everything was dark. But as my eyes adjusted to the gloom I began to see glimmers of daylight coming through a number of narrow vertical slits in the wall to my right. Peering through one I glimpsed the backs of statues and beyond them Cathedral Green below. I knew that the statues occupied a row of niches that ran in a long line across the face of the building, above the west door. But looking around the otherwise featureless passage there was no obvious explanation. Why would any architect take the trouble to incorporate such a thing when all it seemed to do was to connect two staircases that were already connected on other floors? What could be its purpose?

An hour later, standing outside on the grass and looking up through the rain with my binoculars, I could just make out the narrow slits in the dark shadows between the statues. There was nothing to suggest to the naked eye that they were there. In short, if someone had wanted the passage to remain a secret, they couldn't have made a finer job of it. But why would they have needed to conceal it?

There were two potential clues to the architect's motives. One was a curious anomaly. In an otherwise symmetrical structure, the slits were not arranged evenly: there were more of them near the northern end than the southern. There was also a strange coincidence. Behind the west front as a whole were two much larger enclosed musical spaces. At each end of the great facade stands a tall octagonal tower. In the north tower, the upstairs chamber is known as the 'Song School', once used as the classroom for boy choristers. Its equivalent in the south tower is the bell-ringers' loft. Our passageway connects them. Might they have been part of a single musical plan?

The intriguing solution to the riddle is to be found in another famous cathedral church, St Andrew the Apostle at Wells in Somerset, around two hundred kilometres to the south. It turns out that Wells has a very similar passageway, and it too is hidden, and in the same place, crossing the facade just above the west doorway. But this time telltale details in its construction are supported by ancient traditions of the church. It turns out that at Wells the same backstage area – the tower chambers and passageway – was engineered specifically for music; indeed, the engineering extends right up to the height of the roof.

Once again we're lucky enough to have an independent witness: a handwritten fourteenth-century manual for the church's ceremonies throughout the year, which sets out the rules and instructions for how they should be conducted. One event in particular stands out from the rest. It's the celebrations of Palm Sunday.

Palm Sunday, the final Sunday before Easter, commemorates the day when Jesus is believed to have entered Jerusalem with his disciples, before his betrayal, trial and crucifixion. It's one of the most important days in the Christian calendar, and its celebration still includes some of the most elaborate ceremonies. At Wells in the fourteenth century it entailed a complex procession around the outside of the church, and crucially, the manual tells us about the music that was performed during the ritual.

It requires a group of choristers, men and boys, to position themselves high inside the west front of the cathedral – it says that they are to stand *in eminenti loco*, meaning 'in a high place' – and there they are to perform certain chants when the processions converge for the key moment at the west door, a re-enactment of Christ's entry into Jerusalem. It even identifies the chants. *En rex venit* is to be sung by three priests; *Gloria laus* by seven choristers; then the priests are to sing *Unus autem*. It's odd that the writer omits to give the location a name, since he identifies other performance spaces quite precisely. But there can be no doubt that he means the hidden passage – there simply isn't anywhere else it could be. And there's a further clue buried in the detail. It's to do with the number of choristers.

The number seven also connects the chants to the design of the passage itself. At Lichfield there were vertical slits. At Wells they are round portholes, twelve of them, each about eighteen inches deep and conical in shape, with the broader part opening into the passage. To stand in the passage today and speak or sing into one of the portholes feels eerily like speaking or singing into an old phonograph recording horn. The shape of each hole is identical: perfectly plain, with smoothly dressed stone surfaces. But they are placed at two different heights above the floor, seven of them at a hundred and twenty centimetres and the remaining four at a hundred and seventy centimetres. They match the height of boys and men standing.

Anyone singing through the open ports would have been heard down on the Cathedral Green. But if you didn't know they were there, the sounds would have appeared to come not from any human source but from the statues standing in front of them. Traces of pigment have been discovered at various points across the facade, showing that the whole structure would once have been brightly coloured, so much so that in sunlight they would have made an awe-inspiring tableau. If we add to this the mysterious disembodied voices, we can only imagine the impression the event would have created in the minds of medieval believers – no doubt already in a heightened emotional state, caught up in the drama of the occasion and the profusion of holy images spread out before them. But singing is not the only sound that would have been ringing in their ears.

Built into the triangular gable at the top of the facade is a further series of eight circular holes of the same diameter. They form another horizontal row; this time they are penetrating not half a metre of masonry but a wall that's a metre and a half thick. Behind them, in the loft space between the stone ceiling of the nave and the wooden beams of the outer roof, is a stone platform. These holes open at a far greater height above any audience below, but they are perfectly suited to one of the loudest instruments the Middle Ages had to offer: long straight trumpets like the one that was recovered from the mud of the River Thames at Billingsgate and that we've seen in medieval paintings. And as if that wasn't already a telltale sign, there's one final proof. Standing on a ledge just outside the holes are two more limestone sculptures: a pair of angels. Their extremities have long since broken off but if you have a pair of binoculars, even from the Cathedral Green you can see that each angel still has a trumpet mouthpiece pressed to its lips.

For an archaeologist, part of the great charm of the Lichfield slits and the Wells portholes is the way in which their various strands of evidence converge. But there's another curious aspect to the whole phenomenon

In 2012 I was at Yale giving a talk on ancient acoustics, when I met Brian Kane. Brian's particular interest at that time was 'acousmatic phantasmagoria', by which he meant, in the first instance, the concealment of sources of sound, and in the second, their deliberate use and manipulation to achieve dramatic, almost supernatural effects. Delving back to classical Greek and Roman authors, he drew parallels with acoustic screens mentioned by Pythagoras, before bringing the subject back to opera and nineteenth-century theatre designs. He explained Richard Wagner's ideal of the invisible orchestra: that it should be heard but be no more visible than any of the hidden machinery that created the visual drama and magic. Wagner needed a full orchestral sound but he didn't wish the players and conductor to obtrude. In a way, I suppose, he was anticipating a modern cinema-going experience.

Now, up to this point, I'd been focused on establishing the chain of evidence connecting the music with the architecture, and on gauging the scale of the investment needed, as a physical measure of music's importance to communities. But listening to Brian it became increasingly clear that the most remarkable aspect was not so much the designing and building of the passageway and the trumpet holes, but the very fact of their invisibility. There are musicians' galleries inside many places of worship, even some smaller parish churches; and some cathedrals have terraces and balcony-like structures that project from their facades to accommodate musicians. But usually there's no attempt at concealment. What we're seeing at Lichfield and Wells is altogether different, implying a quite different mindset. Like Meschede, it has illusion at its heart. And it's come at a significant additional financial cost.

Such illusion offers another clue to what music does, and is, and may ultimately help explain where it comes from. It amuses us for sure. It can entertain us and move us emotionally. But these attributes also make it a tool, and a very powerful tool for influencing others.

Chapter Twenty-One

Trial and error: tuning bone flutes in medieval Schleswig

North Germany, *c.*1100

Of all the musical treasures that an archaeologist can expect to find, the one that adds most to our knowledge of the past has to be the common bone 'flute' or 'penny whistle'. For as long as people have been making beautiful things with their hands, animal bone has been a favourite craft material. It's plentiful, it's easy to cut and carve and polish; and before modern plastics took over its trad-itional role, it was the material of choice for making all kinds of everyday objects: from toothbrushes and knife handles to buttons and children's toys. It's marvellously tough and robust, able to endure rough and frequent handling; and in times gone by these attributes also made it ideal for making musical instruments. Bone flutes survive in large numbers. In chalky or lime-rich earth, they can be nearly pristine, still burnished, still pale ivory in colour. They survive immersion too, provided that the water isn't aggressively acidic. Many appear complete, or sufficiently complete that even before we've wiped away the dirt there can be no mistaking what they are. And they bring with them the kind of personal detail that reminds excavators why they put up with the heat and cold, the wind and rain, and all the back-breaking discomfort of working on all fours, day after day. When you've been focusing on the technical complexities of stratigraphy and soil structure, on industrial and environmental residues, a flute is a vivid reminder that the places we explore were once trodden by real people, with real voices, whose need for self-expression and consolation was not so very different from our own.

Flutes, and especially bone flutes, also offer a unique perspective on music's buried past. From Ireland to the Western Pacific, from South Africa to North America, it's hard to name a people who haven't made use of them at one time or another in their past. They seem almost as universal as music itself; and this allows comparisons to be made across the world. One of the most fascinating discoveries so far has been a treasure trove of flutes and pipes found beneath the medieval streets of Schleswig, close to Germany's border with Denmark.

Schleswig today is a pleasant town set in rolling countryside on the eastern coast of the Jutland peninsula. It lies at the head of the Schlei fjord, a long, sheltered inlet of the Baltic Sea. During the 1970s and 80s it saw major excavations in three areas of its medieval quarter. One of them was along Plessenstrasse, which was thought to follow the original waterfront. Covering over three thousand square metres, the dig would be one of the largest excavations so far attempted by medieval archaeologists anywhere. 'Plot 83/3' is now hidden beneath smart modern houses and low-rise apartment blocks overlooking the yacht marina. But as work progressed, a medieval quayside emerged, made up of individual parcels of land enclosed by fences and dams, jetties and landing stages. In the saturated ground, timber had been very well preserved, and tree rings dated the wood to 1087 or 1088. Up on drier land further holes, pits and ditches testified to commercial activity there too. Among the many finds in this area were our flutes and pipes – more than fifty of them.

The flutes are eye-catching not just because there are so many. It's because of the information that the excavation process recovered about the circumstances of their deposition and their varying states of completion when they were left there. Often music's archaeology appears to consist of individual instruments deliberately buried, or lost, or abandoned because they've been broken or become obsolete after a lifetime of use. For the most part the

Schleswig finds match none of those descriptions. Like the Oxford tuning pegs, they are the sweepings from the floors of the very workshop or firesides where they were being made. This gives them a very special character as evidence. Archaeologists call such sweepings the 'debitage', the leftovers of processing activities, and from their apparent randomness we can begin to reconstruct a *chaîne opératoire* – the chain of actions charting the manufacture process, from raw material to complete instrument.

Among the finds from Schleswig are examples of that raw material: plain unmodified bones. Most are the shin bones, or tibias, of sheep or goats. There are tibias with their ends cut off, and there are tibias in various subsequent stages of becoming flutes. If we look closely at them we can see how each task played out and how it contributed to the instruments' final forms. But we can also learn from the failures and the errors they embody. They show craftspeople experimenting, trying out alternative schemes, and maybe even teaching each other how the different stages should be accomplished. Of these, the most significant have been voicing and tuning.

Many of the flutes that remain as part of the debitage seem to have been abandoned during the course of being tuned, which is to say during that last, crucial placing and drilling of their finger holes. The fact of their abandonment therefore casts light on the importance people attached to patterns of tunings and to 'being in tune' – preferences which would underpin the very melodies they hoped to play on them. Looking at the diversity of medieval bone flutes today, with their often bewildering variations of tuning, you could be forgiven for thinking that ordinary medieval folk must have had little or no interest in tuning, and no traditions of shared tonal values, and that they simply drilled their finger holes anywhere and accepted whatever they got. Schleswig begins to tell a different story. Preserved in the sequence of actions, trials and errors that it took to tune them, we discover the musical habits, preferences and ambitions, not just of their makers but of musicians themselves. It seems that the act of tuning entailed a whole series of reassessments and 'go/no-go' thresholds.

In the 1980s, after a visit to the Schleswig-Holstein Landesmuseum where all the finds are kept, I made careful replicas of one particular bone, a sheep tibia. It intrigued me because the flute that had been made from it was virtually identical to one I was studying from Great Massingham in Norfolk, across the North Sea. Could they be related in some way? One of the replicas is on the table in front of me now. At just over sixteen centimetres long, the bone is slender from the mid-point to the ankle joint but splays out towards the animal's knee, like a human tibia. In tibias of living mammals there's a natural cavity filled with bone marrow, and with the ends cut off and the marrow removed the bone is ready to make a first sound. But because it's not cylindrical it's a very particular sound. With a little square sounding hole added at the broader end, and a block or 'fipple' pushed inside to direct your breath onto its sharpened edge, the instrument takes on something of the soft hollow tone of a modern school recorder. It sounds even more like a recorder – a sopranino recorder – when the finger holes have been added, and now it can play tunes. Spread in a straight line along the bone, there are four of them, round, with nicely rebated platforms to fit your fingertips. It's at this point that you discover something quite remarkable. By opening and closing them while you blow, you can play a scale of five notes, or even (with practice) a sixth; and although the original is now nearly a thousand years old, the notes that the replica generates are the familiar *do, re, mi, fa, sol, la*. They sound effortlessly in tune. The puzzle is that several other apparently finished flutes from Schleswig do nothing of the sort. In fact they don't seem to conform to any recognisable pattern. What's going on? The solution may be preserved on the surfaces of the unfinished instruments, those bones that have not yet had their finger holes cut.

Look at any of the unfinished instruments through a magnifying glass and you can see little marks left by the maker. One flute has had its topmost hole finished, but where the others should be there's just a row of shallow dots. Someone has clearly taken the pointed tip of a knife and marked out their positions in advance. They've had a plan. But if they knew where each hole should go, why didn't they finish the job? There's one likely reason. In domesticated animals like sheep and goats, bone growth is much more variable than it is in wild animals, both externally and internally, and experiments have shown that it's often hard to predict from outside appearances exactly where a hole should be placed to achieve a particular pitch. You may have a rule of thumb and it may usually work, but there will always be exceptions. If you find the tuning isn't what you hoped and is too far out to remedy, there's only one thing you can do: throw it away and start again. And throw them away the Schleswig makers evidently did. But although the unfinished flutes may represent their failures, by studying them carefully we can see *indirectly* how they defined success.

This discovery has implications that go far beyond Schleswig, and far beyond the Middle Ages. Whenever we dig up a piece of a flute anywhere in the world, it's tempting to assume that we're seeing part of a finished product that fully reflects its maker's intention. So when we're lucky enough to find one that's complete, as we do from time to time, we tend to suppose that the notes we obtain from it must be those that people actually wanted to play. But how can we tell that it's not one of their failures? There's only one way to be certain: we need to figure out if it's actually been played. And the best way to do this is to view the bone surfaces in fine detail under a microscope.

Microscopy had already been applied with success to finds of ancient bone instruments from England and the Netherlands. At even low magnifications, between say ten and twenty times, a wholly new factor comes into view. On an old and much-played instrument, the patterns and textures left by the scraping and sawing movements of the maker's knife are often interspersed with plateaux of high gloss polishing. They are the result of friction-wear: a fragile record of repeated movements of the player's fingertips as they've held and manipulated the instrument. It's particularly noticeable around the margins of the finger holes, and round the back where it would have rested on their thumb. The more wear an instrument exhibits, the more confident we can be that it has met its end user's musical needs, that someone in the ancient past has found it satisfying to own and to play. It may be no coincidence that it turns out to be satisfying for us too.

The idea that instrument-makers and musicians in Schleswig had higher standards to maintain contradicts one infamous eyewitness report. When in the eleventh century a merchant from Cordova in Spain visited this very town, he went away far from impressed by the music he heard there, reporting that the townspeople's singing was atrocious – 'more brutish even than the sound of dogs barking'. He wasn't too enthusiastic about their personal hygiene either. Yet the flutes now offer an opportunity, if not to put the record entirely straight, then at least to show that music in Schleswig may have had a little more to it than a sceptical outsider might guess. It's another illustration of the old adage: that you shouldn't always believe what you read.

CHAPTER TWENTY-TWO

Performing poetry: melody and memory in the Early Middle Ages

Germany, c.1000

Today, written notes are such a large part of a Western musical education that the word 'music' has often come to mean exactly that: sheet music or a printed score. Musicians set great store by literacy: by the ability not only to read and write music but also to sight-read a score in real time, in the same way that we read and write words and numbers. But it hasn't always been this way. It's time now to take a closer look at music at an important moment of transition. We're going to explore some of its very earliest written forms, to see how they might play into the story, not so much of the *history* of performance as of its *prehistory*: in parts of the past (and indeed in some important parts of the present) that lie beyond the scope of formal written symbols.

About ten centuries ago, while the people of Schleswig were tuning up their bone flutes, something new happened. Since time immemorial, people in Europe had been playing and transmitting songs and tunes, lyrics and melodies, from memory. Now, for some reason, what anthropologists call 'the oral tradition' was no longer deemed sufficient. People began to visualise ways of writing down tunes. On the written page, verses came to be annotated with sequences of undulating lines and dots, in which the direction of the text, from left to right, indicated the passage of musical time, and the up-and-down motions of the pen represented the rise and fall of the melody. They were the first experiments in the analogue representation of sound signals in real time. We've already touched on some later manifestations of analog recording technologies, from the undulating tracks of a phonograph to a four-line stave with square notes, scrawled by a fourteenth-century graffiti artist. In this chapter we're going to leave found objects to one side for a moment, to set the scene for a deeper exploration of musical literacy and its wider meaning. It's a material thread of inventiveness that runs parallel to the physicality of our archaeological finds, and sometimes they intersect.

Back in the ninth and tenth centuries, monkish scholars in the British Isles and continental Europe began to write down traditional stories from their remembered past, and they left us some wonderful material, in a variety of European languages. Our challenge today is to work out how on earth they were meant to be read.

The most famous of their early medieval narratives in Old English is the tale of the hero Beowulf. The version of *Beowulf* that survives was composed at around the end of the ninth century. It consists mostly of plain text, handwritten in ink on faintly ruled white parchment, the pages subsequently stitched together in a leather-bound volume. Looking at them today, the lines look exactly like prose. They form a continuous text, with no hint of structure in the layout and no telltale end rhymes to interrupt the flow. But when you read them out loud a pattern begins to emerge. In fact they are lines of verse.

Unlike verses of later ballad traditions, collected in the nineteenth and early twentieth centuries, Old English poets rarely used any kind of rhyme and appear not to have followed a regular metre or rhythm. Instead they've relied on alliteration and assonance, and shifting patterns of stress. Modern scholars have usually read them silently or, if reading aloud, declaimed them in a more or less theatrical manner. They've seen patterns of stress but nothing that could be described as metronomic. This conservative approach has been encouraged in part by the 'blank' nature of the verse, but also by a traditional reticence of scholars to take liberties with the evidence.

On the whole this is no bad thing, but it makes no allowance for hidden depths. Might there not have been more to it than the medium is capable of preserving? Occasionally we come across some curious anomaly that disturbs old assumptions, and one of them is to be seen in another heroic poem that's not dissimilar to *Beowulf.*

Beowulf is generally agreed to be the grandest and most complete of the surviving early Germanic poems. But it isn't the only one. *Heliand* is the work of an anonymous poet composing in the Old Saxon language during the early years of the ninth century. *Heliand* means 'the Saviour', and it's a retelling of the story of Jesus. Expressed in much the same alliterative style and metre as *Beowulf,* it's an adaptation of the New Testament story to appeal to the experience and tastes of the newly converted but still uncertain Christians of northern Germany. In the poet's hands, Jesus has become a great warrior hero and war leader. The text even looks similar to *Beowulf* on the page, and when it's rearranged into lines and half-lines in modern editions, its poetic character becomes equally clear. Teeming with alliteration and assonance, and overflowing with cryptic references and metaphors – known to scholars as *kennings* – the two poems are like two peas from the same pod. Neither shows any sign of a regular metre or end-rhymes, so the challenge for any would-be performer is broadly the same, except for one barely noticeable detail. *Heliand* exists in several copies to *Beowulf*'s one, and in one of the two most complete versions, now preserved in the Bavarian State Library in Munich, there's something unparalleled in the whole repertoire of alliterative verse. Above the words of three short passages there are symbols that resemble an early form of musical notation.

The notes are known as *neumes.* The annotated passages precede the Nativity, where the poet rehearses Joseph's inner debate about Mary's unexpected pregnancy. Why these sections have been singled out for annotation is a mystery, given that there are more dramatic and more obviously lyrical moments elsewhere in the poem. The first two passages concern the threat to Mary's life posed, it's said, by Jewish law and custom; the third describes Mary and Joseph's arrival in Bethlehem. But at any rate, the symbols are neumes, which is to say attempts to represent something of the shape of the music, and are part of a system that would lead in time to the graphic 'staff notations' that musicians use today.

Back in the late eighth century, monkish writers had been thinking about musical theory and experimenting with methods of notation. Their main concern was undoubtedly religious: they needed to find practical ways of ensuring the uniformity of the chants that were being sung in churches. It was important to the early medieval church that different communities around Christendom should be singing from the same hymn sheet, so to speak. Their sudden burst of ingenuity resulted in a number of alternative systems. Some were quite simple: mere shorthand symbols. Others were more complex, and could be very precise. These are called 'heighted' neumes because the dots representing the individual notes rise and fall as precisely as if they are laid on an invisible grid. Among the most elaborate were the neumes developed at the monasteries of St Gallen in Switzerland, Benevento in southern Italy and Metz in northern France. They are easy to read. And it wasn't long before they began to be applied to the preservation and sharing of other kinds of music: popular tunes sung to while away leisure hours in monastic communities or on journeys. Probably the most famous are the Latin and Middle High German poems preserved in the *Carmina Burana*, which are the work of goliards, wandering clerics and university students. Another preserved manuscript contains the so-called 'Cambridge Songs'. In each collection only a selection of poems has been annotated, which seems somehow significant. Was it because they were too familiar to need explaining?

During the ninth and tenth centuries, notation methods would become more and more refined and come to look more like the written music of today, to the extent that we can decipher and perform them with confidence. It's true that the neumes of the Munich *Heliand* are not of this sort. The symbols floating above the text are more like shorthand. They have shapes to them, for sure, some resembling ticks, some an inverted U, while others look like the alphabetical letters v and p. But even if we don't yet know how to make sense of them, they still have something important to tell us. It's in the sheer fact of their presence – and what that says about early vernacular alliterative poetry. It says that one writer at least considered that it could have a musical dimension. It could be sung.

It's a combination of words and music that has support from the poems themselves. The poets are by no means averse to referring to their own kind, and among archaeologists and performers alike, there's been growing awareness of a connection between their recitations and one particular musical instrument. It's a stringed instrument. The vernacular poets call it *hearpe* or *harpa*, among other names; *cithara* in Latin. In *Beowulf*, we see it in the hands of another poet, the *scóp* or *gléoman* (meaning 'shaper' and 'glee-man') at the reflective heart of the drama, rehearsing past heroic deeds before the king and his warriors in the feasting hall. From the cumulative weight of archaeological evidence it seems increasingly likely to be some kind of lyre, an instrument whose traditional purpose in many cultures is specifically to accompany song. And indeed, the Old English verb that's used to describe the way the verse is delivered by the glee-man is *singan*, to sing. So *Heliand* and the evidence of *Beowulf* hold a clear warning: just because we recognise a text to be poetic it doesn't mean there wasn't more going on beneath the surface.

One of the most distinguished exponents of *Beowulf* as live performance today is the American singer Benjamin Bagby, who's made the lyre an indispensable part of his act. For him there's no practical objection to adapting alliterative verse either to the lyre or to a regular metre. The synthesis he achieves is amazing. To listen to him sing *Beowulf* before a live audience is to be transported back to a time when performers didn't necessarily think of poetry and music as separate entities.

And with the question of metre comes something else too. In an anonymous contemporary account of one tenth-century player and performer, St Dunstan of Canterbury, there's a description of a ring dance. It's true that it's being sung and danced by angels in a vision, but the writer adds (with an unexpectedly human touch) that they are dancing exactly as young women do. So if ancient poems like *Beowulf* and *Heliand* were being sung, and could be sung to a regular beat, perhaps they could also be danced to?

Now there's a thought.

CHAPTER TWENTY-THREE

'Flutes' that roar: two double pipes of deer bone from early medieval Europe

Ipswich, England, and Alattyán, Hungary, ninth century

A phone call I took a couple of weeks ago offers a good illustration of the quiet way that most musical adventures in archaeology begin. The caller was a friend from the Museum of London, who told me that her colleagues had recently been exploring a site in Cambridgeshire when they came across a dark patch in the earth. At some point long ago someone must have created a shallow pit, and it had later been back-filled with raked earth in order to level up the ground. The archaeological context suggested a date in the Middle Anglo-Saxon period, around thirteen hundred years ago. Among the items they'd found in the fill was a curious carved bone object that she thought might be of interest to me. It was only small, but it turned out to have something rather important to say, not just about how early medieval people made music but about the origins of music itself.

The fieldwork had been part of preparations for a national road improvement scheme. If you've driven up the Great North Road from London recently or along the A14, and you passed through the new Brampton Interchange near Huntingdon, you'll have driven past the very spot without knowing it. At first glance it's hard to tell now that it was ever a historic landscape. The surrounding fields are open, almost prairie-like, and if the contour of the land varies it's only between flat and very gently undulating. The soils are chalky or gravelly and are intensively farmed for crops like wheat and oilseed rape. But thirteen centuries ago it was a very different place. It would have been mainly pasture, with broad belts of woodland and, here and there, small clusters of thatched wooden houses.

It turned out that the shallow pit was the hollow that had once been the floor or underfloor space of one of these houses. It was a so-called 'sunken floored building'. Towards each end of the rectangular depression a deep hole had been dug for a post to hold up the roof. It was one of a number of similar houses scattered across the site. The people who lived in them were the descendants of the first Anglo-Saxon settlers from north-west Germany, although they'd no doubt mingled with the Romanised Britons who'd farmed the land before them. By the eighth century the villagers would have been talking to each other – and singing their songs – in a dialect of Old English. It was probably similar to the language used by the *Beowulf* poet, though of a more homely sort and no doubt with a less elaborate vocabulary and fewer cryptic references.

The little object they'd left behind seemed equally straightforward at first. It was a short length of worked bone tube, about the thickness of my little finger. It had a D-shaped cross section, and along its surviving eleven centimetres there was a row of four neatly drilled circular perforations that looked like finger holes. But the bone was heavier and more solid than bird bone. The excavator wondered if it could be sheep or goat, like the flutes from early medieval Schleswig.

As soon as I saw a photograph, I knew it was a pipe, in the broadest sense of the word; but although it looked like part of a flute, it wasn't. I'd examined three objects like it over the years and this new find now allowed me to flesh out something of the remarkable story they tell. The dates tallied exactly: the other three pipes were all early medieval, which is to say a century or two earlier than the majority of bone flutes so far found by archaeologists. They were all made from an unusual animal bone: one of the long bones from the lower part of a deer's hind leg. They were therefore by-products of hunting wild animals, not of farming. This might be significant. Being naturally hollow, the bone's length and straightness, together with the narrowness of the bore, also made it uniquely suitable for musical use.

But there was more. I noticed the distinctive way the outside of the bone had been shaved down to form the D-shaped cross section. This indicated to me that it had once been one of a pair of tubes, a mirror pair bound tightly together back to back, so that they could be played simultaneously as a double pipe. When the object itself arrived on my desk, still more of its complex character emerged, together with a first appreciation of the kind of music it would have made. It's a sound that's very different from the airy piping of a flute.

These pipes weren't just flutes made from a different kind of bone: they consistently followed their own distinct design. The story had begun some years earlier, with the discovery of a fragment of much the same size from an excavation in a neighbouring county. With only three finger holes remaining, and the bone in poor condition, it struck me initially as just another example of the perplexing diversity of bone flutes. But when an almost complete single pipe emerged from another excavation, I began to have doubts. They were made from identical bones, deer metatarsus. Then a third discovery showed what they really were. It came to light during excavations around St Stephen's Lane in Ipswich. Sometimes known as the Buttermarket, the site lay at the heart of the earliest Anglo-Saxon trading settlement of Gyppeswic, a stone's throw from the wharfs where the Gipping River flows into the tidal estuary of the Orwell. And during the excavation something rather astonishing had happened. Seen from overhead, stripped back to the subsoil, the surface of the site was criss-crossed with back-filled post holes, trenches, ditches, hollows and pits; and in one of the pits archaeologists had found a pipe of exactly the same kind. But this time it was intact.

It was just over seventeen centimetres long, straight, and its surfaces were polished with handling. The bone itself was mottled in various shades of buff, brown and grey, as bone often is after being buried for so long. It had the same D-shaped cross section as the find from Cambridgeshire, but that was just the beginning. In another pit, some metres from the first, the team found a similar pipe in several fragments. And when the two pieces were placed side by side, the penny dropped. They weren't similar: they were *identical*. They were an exact mirror pair, made from bones so perfectly symmetrical that they could have been sourced from the same deer carcass. After more than a thousand years separated in the earth, they'd now been reunited, and the hard proof that they were intended for each other could be seen under the microscope. Scratch marks on the polished surface of one pipe – some accidental, some deliberately scored – continued straight across the gap to reappear on the other. What's more, there was one significant absence: while both pipes had six well-shaped finger holes, neither had a sound hole or 'window' of the kind that makes the airy whistling sound in a true flute or whistle. These bones required another method of voicing: they needed a vibrating reed. They were relatives not of flutes or whistles, but belonged to the same family as the modern oboe and clarinet, the medieval shawm and more besides. They had all the hallmarks of a quite different musical tradition.

At one end they showed signs that they'd been mounted together in some kind of socket. So could they be the chanters of bagpipes? The origin of European bagpipes ranks as one of music history's holy grails. As early as the eleventh century, pipes with bags are shown in manuscript miniatures, the bag held tight under the player's elbow while he opens and closes the holes with his fingers. But not before. And if any of these deer bones were chanters, then surely we should by now have discovered some trace of the rest of the instrument. So far we have not. In fact the pipes' nearest physical equivalents can be found in living folk-instrument traditions of the Mediterranean basin. It's true that in several Mediterranean countries, traditional bagpipes use double pipes as their chanters, usually made from cane but otherwise closely similar to ours in size, with similar numbers of finger holes and similar musical potential. But other paired instruments tell a different story. Also made of cane, they are connected not to a bag but to a horn, and the player blows directly into the reeds, by mouth: in fact, they are what are known as 'hornpipes'. Which of the two forms might our deer-bone pipes represent? On balance the microscopic evidence around their ends tends to favour the hornpipe. But one thing we can be certain about. They are not flutes. They were never, ever meant to whistle. And that realisation brings with it some important consequences, both for the English finds and for music's deeper origins.

For some years it seemed as if the deer-bone double pipe was going to prove a peculiarly English phenomenon, until I came across an archaeological report that suddenly shone fresh light on the question. As so often happens, the answer came simply by joining up existing dots. The new connection proved to be with finds from continental Europe, but not from where we'd been looking in nearby France or Belgium or the Netherlands. It was nearly twelve hundred miles away, among finds from burials within an Avar cemetery in Hungary. The site was at a place called Alattyán, and the double pipes found there date from exactly the same time as the English finds. The resemblance was almost uncanny. It seemed that in the eighth century Avars and Anglo-Saxons were each using the same bone, metatarsus, from the same kind of animal, deer, and were shaping them in the same way. One of the Anglo-Saxon instruments had six pairs of holes to the Avar instruments' five pairs; otherwise they looked identical.

How could this be explained? Could the English instruments be Avar trade goods, perhaps, or could the Hungarian finds have been traded from Anglo-Saxons? It might be a theory. Could they have shared a common origin, for example somewhere in Germany? That seemed possible too. With only two groups of finds so far identified, it was still too early to say. But there was another and maybe more interesting possibility: that they were each locally manufactured, and that what really connected them was not trade, as such, but a common musical experience, a shared fashion and tradition. However we look at them, they mark another proverbial tip of the iceberg. And since there's no certainty that even England and Hungary mark its outer limits, what an iceberg it might be!

I've yet to examine the Hungarian finds for myself, but I have been able to make a very close study of the English pipes, and under my microscope they reveal something rather wonderful: clear signs that they've been tuned, and not only tuned but fine-tuned. At a magnification of about ten times, each finger hole is framed within a pair of delicately scratched tramlines; and looking into the holes themselves it's possible to see that some of them have been enlarged by undercutting one edge. It's evidence of a tuning adjustment, and once again it's obvious that the adjustment has been successful because the surrounding bone surface has been worn to a high polish with use.

What kind of tuning might we be looking at in these twelve-hundred-year-old reed pipes? It's not yet possible to say with any certainty. We're able to reconstruct tunings in complete flutes and panpipes because they *are* complete, but reed pipes are not: too much depends on the nature of the original reed, and so far in all cases the reed has failed to survive. Having made some replicas of the Ipswich pipes, I can say that they have a deep, clarinet-like tone, and it seems they probably played a more or less heptatonic scale, like the white notes on a piano. But to me it's an uncertainty that detracts little from the discovery. What's exciting about it is the mere fact of its having been fine-tuned. Fine-tuning shows intention. Someone has had an acute ear and a clear tonal preference: a precise sense of what sounded 'in tune' and what was 'out of tune', and they've known how to adjust for it. So once again, there's nothing 'primitive' about this instrument, and it supplies a ready answer to a riddle that we're going to encounter later in this book: is a bone 'flute' always a *flute*?

Chapter Twenty-Four

Water music: a terracotta flask with warbling bird from South America

Peru, Moche Culture, c.700

One of the earliest encounters I had with a truly ancient sound came about in an unusual and, on the face of it, rather improbable way. I must have been about ten at the time. On a Sunday afternoon we would sometimes visit my great-aunt Alexandra, or Alec as she was known, in County Durham. Her house was on a hillside in a colliery village that looked out over the wooded valley of the River Derwent. Beyond the woods, the hills of Northumberland rolled northwards to the Tyne, to Hadrian's Wall and beyond, and on clear days the distant Simonside and Cheviot hills of the Scottish Border could be seen floating on the edge of sight. Alec's husband Bill had been a collier. I don't know if he'd ever travelled; but according to family lore his uncle, a mining engineer, had worked overseas, and one of his trips had taken him to Peru. When he died he left some Peruvian souvenirs to Bill, and they included various pots. They were known in the family as 'Bill's Inca pots' and they lived in a cupboard in the front room. They rarely saw the light of day, but sometimes Bill could be persuaded to get one out. They seemed strange to us children, and slightly sinister, but they were obviously very ancient.

Most of them were a rich red ochre colour, decorated with a cream slip and burnished to such a shine that they almost resembled ancient Greek vases. The decoration was skilfully done. Some were moulded in the form of human faces or figures, with weird

146

costumes and distinctly Andean features. To me they looked like portraits or caricatures of real people. Others resembled cats or monkeys. Alec's favourite, and the only one that was ever on display, was a crouching chihuahua dog, life-sized, with large ears and a snarl, which lived a precarious existence on the living-room mantelpiece. But one pot attracted me even more than the dog. It was a brick-red double flask consisting of two conjoined grapefruit-sized spheres, painted with cream lines and spirals. On top of one sphere was a hole where a chimney-like spout had been broken off. Perched, or rather moulded, on top of the other was the small compact figure of a roosting bird with speckled breast and striped wings and tail. It held its little head tucked back over its shoulder, its eyes closed as if it was asleep. It was a beautiful creation. But one thing made it stand out from all the rest. It whistled.

Years later, it's on my desk in front of me as I write. If I peer closely at the side of the bird's head, just below the sleeping eye, I can see two tiny holes. And if I blow into the broken top of the other sphere, the holes emit a gentle fluting tone. But that's only the beginning. I remember that when Bill poured water into the pot and then blew it, the air could be heard bubbling from the first chamber to the second, and then the bird would begin to chirrup. By carefully adjusting the amount of liquid, he could even make it warble and trill. It's what's known today as a 'water nightingale', a toy for children – except that this one isn't just a toy: it's also a fully functioning flask, and a remarkable work of art.

What sort of people could have made ingenious objects like Bill's Inca pot? Well, to start with they were definitely not Incas. The potter's style dates from a much earlier period: it belongs to a people known today as the Moche, or the 'proto-Chimú' culture of northern Peru. The Moche farmed and fished along the tropical coastlands of the Peruvian north, especially around Trujillo in the Moche Valley, where they lived from around AD 100 to 700. It makes them roughly contemporary with the 'Six Dynasties' in China and the late and post-Roman periods in Europe. The Moche created a highly civilised agricultural society, supporting skilled craftspeople and artists of all kinds. And nowhere is their skill and artistry more evident than in their beautiful ceramics. Examples of their pottery are generally discovered when excavating temples or cemeteries. Perhaps Bill's collection was unearthed when some mining project disturbed one of them. At any rate, that's the story I heard as a child.

It turns out that whistling pots are common to many early Central and South American peoples, living as far apart as southern Peru and Mexico. For the American artist and musician Susan Rawcliffe, who makes and experiments with them, one of their most intriguing aspects is the contrast between their external appearance and their internal structures. Outwardly, the designs show great individuality, varying from region to region; yet inside they all have the same set of acoustical adaptations. The principal device is a little spherical vessel, about the size of a walnut, with a single round sound hole and a little tube to direct the air across it – rather like the *Mary Rose*'s bosun's calls but moulded from clay. These devices have not been discovered anywhere in Europe or Asia at such an early date; they seem to be unique to the New World. If there is a global connection, it's not so much in the technical detail as in the way it taps into our shared human psyche: our eagerness to mimic the sounds of nature.

As my uncle Bill seems to have worked out, liquid played an important part in the way these whistling pots were used. The Chilean archaeologist José Pérez de Arce thinks that they evolved specifically to accommodate liquids and to exploit the properties of air and liquid when mixed together. When such pots are empty, they merely toot or hoot like a flute or an ocarina, but when they are suitably charged with water (or some other drink) the sounds and textures they produce are delightfully varied: from trills and warbling tones to bizarre and disconcerting subterranean rumblings. Susan Rawcliffe has shown how replicas of double flasks like Bill's can even be made to play by themselves: if she half fills them with water and then tilts them to one side, the liquid surges through the tube connecting one sphere to the other, causing the tone of the whistle to change. When bubbles pass through, and especially if liquid is drawn through the whistle itself, the effect of the oscillation is rather like someone trying to sing a note while swimming underwater.

Quite what these pots meant to the Moche remains a puzzle to us – perhaps as the design of a modern novelty teapot might mystify anyone finding it twelve hundred years from now. By the time the earliest Spanish chroniclers arrived in Peru, some eight centuries later, Moche traditions had long been forgotten. So all we have to go on are the objects themselves. Still, the pots and their contexts have quite a lot to tell us. It's long been suspected that they must have had some ritual dimension in ceremonial feasts, when alcoholic and hallucinogenic drinks would have been shared. It's also possible that the unpredictability of the sounds they made would have encouraged their use in divination. The element of randomness in their music-like phrases might have been interpreted in the same way as oracles, or tea leaves, to help foretell the future or suggest future courses of action. But part of their charm and power must also have lain, then as now, in the cunning way they conceal their ingenious mechanisms. Hearing the little bird warble was a magical experience for me as a child, and in this sense it's another example of an acoustical conjuring trick to compare with the Meschede pots and the Lichfield singers' gallery. If such things retain the power to surprise, delight and entertain us today, when we have so many more ingenious devices of our own age, it's not hard to imagine that this would also have been a large part of their ancient appeal.

Bird whistles and water nightingales of one kind or another can be found almost anywhere in the world and reveal to archaeology our ancestors' near-universal fascination with birds and the sounds they make. To modern science, birdsong is perhaps no more 'musical' than their ritualised bobbings and struttings can be considered to be 'dance'. But of course ancient people were not yet burdened with this kind of knowledge and were free to respond to it in whatever ways occurred to them. Mostly, it seems, they responded with curiosity, admiration and delight. Birds have been widely revered not only for the beauty and complexity of their song, but for the meanings it seems to convey. Some traditional peoples, for example in New Guinea, still regard birdsong as the voices of dead ancestors speaking to them. Others in East Africa imitate them in their songs, by inserting short 'signature' phrases like the call of the bean goose or the cuckoo, and sometimes by building whole compositions around them. And don't forget, songbirds (and indeed other 'musical' animals, such as cicadas) were traditionally caged and even trained or encouraged to sing, as a way of enlivening and beautifying households before the invention of modern music technologies.

The beauty of birdsong is celebrated in early literature too, all over the world, where the birds' impulse to sing is frequently given a spiritual motive. We now know that it's hormones and the changing length of day that set our garden birds singing, but to Geoffrey Chaucer, writing in the fourteenth century, it expresses the gladness they feel at the approach of springtime:

The byrdes that haven lefte her song
The birds that had left their song

While thei han suffride cold so strong
While they had suffered cold so strong

In wedres gryl, and derk to sight,
In weathers grim and dark to sight,

Ben in May, for the sonne bright,
Are in May, with the sun so bright,

So glade, that they shewe in syngyng
So glad, that they show in singing

That in her hertis is sich lykyng,
That in their hearts is such liking

That they mote syngen and be light.
That they must sing and be light.

The archaeological evidence isn't limited to bird whistles. Archaeologists have recovered many musical objects that are either made
from the bones and feathers of birds or resemble birds in some
other way. Pipes made from bird bones are among the most beautiful and ancient of human artefacts, from the swan- and goose-wing
bones used in medieval pipes to the crane-bone flutes of Neolithic
China, nine thousand years ago. We assume that bird bone was
chosen for purely practical reasons: it's perfect for forming long
slender tubes. But sometimes small details hint that its relationship
to the living animal hasn't been forgotten. One medieval bird-bone
pipe from Lincolnshire has been fitted with a little collar for the player's fingers to grip, fashioned out of slender bony rings taken from a
bird's trachea: the very part of its anatomy that powers its song.

While objects like the Moche double flask bear witness to the ways
in which ancient people were accustomed to making music and
entertaining themselves, it could of course be argued that 'real'
musical instruments, such as flutes and panpipes, harps and trumpets, are far more eloquent witnesses. What can whistles possibly
add to what they tell us? The answer is simple enough. It's true that
the 'music' of water nightingales and devices of a similar sort is far
less complex than the music we play or listen to today, but we
mustn't let this confuse us. To the archaeologist they're about
something much more than making and performing music.
They're also about hearing and listening, and the ways people perceived and observed their world through sound. If we humans
want to mimic a bird's call today, whether we're hunting for our
next meal or doing it simply for fun, we first need to listen and pay
attention to what we hear. We need to attend to the particular tone
of the bird's voice, to the patterns of rise and fall in the melodic line,
and to the pace and phrasing of the song as a whole. Birds themselves do exactly the same. A singing blackbird or robin alternates

its sung phrases with periods of listening to other birds performing nearby; and what it hears affects its own song. It's a competitive, adversarial thing, of course; but it's also a learning experience, in which younger birds develop their technical skills and repertoire by imitation. This is no less true of humans. Many traditional forms of musical performance depend on listening to each other and learning from what we hear. And in the end, that's a large part of what music is all about, as a medium of creative expression and communication. We listen. We learn. We emulate, and we play.

PART SIX

Light in an Age of Darkness

The Eighth to the Fifth Century

Sandwiched between the European Middle Ages in the ninth century and the end of the Western Roman Empire in the fifth is the period that we used to call the Dark Ages. Today archaeology is revealing how misleading this was, as excavation after excavation testifies to a cultural complexity in which music and musicianship play an increasingly visible part. We're now more than a thousand years into our journey, and we're going to be shuttling between Ireland, Germany and Egypt, exploring musical remains that have been preserved by waterlogging, by desiccation and, strangest of all, by toxic chemicals. Among the most remarkable finds are three graves that could hardly be more different from one another and yet tell parts of the same story: that of ancient poets and musicians. In Ireland another trumpet will be dredged out of a river, this time a wooden one with a surprisingly lyrical voice.

The message that each of these objects will carry is that here on the cusp of our prehistoric past we have to set aside our preconceptions – and our old textbooks, with their tendency to generalise and rationalise – to look instead at the details of the primary evidence, in whatever forms they survive. We're first going to pay a visit to an Italian seaside town and an ancient English library, comparing two artists' attempts to portray not so much the act of music-making as the phenomenon of sound itself. The modern image has been captured in spray paint, in a dramatic piece of street art; the other survives in pen-and-ink in one of medieval Europe's oldest illuminated manuscripts. What they have to say will hold clues to ancient people's musical perception and the value they placed on the act of hearing and listening.

CHAPTER TWENTY-FIVE

Images of sound: capturing voices in an early medieval painting

England, c.750

Driving through a small Italian town one afternoon last summer, a piece of street art caught my eye, spray-painted on a high concrete wall. The images were so striking that I had to stop the car and take a closer look. Only that morning I'd been musing about the way that, down the centuries, artists have sometimes tried to capture images of sounds and music. I don't mean the act of creating music, with voices or instruments: I mean the sounds themselves as they invisibly fill and stir the air. A detail of the mural suggested that this Italian street artist had been entertaining a similar thought.

The work was a little faded in places where the sun and rain had weathered it. Moss and algae were slowly encroaching on the upper parts. But it was expertly drawn and coloured, and very large – about three and a half metres high and about eighteen metres from left to right. Dominating the left-hand side was the figure of a jazz trumpeter, a jovial, rubicund, middle-aged figure, caught in the very act of playing his instrument. He seemed to be reclining in the laid-back posture of someone sitting in a comfortable armchair, but floating on air. He was still putting a good deal of energy into his blowing, however: his cheeks were puffed out, his eyes comically crossed. To his left were some weird rectangular shapes, looking like animated note pads, open at the page to reveal gaping mouths with shiny white teeth. From each mouth something seemed to be escaping: they were arrows, of the kind you might see printed on a sheet of instructions for assembling flatpack furniture. The trumpet also showed something perched inside the trumpet's open bell. Looking closer I saw that, bizarrely, it was a little bird, with its beak wide open. The meaning seemed obvious: both the arrows and the bird were visual metaphors for musical sounds.

But what exactly was the artist trying to convey? The question takes us into the realm of historical iconography, for hints of symbolic meanings in musical scenes are by no means a modern phenomenon.

The library of the great Romanesque cathedral church of Durham, in the north-east of England, houses an ancient manuscript volume, handwritten on leaves of crisp white vellum. It's an eighth-century illustrated Anglo-Saxon copy of a still earlier book, a Latin *Commentary on the Psalms* by the fifth-century Roman writer Cassiodorus. It contains three portraits of the Old Testament King David. In one of them he's depicted in the very process of creating the Psalms, which is to say the biblical collection of religious songs and poems that make up the Christian *Book of Psalms*, the Hebrew *Tanakh* and the Muslim *Zabur*. The king is sitting on his throne, which has wolf heads carved on the top of its two back posts, in the early medieval manner. On his lap he holds a lyre, a symmetrical instrument with five strings, a shallow sound box, two upright arms and a curved bar mounted across the top.

Lyres are often shown in early medieval images of David, and occur more frequently than the triangular harps that later artists attributed to him. Here it's being shown from behind, which means that we can't see how the strings are fitted, but it gives us a splendid view of the fingers and thumb of his left hand. We can even see his fingernails. He's supporting the instrument with a strap attached to his left wrist, and the way he's touching the strings suggests that he's delicately stopping or damping them while he raises his right hand to strum. Archaeological finds include some splendid instruments of precisely this type. But here it seems the artist is also trying to tell us something about the performance and its context.

The beauty and meaning of the image are in the detail: the red of the strings and of David's hair, the vivid blue of his eyes, the nimbus around his head. But it's the wolf-headed throne or *cathedra* that keeps catching our eye. And it has one very curious detail, which may be a visual metaphor.

On the posts of early medieval wooden chairs and benches that have survived, the animal heads generally face outwards. Here they point inwards, directly at David's ears. What's more, from their open mouths emerge weird tangles of ribbon-like interlace. If we zoom in closer we can see that they are elaborated extensions of the animals' tongues. And when the picture is compared with other early medieval manuscript images of David, we find similar paired-animal motifs. In a tenth-century book of the Psalms in Klosterneuburg, Austria, one image of David shows a pair of birds perched on his shoulders, apparently whispering into his ears. They may be even singing to him. Such birds aren't the sole preserve of manuscript images. At least two of the early medieval lyres so far excavated have had a pair of beautiful little bird-headed plaques attached to the tops of their arms, again facing inwards, and gilded and inlaid with semi-precious stones. They are a reminder of tales of the old northern god Oðinn, the patron of poets, listening to his winged spies: the ravens Huginn and Muninn, 'Thought' and 'Memory'.

Such strange collisions of ideas are among the dualities that play such a prominent part in early medieval culture. The wolf heads could, of course, be included here simply because they would naturally adorn any royal throne. But in medieval art things can seldom be taken at face value. Art historians know that nearly every detail serves a purpose, for someone: it re-enforces part of the message that the picture is intending to convey. Dual meanings were one of the stocks-in-trade of vernacular poets. And poetry calls other anomalies to mind: scenes from the life of the pagan hero Sigurd, for example, carved around the doors of Romanesque churches in twelfth-century Norway. What's so interesting in the Durham manuscript is that the artist hasn't just pointed the animal heads towards David's ears: like the figures on the Italian mural, there is that detail emerging from their mouths. It's hard not to see it as a symbol of their breath and, by extension perhaps, of their voices.

The wolf has a rather odd relationship to early medieval music. Wolf heads with gaping jaws are often carved not only on wooden furniture but on triangular harps. To us it feels somehow incongruous: the howling of real wolves can't have made comfortable listening, especially as the animal posed a real danger to people and livestock in the countryside. Yet as with many aspects of medieval art, their significance may have held some positive meaning, and part of that meaning may have been scriptural. As usual, the evidence is a little convoluted. *Wulfas sungon atol æfenleoð ætes on wenan,* wrote the Old English translator of the biblical Book of Exodus, meaning 'the wolf sang its terrible Evensong, longing for its next meal'. A 'terrible Evensong' is already a peculiar juxtaposition. And there's another interesting aspect to a wolf's head that would have been familiar to Christians in Anglo-Saxon England. The Old English expression 'wolf-head' meant an outlaw, and a 'wolf-head tree' (*wulf-hēafod-trēow*) was the common gallows where criminals were hanged. Could our wolves-with-tongues be a reference to Christ's crucifixion?

The answer may lie partly in the setting of the Durham image within the manuscript. The text it faces is Cassiodorus' commentary on Psalm 51, the supplicatory psalm that begins: *Miserere mei, Deus, secundum misericordiam tuam; et secundum multitudinem miserationum tuarum dele iniquitatem meam . . .* ('Have mercy upon me, O God, according to thy loving kindness; according to the multitude of thy tender mercies blot out my transgressions . . .') In verses 14 and 15 the psalmist invokes voices and tongues when he sings:

Libera me de sanguinibus, Deus, Deus salutis meæ,
et exsultabit lingua mea iustitiam tuam
Domine, labia mea aperies, et os meum annuntiabit laudem tuam

Deliver me from bloodguiltiness, O God, thou God of my salvation;

and my tongue shall sing aloud of thy righteousness.

O Lord, open thou my lips; and my mouth shall shew forth thy praise.

Visual cues of this sort are potentially important in that they imply that ancient peoples may have had a pretty shrewd practical grasp of what we think of as acoustic phenomena. And it's not hard to imagine some of the ways they could have acquired it. When they played stringed instruments like the lyre they would surely have sensed them vibrate. You can't pluck a string and fail to notice the movement that accompanies its ringing: the source of the sound is plain to hear and feel, and even to see. They would have felt vibrations too in their trumpets whenever they held their hand across the open bell. And on a freezing winter's day they would have been familiar with the sight of warm breath escaping from their mouths as they sang. The challenge for archaeology now is to try to discover whether from these purely practical observations they could have reached a more theoretical understanding of its physical nature.

In the next chapter we're going to step back into the physical world, to explore some of the hard archaeology that lies behind the image. In the process we're going to find some real-life poet-musicians who could almost be the Durham artist's models, and discover signs that connect them to their instruments – and their instruments to long-lost traditions of vernacular poetry and song.

Chapter Twenty-Six

Poetry's dark matter: the Prittlewell prince

England, *c.*600

Anyone who's read John Preston's 2007 novel *The Dig*, or enjoyed watching Ralph Fiennes and Carey Mulligan in the 2021 film, will have some idea of the magnificence of the fourteen centuries-old treasures from the Sutton Hoo ship burial, the final resting place of one of the last pagan Anglo-Saxon kings. On the cusp of England's conversion to Christianity – in which he himself was probably an important player – he'd been interred with his gilded hoard in a wooden chamber, set in the centre of an extraordinary longship. The ship had then been buried under a tall mound of earth, a barrow, and when it was investigated in 1939 by landowner Edith Pretty and local archaeologist Basil Brown, the treasure was still intact. It's utterly magnificent. But among all the gold and the glittering glass and blood-red garnet inlays, among all the fine weapons and symbols of kingship, there are some still greater cultural treasures. What makes them more valuable even than gold is that they offer us a glimpse of the material reality that underpinned Northern Europe's musical and literary traditions – ancient legends of kings and queens, ogres and dragons, and the deeds of heroes of old. And those cultural treasures included the decayed wooden remains of a medieval storyteller's most prized possession: his stringed instrument.

Only the solid upper part of the frame survived – the part that held the tuning pegs for tensioning the strings. It owed its survival in part to the care with which it had been buried, but above all to an astonishing stroke of good fortune. The site of the Sutton Hoo burial mounds is in open pasture at the head of a long wooded slope, and beneath the grass the earth is just ordinary, well-drained English soil. It's light enough to contain air, and when it rains the water can trickle through it and moisten it. This makes it a biologically active environment, in which all manner of organisms are free to break down dead plant and animal matter, and sadly this includes wooden objects such as ships and furniture. By rights, therefore, hardly a trace of a wooden instrument should have survived. But there had been a freak accident. From its position hanging high on the wall of the closed, damp burial chamber, the instrument had fallen down, only to land upside-down in a large bronze bowl. It was a fine bowl of Near Eastern origin, and it was probably already full of water. The water had begun reacting with the copper in the bronze, and this was to be the key to a musical miracle. When alloys of copper corrode, the products of the chemical reactions are poisonous. Anything organic that lay inside or even close to the bowl was effectively pickled. And with this discovery inorganic chemistry became a new ally in the search for ancient music.

As only the upper parts of the instrument were fully immersed, only they survived in good condition. But the upper parts were substantial, and when a sample of the wood was analysed it was found to be maple. The tuning pegs proved to be poplar or willow. When all the pieces had been treated and were carefully laid out, it seemed at first that they must belong to a small harp – but it was hard to find any medieval pictures of harps that matched them. It was about to become one of the greatest musical mysteries in European archaeology.

As time passed, it became apparent that in fact the pieces didn't add up to a harp at all. They belonged to a different type of instrument entirely, with a different musical history: they were parts of a lyre like the one in the Durham manuscript. Harps, like the one we saw at Carncoagh in Ireland, are essentially triangular, or at least angular, in construction. One edge forms the long hollow sound box; another is the 'neck' that carries the tuning pegs. The triangle is completed by a third piece of wood, a kind of prop known as the forepillar. The strings range in length according to where they cross the triangle: smallest in the angle between the neck and the sound box, longest near the pillar.

Although it shares some features with the harp – open strings, lack of a fingerboard – the structure of a lyre is quite distinct. For one thing, it's usually symmetrical, like a violin or a guitar. Visualise one of those instruments, with its hollow sound box; then imagine it's been fitted with two necks instead of one – two parallel necks – connected across the top by a crossbar. That's a lyre. From the bottom of the instrument the strings fan upwards to the crossbar where they are wound around the tuning pegs, so they all tend to be the same length. You can strum them with your thumb, just as you would a guitar. You can finger-pick individual strings as you would a harp. But you can't stop a string with your left hand, in the way that a guitar or fiddle player can. This is because there's no fingerboard.

Armed with this new identity, the Sutton Hoo lyre fragments now took on a very different appearance, and when in 1970 a new reconstruction was completed, making music with it proved to be very different too. Lyre playing was a lost art, at least in Western musical traditions: to all intents and purposes, the instrument was long extinct. This would pose some fascinating musical challenges.

Soon afterwards, a second lyre came to light, fragmented but unmistakable, among pieces from another aristocratic mound burial. It had been found at a place called Taplow by the River Thames in Buckinghamshire. Since its discovery in the 1880s, no one had imagined that it had anything to do with music – the original finders had labelled it a 'crescentic ornament', perhaps a handle detached from some larger structure. With its resemblance to the top of the Sutton Hoo lyre its true identity was now revealed. This would become a pattern for subsequent discoveries.

With their aristocratic connections, the shapes of both lyres were consistent with the instrument played by King David in the

Durham manuscript. But the next find showed a different side to the tale. Found at Abingdon in Oxfordshire, it was part of the top of another lyre, but the man in this grave was no king or prince. He was armed with a sword, which shows that he was no peasant either, but the grave was hardly longer or broader than he was. There was no other sign of conspicuous wealth. Who was he, and why had a lyre been put in his grave?

Back in the 1970s, the Abingdon pieces seemed to be the least significant of the three finds. But they increased the complexity of the archaeological puzzle. As we've seen, Old English poets occasionally mention someone called a *scōp* or *glēoman* – 'maker' and 'glee-man' – who composes verses while playing a stringed instrument. Could Abingdon Man have been one of these? It was too early to say. Clearly more detective work needed to be done. The first task was to extend the search, to try to reconstruct more of the lyre's sixth-century backstory.

Step by step, and excavation by excavation, archaeology began to reveal the instrument's secrets. Next came some pieces of wood from a grave on the edge of a gravel pit near Bergh Apton, in Norfolk. It was another early Anglo-Saxon lyre and it too had been preserved by the toxic corrosion leaking out from little metal fittings. It was in even worse condition – it resembled strips of dried meat – but showed some telltale structural details. One of the fragments still bore the edge of one of the tuning-peg holes. Another held the attachment for a wrist strap. And as we became more familiar with the type more fragments came to light, from equally ordinary graves within other community cemeteries. Slowly more and more dots appeared across the map of England, making clear how widespread the instrument must have been among the early Anglo-Saxons.

Building replicas helped to make sense of how they might have been meant to function, and how their sounds could have added to the quality of people's lives. But these steps forward came with a headache. In their ancient verses the Old English poets refer to an instrument called *hearpe*, which was sometimes also known by various bye-names or 'kennings'. *Gomen-wudu* was one of these, meaning 'joy-wood'; another was *glēo-bēam*, 'glee-beam'. There's no mention of lyres.

Even the verb used, *hearpung*, suggested a harp, and after years spent imagining poets with harps, it was difficult to persuade scholars that they hadn't meant harps after all. Yet the hard fact had to be faced: archaeology was finding lyre after lyre and the harp was nowhere to be seen. Some ingenious counter-arguments were put forward. These dead lyre players, some said, must have been merely musicians; real poets would still have played harps. Well, maybe they would. But as more and more lyre fragments emerged, in quite different settings, the harp theory began to lose traction.

It's a feature of archaeological excavation that fortunes can change in the twinkling of an eye, and you never quite know what's round the corner. Even twenty years ago we still had no proof – beyond a handful of more or less enigmatic images – of the lyre's overall shape and length. It was still just a glorious jigsaw puzzle of fragments. But then in 2003, archaeologists from the Museum of London at last found the missing link.

Luck had intervened in a most dramatic way. In an early Anglo-Saxon cemetery at Southend-on-Sea in Essex, a major princely tomb was discovered. Around fourteen centuries ago, a large square chamber had been dug down into the sandy earth, and walled and roofed with timber. It had then been covered with a broad circular mound. Over the intervening centuries the roof had caved in and the mound had collapsed, so that as our present millennium dawned, no one suspected that it had ever been there. But its invisibility had had an important benefit: it had preserved the contents from the attentions of antiquaries and treasure hunters.

As they pared away the earth, the archaeologists were in for the surprise of their lives. They found pieces of household equipment where they had been left hanging on the timber walls, still held in place by sand from the collapsed roof though the walls themselves had long since rotted away. As the excavation neared floor level, the remains of wooden and iron furnishings began to appear as stains and concretions in the sand. They included a large wooden coffin, an iron-framed folding chair and traces of a large wicker basket. Stacked along the base of the walls was a showroom display of expensive metal and glass vessels of the kind used for feasting. And as the team reached the floor, other items began to appear. One was a sword in its scabbard. At the foot of the south wall was a curious iron concretion, which proved to contain a bundle of rusted spear and arrow heads. But beneath them, flat on the floor, was a strange dark patch that looked like powdered charcoal. With the greatest possible care, the overlying earth was gently cleared away, to reveal the outline of a lyre exactly like the outline of the instrument in the Durham manuscript.

It had benefitted from another stroke of luck. The pale yellow sand that had filled the chamber from above was so sterile that it had been shunned by worms and other small burrowing animals. It remained quite undisturbed, and so were the decaying wooden objects within it. Against its pale background their dark residues now stood out. And embedded within the ghostly lyre-like shape were small metal fittings, with here and there a glint of burnished gold.

Realising its potential importance, the team lifted out the whole block of earth in one piece and carefully removed it to the laboratory. And there any remaining doubts that it was a lyre were dispelled by CT scans. Still hidden in the sand, on the screen we could see the rest of the instrument in remarkable detail. It had evidently been fixed together with pins and rivets and little rectangular metal plates, each of them still in its proper place, each with mineralised wood still attached. The lyre's strange story was finally beginning to reveal itself.

If we'd been expecting to see a snapshot of a single musical moment we were in for a surprise: what we found was a whole movie. It was virtually the life story of a long-cherished working instrument. There were clues as to why it was in the grave. We could see that it hadn't been made just to be a token addition to the funeral tableau. It had been a much loved possession. It had seen life. At some point in its past it had been smashed into pieces, with great violence, then cunningly stitched back together again. Little gold and silver staples had been added to rejoin the splits and under the microscope they showed patterns of wear which indicated that the repaired instrument had gone on being used. What might this tell us about the man in the tomb?

The sheer size of his monument and the grandeur of his equipment mark him out as someone of rank, a warrior and a major householder, buried with full pagan honours. But he's equally identified as a Christian: as he lay in his large coffin, someone has laid a pair of little gold foil crosses over his eyelids. The lyre now proclaimed him as someone who made music an important feature of his life. Could it also mark him as a poet?

The discovery brought an end to nagging doubts about the other fragmentary lyres and their musical identity. As ever more fragments emerged it seemed that lyres and song must have been almost everywhere in Anglo-Saxon England. And this is how, like crime detection, music's archaeology works at its best: by the slow, patient assembling of clues, many of them negligible in themselves perhaps, but together slowly and steadily building up a case. We were now moving beyond the instrument's shape and construction, to apply an archaeological eye and ear to its role in society. The question now was: what might we find if we continued the same painstaking search across a wider geographical area?

CHAPTER TWENTY-SEVEN

Horns of Elfland: a wooden trumpet from the bed of the River Erne

Ireland, eighth–seventh century

Music-making can sometimes be a dangerous business, and it's alarming the number of ways you can hurt yourself while you're making it. It's especially true in music's archaeology. One day in March 1857, the eminent Dublin naturalist Robert Ball was testing an ancient bronze horn that had been found in an Irish peat bog. It was to be his last experiment. Although the instrument seemed complete, it lacked anything resembling the long narrow bore and small, carefully shaped mouthpiece that allows today's horn players to articulate the multiple notes of the harmonic series. All he had to work with was a broad conical bore and a rather large oval hole moulded into the side of the horn towards its narrower end. Sounding it in the modern way would have been a severe test of any player's lungs, to say nothing of his diaphragm, windpipe, facial muscles, lips and general circulation. Nevertheless, 'By a strong effort of the lungs and lips,' we're told, 'he was able to produce, on a smaller trumpet of this form in the Academy's Museum, a deep bass note, resembling the bellowing of a bull.' So far so good. His mistake was to try to obtain a clearer tone. 'In the act of attempting to produce a more distinct sound on one of the larger trumpets,' the report continues, 'he burst a blood vessel.' He'd suffered an aneurysm. No amount of nursing could save him, and a few days later he died, at the age of fifty-five: the first known martyr to our cause.

Thankfully, such fatalities are rare, but even today experiments are not without their attendant hazards. Equally perilous in its way – and far more insidious – is the danger posed by workshop fumes and dust. If the seasoned flint knapper can eventually succumb to silicosis, the fumes from hot metal can be every bit as nasty, and their effect is immediate. When copper is smelted from its natural ores, one of the harmful vapours given off is arsenic trioxide. Plastics used for moulding copies of objects can emit carcinogenic styrene vapour as they cure. So all in all, you might think, it would be safer to concentrate on building wooden instruments. After all, what could be more innocent than a piece of clean fresh timber? The answer, it turns out, depends on which timber you have in mind.

In this chapter we're going to meet two rather special instrument finds, and they were both made from a particular timber: yew. It's the coniferous tree with the dark glossy needles and attractive pink berries that's popular for garden hedges and grows to a great age in so many ancient British and Irish churchyards. It's a wonderfully strong, resonant wood, and since time immemorial these qualities have recommended it to makers of traditional archery bows and certain types of musical instrument. But it's a material with a dark secret. 'Every part of this tree,' the textbooks tell us, 'is poisonous.' It's especially dangerous when it's dried. At least two archaeologists I've known have fallen ill while experimenting with yew, one of them needing hospital treatment. The cause of the trouble proved to be the fine, airborne dust created by machining. Yew sawdust contains taxane alkaloids, and they are particularly strong in the European species *Taxus baccata*. Breathe in enough of it and you can find yourself in serious trouble. So if you ever think of making copies of either of these two finds, think very carefully first.

The instruments are again Irish horns, but this time they aren't prehistoric like the bronze one that killed Robert Ball. They are early medieval. And the sounds we get when we make and play accurate replicas are surprisingly sweet.

Show most people the silent remains of an ancient horn or trumpet, and they'll imagine something rather loud and strident, even brassy. They'll think of the instruments echoing through forests, or calling to each other across mountainous seas, or the clash of arms. And it's true that, along with drums, horns and trumpets have long been famous for being able to penetrate the din of storms and battles. Indeed, early writers emphasise this aspect, and for military historians especially, loudness and clarity have been the instruments' single most important attribute. It's a reputation that's stuck. Today, almost every new find of a prehistoric horn or trumpet is greeted by archaeologists as a 'war horn'. But new evidence suggests that even before their adoption by modern musicians and orchestras, trumpets and horns were already showing a gentler, more personable, lyrical side. And this brings with it some clues that are going to have a bearing on how we read parts of music's deeper fossil record, when the time comes.

The first horn was found in 1791 by local people cutting peat for winter fuel from a bog near Bekan, between Knock and Ballyhaunis in County Mayo. The instrument duly found its way to the National Museum in Dublin, where it remains to this day. Among those who've made it their particular study is Simon O'Dwyer, who specialises in prehistoric Irish music. In 2000, he was part of a team that subjected it to a detailed scientific reassessment and afterwards he produced a replica, accurate in every possible detail.

The remains are nearly two metres in length, expanding at one end and narrowing gently towards the other. The wood is dark, like most organic materials that have spent centuries buried in bogs, and for almost its entire length it's been wound about with a kind of spiral binding: five lengths of now corroded and fragmentary bronze ribbon, that originally formed parallel helixes like the stripes on a barber's pole. The replica reveals a strikingly beautiful combination of dark wood, pale wood and glittering bronze. The hardness and thinness of the wood provide the first hints of its likely musical character. Its long, narrow bore and its lack of finger holes make it in some respects acoustically similar to the medieval trumpet found at Billingsgate and to the traditional tree-bark flute. Radiocarbon dating has put its age at around thirteen hundred years, so around AD 700, give or take a few decades.

The second instrument was found in 1956. Workmen were dredging the bed of the River Erne, in the townland of Coolnashanton, four miles south of Enniskillen in County Fermanagh, when someone noticed fragments of wood and metal in the mud and silt. It's preserved today in the Ulster Museum in Belfast, where we can see a display of all the pieces the workmen were able to retrieve. According to the standards of the late 1950s, once the wood had been treated to prevent it from shrinking, they were glued back together and the gaps made up with balsa wood and wax filler, suitably stained. It's not how we'd treat such an important find these days: now we would prefer to exhibit the fragments with a reconstruction alongside. But that was then. The first person to make a proper reconstruction, as far as I know, was a colleague of mine, the Scottish musicologist John Purser, who published an account of his results in 2002. Like the Bekan instrument, the original seems to have been made of yew, but at fifty-eight centimetres long, it's around a quarter of the Bekan's length. Once again it's been bound with bronze ribbon, this time formed into hoops like the hoops of a barrel. A simple bronze mouthpiece built into its narrow tip completes the structure.

Both ancient makers have used the same method to achieve their instrument's hollow shape, and it turns out to be an object lesson in itself. There are essentially three traditional ways to achieve a wooden tube, all of them still in use today (if you know where in the world to look). The simplest and we might suppose the most primitive method is to select a naturally hollow plant stem, as you would a naturally hollow bone for a bone flute. But of course the shape and size of the instrument can't be developed beyond the limits set by nature. A more flexible (and more time-consuming) method is to start with a rod or baton of solid wood and drill a hole straight through it, lengthways. This is how a modern orchestral clarinet begins its life. The bore is then expanded, or 'reamed', to form the desired cone shape, and the outside shaved down; but it takes a great deal of planning and skill, as well as specialised workshop equipment. The third way lies somewhere between these two, and it's the method that's been used in both horns.

Instead of drilling through the initial baton, the maker has begun by sculpting its external shape, then split it in half lengthways and hollowed out each half. When the work was finished they've reassembled the two parts. If you can imagine scooping out the flesh of a coconut, then fixing the two halves back together, you've grasped the general principle. All that's needed now is a way of securing the join, and a suitable paste or gum to caulk it. It's simple, and it's flexible. Unlike natural bores and bores that are drilled out, there are no limits to the hollow shapes you can make with it. It's how later medieval makers made curved horns of elephant ivory (so-called oliphants) and Renaissance makers made their curved krumm-horns and cornetts. But it wasn't just medieval and Renaissance makers who found it useful. The same method is still in widespread use today, from the long straight birchwood horns of Scandinavian and Central European folk traditions, tied together with strips of birch bark, to the enormous curved alp horns of Switzerland, bound with reed or cane of the kind that's used in basketry and wickerwork. It's a technique that has extraordinarily deep roots. But that wasn't the biggest surprise to come from John's and Simon's studies. Hewn from solid wood, the Bekan and River Erne finds may be mere horns, but it doesn't mean that they can't also make fine and delicate music.

The clue is to be found in an eighth-century miniature from Canterbury, closely related to the image of King David and his lyre in the Durham Cassiodorus manuscript. Occupying the centre of a colourful tableau, David again sits on his throne, playing his lyre. This time, however, he's not alone. Around him are other musicians. Two are preparing to take notes, with quill pens and a scroll. Two more at his feet are dancing and clapping. Two to his lower right (our left) are playing what look like cow horns while two more to his left play straight horns of exactly the River Erne shape, with metal bindings picked out in silver leaf. Are we looking at a more or less random compilation of eighth-century instruments?

Or could the artist be attempting to portray a genuine musical ensemble? To art historians and musicologists the answer has always seemed perfectly clear: it's a case of imagination rather than reality. Even those of us familiar with the more vigorous techniques of lyre playing have doubted that they could seriously have competed with horns and trumpets. But it turns out we were wrong.

Just how wrong was revealed in 2002 at a conference in Germany, where one of the underlying themes was experimental performance. John was there with his replica, and I was there with one of my lyres. Joachim Schween, from Hamelin, had been dazzling us with his performances on Bronze Age horns (of which more later), and Simon, a passionate advocate of the Canterbury manuscript, decided to set us a challenge. Could we make musical sense of the image? It seemed unlikely, until we started to improvise. Suddenly, in Joachim's expert hands the River Erne horn began to emit the sweetest lyrical sounds. It in no way drowned out the lyre. So much for all our old, lazy assumptions. So much too for that old cliché, the 'Celtic war horn'. It seemed it could be a proper ensemble instrument after all. It had an important benefit too. Playing the horn quietly as Joachim did entailed minimal risk to life and limb. There was no need to strain in order to hit the notes. And remembering what happened to poor Robert Ball, that's surely no bad thing.

CHAPTER TWENTY-EIGHT

Hidden meanings: a traveller's lyre from Dark Age Germany

Trossingen, Baden-Württemberg, 580

Along with the thousands of little mouth harps that are now familiar to archaeologists all over Europe and America, the remains of harmonicas like the one from the Alamo Mission seem to owe their origins to the busy craft workshops of late-eighteenth- and nineteenth-century Austria and Germany. One of the most prolific brands, and certainly one of the most respected, is that of the Hohner Company, of Trossingen in the southern German state of Baden-Württemberg.

Today, the nature of Hohner's business is changing. Production has moved to other sites, and the factories and offices are being converted to smaller business and domestic uses. But conversion has inevitably involved groundworks, and it was during one deep excavation in the winter of 2001–2 that a stunning musical discovery was made. Paradoxically, it had nothing at all to do with harmonicas, or indeed with any of the other instruments made nearby. It was entirely coincidental. Under part of the site an ancient burial ground came to light, dating from the late sixth century. It was waterlogged, and in the saturated earth at the bottom of one of the graves, archaeologists discovered the bones of a man, still stretched out on the ruins of his wooden bed. In his arms he held a wooden stringed instrument. It was another lyre, closely similar to the ones from Anglo-Saxon England. But where circumstances had reduced the English lyres to fragments, here its preservation was nearly perfect. Every last structural and decorative detail had survived.

The archaeological project had been a professional all-seasons 'rescue' excavation. The conditions were tough. It was the middle of winter, and there was snow on the ground. Rain is rarely good news for archaeologists, but snow is especially challenging. Quite apart from giving you cold hands and feet, falling snow and failing light hinder the whole scientific process. They make it hard to spot the subtle changes of colour and texture that separate one soil layer from another. If temperatures drop further and the ground freezes, digging becomes impossible. And when the thaw comes, most sites quickly turn into quagmires. Special methods are needed. For the Trossingen team the first priority was to put up a canopy over the grave and to secure the objects that were already exposed. Flooding remained a constant problem. The ancient gravediggers had dug below the natural groundwater level, which explains how the wooden elements had come to be so finely preserved: the grave had soon filled up with water and silt, like some landlocked shipwreck. A way had to be found for the bed and its contents to be removed in one piece for investigation elsewhere.

The engineering solution was to widen and deepen one side of the shaft, allowing a steel plate, like a gigantic cake slice, to be lowered into place. Hydraulic rams were then attached, and the plate was driven sideways, cutting through the underlying clay. Then the whole undisturbed structure – bed, objects and body – could be craned out on the plate, lowered gently onto the back of a truck, and driven slowly to the laboratory. Happily, it went without a hitch, and now the science could really begin.

In a controlled environment, kept constantly moist, the earth was carefully pared away. One by one the objects were drawn and photographed where they lay, then lifted out, to be washed clean and prepared for freeze-drying. The silts between them were examined for microscopic residues, and samples of the timbers were taken for scientific dating. The lyre was relieved of its remaining coating of fine grey clay. But as the work progressed, some amazing details began to emerge. I flew down to Lake Constance and met Barbara Theune and some of her team, with the pieces of the instrument laid out on the laboratory bench in front of us like a scene from an air accident investigation.

There was a great deal to consider. The original maker had carved the sound box from a single piece of hardwood: a flat, probably rectangular plank of maple about eighty-one centimetres long, twenty centimetres wide and two centimetres thick. One end of the plank had been shaped to form the instrument's elegant upper works: two slender arms with a delicate crosspiece spanning the top, the yoke. The lower half had been hollowed out from the front to form a shallow trough. This was where the vibrations of the strings would be converted to audible sound. The hollowing had been extended right up into the arms. The yoke had next been supplied with six little drill holes for tuning pegs –five of the actual wooden pegs were still in place – and the open box had been covered with a tight-fitting lid of thin wooden sheet, the sound board. It tapered from just under seven millimetres thick in the centre to about a millimetre at the edges, which compares very favourably with the sound board of a modern guitar; and when it was new the whole lyre could have weighed no more than a violin or a viola does today.

Having built a few lyres in my time, I could see that its lightness would have given it a bright and resonant tone. But fascinating as it all was, it was nothing compared to the surprise that was now staring out at us from the cleaned surface of the wood: the whole structure was covered in finely scratched decorations. Nothing quite like it had ever been discovered – or even imagined – on an instrument of its age.

Occupying most of the back is a splendid panel made up of forty-four interlaced beasts, in the form of serpents. Their ribbon-like bodies resemble a woven mat, with their outstretched heads making a fringe around the edges, like the tasselled border of a Persian carpet. Each little head has a beady eye and a tiny tongue that projects from the tip of its crocodile-like jaws, and each set of jaws is clamped onto the tail of another animal. The decoration on the front is even more powerful. On each arm are two more panels of interlacing serpents, in contrasting styles. But spread across the centre of the sound board, and arranged lengthways in landscape format, is a dramatic scene. Twelve standing human figures are arranged in two rows of six, each row to either side of a firm dividing line: a tall vertical object that could be a spear or a mast or a standard. It's shown planted on the ground, pointing straight upwards, and it has something like a spearhead at the top. The two nearest figures extend an elegant hand to support the shaft.

None of these details had been obvious when the lyre was first brought into the laboratory. Beneath its film of wet clay, the wood had swollen and the fine scratches had closed up. It was only when the air began to get to them that they started to open again. What did the imagery represent? Why had the designs been cut so delicately, barely visible to the casual eye? And why had no attempt been made to colour them?

The interlaced serpents might be no more than decorative motifs. Their geometrical patterns are common to many early medieval artistic traditions. But the warriors look as though they ought to represent something particular. They are dressed for action, each with a tall cap or helmet on his head, each carrying what looks like a pair of circular shields, and a staff resting against his shoulder. Are they just a generic group of warriors? Or could they allude to some well-known story? Could they be the confirmation we've been searching for: that lyres were not just used to play tunes but were also engaged in singing and storytelling? We've seen in earlier chapters how, over in Anglo-Saxon England, Old English poetry may have been spoken or sung to the accompaniment of lyres of just this sort.

The number of the warriors provides the first clue. Unless that figure is purely coincidental, it calls two powerful stories to mind. The first is the funeral of the eponymous king at the end of the Old English *Beowulf*. After the death of Beowulf, mortally wounded in his fight with a dragon, the Anglo-Saxon poet paints a vivid picture of his royal funeral. At its climax, warriors of the king's *comitatis*, his personal entourage, form a procession around his flaming pyre, singing a heroic lament. The second is the Christian story. We know from the New Testament that Jesus was throughout his ministry accompanied by his twelve Disciples. We've already seen from the Old Saxon poem *Heliand* how early Christian converts among the Germanic tribes saw Jesus in terms of a militant prince supported by his loyal henchmen. What's more, in late Roman and early medieval art the Disciples are often shown in a similarly symmetrical arrangement: in two groups of six, separated by a cross or by the figure of Jesus as the risen Christ. There's no Jesus to be seen on our lyre, and no cross as such, but could the enigmatic central feature be some other Christian symbol? The solution to the riddle – and perhaps it was indeed *meant* to be a riddle – may hang on the lyre's cultural background, in particular on the Trossingen musician and the divided nature of his world.

In the laboratory the team began to piece together important details of his lifestyle. DNA sequencing proved inconclusive, but mineral isotope analysis of his tooth enamel showed that he'd grown up in the local area. He'd been smartly dressed in red and yellow cloth, with leather shoes and gloves, and someone had strewn the grave with flowers. There was also his equipment. Besides his bed, it included a wooden candlestick, a large chair, and a three-legged table dismantled to fit the space. He also had a number of possessions of the sort that a man might have taken with him when travelling. He had a fine steel sword, a shield, a lance, and two wooden drinking flasks, one still with honey residues inside. There was also a piece of carved wood from a horse's saddle. The larger timbers could now be dated scientifically, and this produced another surprise. Ordinarily radiocarbon analysis would have been the team's first port of call, but here they were so well preserved that a far more precise method could be brought into play: dendrochronology, or tree-ring dating. Taking all the samples into account, they were able to pinpoint the exact year in which the burial had taken place: it was 580. We can be even more precise: it was the autumn of that year.

What kind of world did he leave behind? It was a fractured world for sure. The end of the sixth century was a time of turmoil. Germanic kings and chiefs controlled most of Rome's former western provinces, from Italy to Spain and England. Some ruled more firmly than others and they were apt to fight among themselves. While the territory around Trossingen was populated by the Alamans, further to the west loomed the growing power of the Franks. History preserves occasional glimpses of the music of their time, but one story in particular stands out. In around 567, just thirteen years before the funeral in Trossingen, one Frankish king, Sigebert of Metz, announced his forthcoming marriage to the Visigoth princess Brunihildis. Sigebert and Brunihildis would themselves become names for a storyteller to conjure with, but in the meantime a young poet from Italy, with an eye to the main chance, decided to travel north to take part in the festivities. His name was Venantius Fortunatus and he may even have passed through Alamannia on his way, since by coincidence it would have been on his direct route into north-eastern France.

Fortunatus' life story may hold a useful lesson, and it's this: that finding a piece of fancy musical equipment in someone's grave may be referencing something bigger than just their fireside pastimes. Even today, a singer-songwriter can be far more than just a jobbing performer. Some reflect and comment on current social issues; their lyrics can even be politically explicit. Their art puts them in a position to entertain, certainly, but they also 'speak truth to power', and this was no doubt true for the young man from Italy. We can see it in his lyrics: how he appealed to the Frankish ruling class for patronage and how, not to put too fine a point on it, he played them for all they were worth. His songs were the foundation of his diplomacy, and he did supremely well out of it. In spite of dangerous times he kept his head firmly on his shoulders, rising to a prominent position in the Frankish kingdoms and securing considerable estates for himself near Poitiers. My colleague Peter Godman has summed up his achievement neatly: 'Panegyrics,' he writes, meaning flattering political verses, 'were not the cosy occupation of an armchair versifier but a political act with its special attendant dangers.' If we read contemporary writers like Gregory of Tours, the sixth-century historian of the Franks, we can see just how grave the dangers were that he faced.

He maintained his position by making his services indispensable. He clothed his messages in honeyed Latin that represented everything his aristocratic patrons aspired to. And one of the striking things to emerge from his verses is a sense of his audience's divided sense of who they were. These were Germans who had only recently converted to Christianity and were still anxioius to be associated with the language and customs of Rome. Their transition was by no means complete, and they yearned, if not to shake off their Barbarian identity – because they showed no sign of forgetting their old Northern folk traditions – then at least to add to it some of the trappings of civilisation. But the process was politically sensitive. Our man in Grave 52 is unlikely to have enjoyed Fortunatus' exalted status, but could it be that sensitivity of this sort is the real backstory to the Trossingen warriors? Could the ambiguity of the central picture be intentional? Like anyone else in troubled times, poets would have needed to express their own private allegiances and beliefs with discretion.

So perhaps when we ask whether the warrior tableau represents a prince's bodyguard or Jesus' disciples, we're asking the wrong question. Perhaps they are both at the same time. Perhaps they are an admission that, like politicians and diplomats the world over, a traveller and musician needed to be able to become all things to all men.

CHAPTER TWENTY-NINE

Woman in the saffron robe: tuning the lute in the Byzantine East

El-Sheikh Ibada, Nile Valley, Egypt, sixth century

We can picture the scene. It's morning, and from across the broad river an ancient ferry boat glides silently into the eastern bank, lit up by the bright Egyptian sun. In the bow, mirrored in the dark surface of the Nile, stands a figure waiting to disembark. Upright, slim, elegant, in her mid-thirties: she's the epitome of a prosperous, fashionable modern woman. She wears her long hair tied up beneath a red cap. Beneath her shawl a robe of fine yellow wool, exquisitely tailored and embroidered, is gathered at the waist by a red-and-blue woollen cord. On her feet she wears delicate sandals of brightly coloured leather, and as she steps out onto the wooden stage her robe parts to reveal an ankle-length linen skirt, white with a thin carmine stripe. Behind her shuffles a small boy clutching a long, narrow bundle. The people waiting on the jetty adopt a deferential posture, standing aside to let her through into the town; then the crowd draws together again.

It's a scene that must have been played out many times at riverside landings up and down the Nile, as people paid their respects to a passing celebrity. But if this figure was someone special to local people, she's quite special to us too. She, at least, is no figment of our imagination. She's a real person, and the precious object hidden inside the boy's bundle is a delicate three-stringed lute.

We have a man called Albert Gayet to thank for introducing us to her in such detail. He's from Dijon, in France, and in the winter months of 1906–7 he's already in his twelfth season of explorations at the site. He's especially interested in tombs and *objets d'art*, because back home that's what excites museum visitors and impresses the people who bankroll his expeditions. This season he's working to the east of the old city, in the space between its outer walls and the hills. Of the city itself it's surprising how little has remained standing: hardly more than a jumble of rubble to show for all its once-grand buildings, elegant colonnades and broad avenues. The nearest settlement is a modest riverside affair of mud-brick houses, known in Arabic as el-Sheikh Ibada. Yet once upon a time elaborate buildings of one sort or another occupied much of the narrow plain. The place had been a major commercial and cultural centre, and its name was Antinoöpolis: the City of Antinoë.

Founded in the second century AD, it had quickly grown into a vibrant multicultural hub within the Roman world. A metalled road, the Via Hadriana, led directly over the hills to the eastern desert and the Red Sea, where ships would arrive from Persia, India and East Africa. The Nile brought shipments of goods and raw materials from the highlands of the African interior, while upriver from Alexandria and the Mediterranean came all the luxuries, news and fashions of the Late Roman Empire. Towards the middle of the sixth century, when our local celebrity seems to have flourished, the Eastern Roman Empire was at the height of its power and influence. By now Antinoöpolis was a place of Christian churches and monasteries, but it also boasted a theatre, a race track, stylish boulevards and a busy marketplace. And just outside the city limits its citizens buried and commemorated their dead in spacious cemeteries and ostentatious necropolises.

Since 1896 Albert Gayet has been systematically rummaging through these sacred outer spaces. With members of his Egyptian staff he's been unearthing dozens, sometimes hundreds, of tombs at a time, and crating up the bodies and the things found with them. It's a kind of archaeological gold rush. There's little actual gold but a stunning treasure trove of Roman and Byzantine cultural objects.

What makes the site so productive is the dryness of the earth. The valley might have one of the world's greatest rivers flowing through its middle, and the land may once have been fertile, watered by irrigation, but the natural climate is arid. There's none of the steady rainfall that moistens the ground in more temperate climes, and any raindrops that have ever touched the parched upper soil have quickly evaporated before they could sink deeper. Underground the earth has remained cool and, most importantly, dry – so dry, in fact, that bodies buried here have slowly dried out, remaining otherwise intact, while any organic objects buried with them have largely been unaffected by the processes that would otherwise have destroyed them. There have been few fungi and bacteria to cause them to rot. There are no woodworm or other insect pests. Desiccation has preserved all the objects in their original condition.

Among the finds is a beautiful lute. It's miraculously intact. The wood remains solid, and heavy. Its surfaces feel exactly like the surfaces of a modern wooden instrument. The neck and sound box have precisely the appearance and feel of the neck and sound box of a guitar or a mandolin. It's as though it's just come out of storage. There's also much we can learn about the person who played it. Inside the tomb where it was discovered, the arid climate has also preserved the clothes and other belongings of the woman who was buried here. And while most of the finds we've seen so far give a sparse and largely monochrome impression of people's lives, here everything bursts into colour.

In 2006, archaeologists conducted a 'cold case review' of Albert Gayet's surviving materials, particularly the finds from what, for promotional reasons, he'd nicknamed 'the Tomb of the Prophetess'. For many years no one had looked at them as a distinct group: they'd been dispersed around the museum as examples of the various arts, crafts and industries of Late Roman and Byzantine Egypt. But the team now began to gather all the threads of evidence back together, and to interrogate the remains using the latest scientific techniques. They examined the woman and her lute in the finest possible detail. Her body was scanned using the latest X-ray tomography, and the lute was subjected to further microscopic examination and analysis. Radiocarbon dates were obtained for the body, the coffin and the lute, and the species of wood were identified along with plant fibres and residues from the floor of the tomb. To compensate for Gayet's omissions – he hadn't bothered to draw a grave plan – they searched the museum papers and early visitor guides for clues to the tomb's construction, its approximate location within the necropolis and how the body and the objects would have been set out within it.

A black-and-white photograph from 1907 shows the body and finds laid out in a glass case in their first new home, the Musée Guimet in Paris. The woman is lying on her back, fully dressed, supported by a shallow bed of dried plant stems, perhaps the remains of a mattress. Her legs are straight, ankles together, and her hands placed close to each other over her lower abdomen. Around her we can see a number of objects, including a pot to the right of her head and another by her left foot. The lute lies alongside her left leg.

The pots are painted with red and black designs on a white background, with touches of lime and apple green here and there, and one has three little figures of songbirds running around a central band. They resemble Eurasian sparrows or robins, or maybe skylarks. A bundle next to the bed contains the remains of a real bird, an ibis, revered by generations of earlier Egyptians as the living embodiment of the god Thoth. There are still more birds on her tunic, framed in six square panels of red, white and blue embroidery. The colours contrast dramatically with the tunic, which is made of bright yellow wool with a weft of white linen threads arranged in bands. The facing strips, cuffs and strips down the back are also embroidered in red, white and blue, with blue oblong panels containing white lyre-like motifs. Beside her head is a straw hoop the size of a coronet or tiara, evidently the armature from a wreath of living, scented citrus flowers.

She must have cut a splendid figure. A tomography scan of her skeleton shows that she was about forty years old. Radiocarbon dating indicates that she probably died some time between 520 and 610, during the reign of Justinian or one of his successors. There's no obvious cause of death.

But of course, for us the most fascinating object in the whole assemblage has to be the lute. It's not just that it's in near-perfect condition; it also preserves for us the musical scale or mode that its owner was accustomed to play. Like the fingerboards recovered from the wrecks of the *Trinidad Valencera* and the Lelystad ferry boat, it retains a series of transverse slots that originally held frets: matchstick-like strips of hardwood that define the *do-re-mi* framework on which all its music would have been based. Experiments show that, like the tones of medieval bone flutes, it's not exactly *do-re-mi* as we know it today.

On a modern keyboard, adjacent notes should all be precisely one semitone apart, or a hundred cents as musicians measure them, so that a normal major scale *tone, tone, semitone, tone, tone, tone, semitone* measures 200 + 200 + 100 + 200 + 200 + 200 + 100 cents in ascending order, giving an octave of 1,200 cents. This lute has no semitones, as such. Its slightly larger octave of 1,300 cents is made up of seven intervals of various sizes: in ascending order they are a full tone of 198 cents, a diminished tone of 160, another diminished tone of 176, another diminished tone of 168, then a full tone of 197, an augmented tone of 221 and a full tone measuring 195. They sound strange when the instrument is played for the first time. They seem distinctly off-key, out of tune. It's what my grandparents' generation would jokingly have called 'playing in the cracks'. But if we take the trouble to persist and become familiar with it, something even stranger happens. The tuning gradually begins to attract its own distinct musical flavour: it sounds less like an error or an accident and more like some of the scales we hear in non-Western traditions today. And as we become attuned, so to speak, the music takes on a charming character of its own.

It's amazing how quickly the human ear can adapt in this way, and if only we can free ourselves from a lifetime's exposure to rigorously uniform keyboard scales, new possibilities open up for personal musical expression. It's a revelation that we'll do well to remember as we dig ever deeper into music's remote past.

What might this elegant lady have been doing with such a lute? Did it belong to her and was she therefore a musician? Or has it simply been placed in her tomb as a parting gift? Certainly it's a real instrument: it's been played. It's also been damaged at some point and quite badly: broken in two like the Prittlewell lyre, then glued back together. The repair has been pinned through with an iron nail and wound about with a tight cord binding. But the vital clue is preserved in patches of polish that can be seen along the neck and fingerboard, and in the degree of use they reveal. This is how we know that it has indeed been a working musical instrument, but they reveal something else as well.

Experiments with replicas show that the areas of polish indicate the places where it's most comfortable to hold the instrument when playing it, or to grip it when tightening the strings. Because the polish is very glossy, with little of the coarser abrasion that normal wear and tear would have imparted to it over time, it's tempting to conclude that it's only been played for a short time or very occasionally. But that would be to ignore its owner's pathology. Almost uniquely in the archaeology of music, here we have not only the instrument but also the fingers of the person who we believe played it. And the pathology report shows that they have been surprisingly well manicured. Isn't this light polish exactly the kind of wear we ought to expect from such soft and sensitive fingertips?

So who exactly was our lute player, and what has been her role in the life of her community? Albert Gayet supposed her to have been a 'prophetess.' Others since Gayet have proposed less noble professions. But today it's hard to think that we oughtn't to imagine someone more like her near contemporaries, the men buried with their lyres at Prittlewell in England and Trossingen in Germany. As we reflect on her identity, gender and intimate relationship with her instrument, it's important that we don't forget poetry, and song, and the crucial part that women have always played in humanity's musical traditions.

PART SEVEN

Empires East and West

The Fifth to the First Century

On the far side of the world, twelve thousand kilometres from the deserts of Byzantine Egypt, lie the equally arid foothills of southern Peru. There, in the thirsty landscape between the High Andes and the Pacific Ocean, music's archaeology presents us with another fascinating brain-teaser. From around fifteen hundred years ago, a thousand years before the arrival of the Spanish, it's another New World instrument that looks and sounds strangely like something from the Old. The resemblances between the 'flower flutes' of Aztec Mexico and the end-blown flutes of ancient Eurasia have already shown how the New World and the Old have fostered independent yet somehow parallel concepts in music technology. In our next group of chapters we're going to sift through the precious sediment of another five centuries, to seek out further musical coincidences and discover what light they might shine on music-making as a global human phenomenon.

We'll see how, despite the gradual thinning-out of written records within this earlier timeframe, human musical and poetical sensibilities are gradually being mapped by archaeology. And we'll see how the meeting of East and West that we saw in early medieval deer-bone reed pipes is outmatched by a still more astonishing new discovery, not in Europe this time, but on the semi-desert steppes of Kazakhstan.

We'll discover too how mechanical aptitude and ambition combined to create some of the earliest musical keyboard mechanisms, while a grave on the shores of the Black Sea will reveal an instrument that was once thought to be another type of lyre but may now be something else entirely. Finally, in the far north of England we'll hear a dog that didn't bark, and what it could mean for military communications in and around the Roman Empire.

CHAPTER THIRTY

Sealed with music: panpipes in the final days of a Nasca temple

Cahuachi, Peru, c.500

One of the most mysterious of all our ancient civilisations has to be the Nasca culture of southern Peru. Its decorative pottery and beautiful landscape art have left us with a tremendous wealth of archaeological evidence that paints – sometimes literally – a colourful record of its people's lives and times. And yet so much about the Nasca is still a puzzle. Central to questions of their identity, and key to some of the Nasca enigma, is the vast ceremonial site of Cahuachi, in modern Ica Province. Thanks to excavations, we now know that music lay at the very heart of rituals that were conducted there some fifteen hundred years ago.

Like their near contemporaries the Moche of northern Peru, Nasca craftspeople were producing great numbers of fine ceramic wares. And preserved among the remains of pots and bowls are some elaborate drums, whistles and flutes. Pottery is a robust material, especially when it's buried in dry earth. It may break, it may be trampled into fragments, but as a rule it doesn't dissolve through chemical corrosion or biological decay. So, unlike instruments made of wood or bone, or even metal, almost all pottery drums, whistles and flutes ever produced must still survive in some form, waiting to be discovered. In the arid climate of the foothills that separate the snow-clad Andes from the blue Pacific Ocean, that's likely to be a very large number.

The most remarkable of all the ancient Nasca instruments are their panpipes, known today as *antaras*. Those that survive complete, or nearly so, offer glimpses of the kinds of music the Nasca valued, and what they could have sounded like. But like the flower flutes of Aztec Mexico they also take us right to the heart of one of the world's greatest musical puzzles: how do musical traditions begin? A quick glance is enough to reveal that the pipes from Cahuachi resemble panpipes played all over the world: in Europe and North Africa, South Asia and China. So how are we to account for the similarities? What kind of thread, what mechanism of communication or shared experience, what necessity or ambition, could explain their emergence in both the Old and New Worlds?

Some four hundred and fifty kilometres south of the Peruvian capital Lima, at around sixteen hundred metres above sea level, Cahuachi sits on a bare, stony plateau in one of the most arid landscapes in the world. The archaeological complex is hugely impressive, spanning some forty-two square kilometres in all, and instrument fragments have been found there in a number of different locations. Two discoveries have been particularly dramatic.

As archaeologists sifted through the soil and rubble of the courtyard of one temple building, they came across a shallow trench that contained a deposit of twenty-seven beautiful panpipes, each moulded from fine clay, carefully burnished to a gloss and then fired to a rich ochre colour. They all share the same shape: a long right-angled triangle, and each instrument has twelve to fifteen tubes, moulded inside the clay. Their openings form a row along the narrow, squared end. It's a masterclass in the potter's craft. But to anyone familiar with panpipes, the most striking thing about them is their unusual size. In spite of their inherently fragile construction and their slender, flat cross sections, they can be anything up to ninety centimetres long. This makes them some of the largest pottery instruments ever found – and arguably the pinnacle of Nasca ceramic technology.

How did they end up lying in a shallow trench? It seems they've been placed there quite deliberately, following an earthquake. On the south side of the excavated space, the remains of a wall and the floor next to it show signs of structural damage. The trench has been dug along the wall's footing. The instruments have then been arranged inside it in order of their colour: those of a browner cast towards the east, followed by blackish ones, then greyish ones, then yellow and finally polychrome. Each has been broken in half, and this too was clearly deliberate. Someone has then kindled a fire above them, before dousing the flames and backfilling the trench with earth. Radiocarbon dates for organic materials in the fill place the whole strange event somewhere between AD 380 and 540.

At another temple mound archaeologists again discovered a surprising number of panpipes, buried in groups. An access stairway inside the northern part of the mound was found to have been blocked up with unfired clay bricks, and close to the blockage were a hundred and seventy fragments of similar instruments, representing around thirty separate sets of pipes. Still more were found in a passageway on the mound's western side. But although they were in pieces, again there was nothing random or chaotic about the way they'd been placed. The fragments had been carefully arranged so that all their tubes aligned in the same direction. Nearby was evidence of a sacrifice: a polychrome textile ribbon, rolled up, and a length of braided cord made from human hair.

Archaeologists believe that both sets of finds were deposited during so-called 'closure ceremonies'. In the fifth century, Nasca culture seems to have been in decline and the ceremonial life of the complex was coming to an end. We don't know why, but instead of simply abandoning their religious buildings the Nasca evidently decided to shut them down and mark the moment with sacrificial rites. The rituals themselves must have been awe-inspiring – at least to Nasca tastes. Today the extent of the bloodletting involved can seem shocking. Across the floor of the temple courtyard, pits have been dug and filled with things of value, including the decapitated bodies of sixty-four llamas. And the body count doesn't stop there. The remains of a man and a woman were discovered in the south-east corner. They were buried sitting up, and they too have been beheaded. Nearby were other detached human skulls.

It's by no means the last time we'll come across such gruesome finds; but for archaeology at least, it has a benefit. It may explain why the instruments were deliberately broken and the pieces rearranged. Perhaps like the Aztec flower flutes that we saw earlier, they were broken to ensure that their voices would never again be heard in this world.

With the aid of reconstructions we can hear that the essence of those silenced voices lies partly in the quality of the sound they made – their 'tone colours' – and partly in their tunings. Whether the pitch of a pipe is high or low depends on its length; and from the ranges of lengths that the Cahuachi instruments show, whole series of tunings emerge – in effect, musical scales.

But these are not quite the scales we know from European and Asiatic traditions. Old World panpipe scales are generally configured to allow melodies to be played, and this explains why their ancient equivalents are such a source of fascination for scientists and musicians alike. We may not be able to say for sure how the Nasca spoke to one another, or how they sang, but in their panpipes we have an opportunity to examine at least one aspect of the way they organised the sounds they made. However, it comes with a mystery attached.

Some of the intervals, the spaces between the notes, are appreciably bigger than those found on most instruments of modern Western music. In one set of pipes they are made up of alternating large and small intervals, somewhere between small semitones and modern ditones (otherwise known as major thirds). Variable as they are, they are still grouped more or less as we arrange notes, in octaves. But while some of the pipes have been made and tuned in pairs, different pairs express quite different tunings.

Randomness is always troubling; we hope to find patterns, partly because we're conditioned by our own musical experience to look for them. In our modern world we tend to express ourselves through melody when we sing or play together, and broadly speaking that means in combinations of tones and semitones, or small increments of similar sort, arranged in fourths, fifths and octaves. It's a social thing. So wouldn't this have naturally militated against random tunings? Well, it seems not necessarily.

Musical traditions still prevalent in modern-day Chile suggest that people aren't always interested in tunings, or even in tunefulness. The satisfaction they get from ensemble playing may simply be the combinations of colour and texture in the sound they are able to make together. In central Chile, groups known as *chinos* practise a form of traditional pipe playing in which each member of the ensemble plays just one detached tube, their own separate pipe. It's as if a set of panpipes has been broken up and shared out among the players. And remarkably, the players make no attempt to play anything resembling a melody. Like the constant noise generated by the massed plastic *vuvuzelas* at the 2010 Football World Cup in South Africa, it seems the aim is simply to produce a 'wall of sound' when walking in processions. It's an intensely social, and amazingly inclusive, way to perform – everybody is doing their own thing – but it doesn't produce melody as we know it. And to make matters more random still, I'm reliably informed that the pipes themselves are never fine-tuned.

It's not known for sure whether this was the case in ancient Peru, but it certainly gives us some food for thought. It's just another warning to the modern musical time traveller not to be guided, or misguided, by our comfortable Western preconceptions. Like birdsong and other sounds of nature, human sound-making can be sonorous, engaging, inclusive, meaningful and intensely creative, without necessarily conforming to traditional Western concepts of lyricism and harmony, and indeed, purpose.

It's easy enough to identify points of difference between modern South American panpipes and some of their modern Eurasiatic equivalents, and between Nasca instruments and the panpipes depicted in ancient Chinese pictures and the art of the Ancient Near East. Apart from anything else, the Nasca pipes are much longer. But the true enigma lies in their similarities. In both hemi-spheres we can see two broad types: instruments made by joining together sets of hollow plant stems of different lengths; and instru-ments made by drilling or moulding multiple tubes into a solid matrix. The pipes are mostly arranged in the same logical way in both: shortest to one side, longest to the other. We voice them all by blowing across the open ends. There's no block, no duct, no beating reed. Does this mean that they (or some primitive ancestral form) were brought to the Americas by the first migrants from Asia to Alaska around twenty thousand years ago? Or could we be look-ing instead at a wholly independent invention that – like agriculture and urban organisation and ceramics – has been able to evolve sep-arately because it seems the simplest, most natural solution to a shared problem: in this case, creating an instrument with two or more pitches by the simple process of attaching two or more pipes together?

These are questions that have long exercised archaeologists' minds – the choice between the diffusion of ideas and independent invention. But there is one more curious fact for us to ponder. While there were wind instruments, drums and rattles in the Americas long before the Spanish and Portuguese arrived and introduced theirs, there seem to have been no stringed instru-ments. Why not?

CHAPTER THIRTY-ONE

Silken threads: a lyre from the steppes of Central Asia

Kyzylorda region, Kazakhstan, Late Antiquity

What we read in the pages of our history books has usually been worked over by generations of historians, with infinite attention to historical documents. Compared to archaeologists, historians have that one great luxury: the written word; and by and large they talk about things and events that are well documented. For recent history in particular, this can involve them in processing vast amounts of information. Their challenge is therefore to draw meaning out of superabundance. The archaeologist working backwards in time rarely enjoys the same luxury. Nevertheless, archaeology has one great advantage. It's a growing asset. We keep adding to our knowledge with every random find we make. And because of this we often find ourselves confronted with things that are quite new and unprecedented. Fresh discoveries seem to come at us out of left field, so to speak, when we least expect them, and theories can be made or unmade in the twinkling of an eye. My next discovery offers a curious and intriguing variation on this perennial theme. This time it's a type of instrument that we're already familiar with, and its shape and function are perfectly well understood. What's so unprecedented is not *what* archaeologists found but *where* they found it.

The *what* is straightforward enough. It's part of another wooden lyre, which is to say an instrument very much like the ones we saw at Trossingen in southern Germany and at Sutton Hoo and

Prittlewell on the east coast of England. The *where* is less so. This particular lyre would have excited little comment if it had been found anywhere in Western Europe. But it wasn't. It wasn't in Europe at all.

On the north-eastern shore of the great dust bowl that used to be the Aral Sea in Western Asia is the dried-up delta of a once vast river, the site of one of the worst environmental disasters of the twentieth century. The river's name today is Syr Darya. To early Islamic writers it was the Seyhun. The ancient Greeks and Persians knew it as the Pearl River, the Jaxartes, and the Greek historian Xenophon tells us that Alexander the Great paused here in 329 BC, after conquering Bactria and Sogdia. Its headwaters rise among snow-capped peaks more than fifteen hundred kilometres away in the Tian Shan Mountains, where Tajikistan and Kyrgyzstan border western China. Near its mouth stand the massive ruins of a deserted fortress, the caravan city of Dzhankent. Once the ancient capital of the Oğhuz Turks, from its now-silent gates a caravan route stretched like a pale ribbon into the distant East: the legendary Silk Road.

When in the 1970s Soviet archaeologists were excavating in another ruined caravan town nearby called Dzhetyasar, they found an ancient cemetery, and in one of the graves there was something astonishing – so astonishing that when I first saw a picture of it I could hardly believe my eyes. It was a lyre. There's nothing especially unique in either its shape or its construction. It so much resembles instruments like the Prittlewell and Trossingen lyres, and it's so close to them in date, that if it had been found in the fields of eastern England or southern Germany no one would have raised so much as an eyebrow. It wouldn't have occurred even to an expert that it wasn't English or German in origin. So what on earth could it be doing in Central Asia? It proves to be another timely lesson in not jumping to conclusions.

Between 1945 and 1976, a number of archaeological and anthropological investigations had taken place in the region formerly known as Khorezm, or Chorasmia, and in 2019 the Kazakh archaeologist

Azilkhan Tazhekeev wrote an article drawing attention to two musical finds that had caught his attention. One was the lyre from Dzhetyasar. At sixty-five centimetres long, it's about the same length, breadth and depth as its Western European counterparts, and it's been made exactly like them, from a single wooden board, hollowed out from the front. It has exactly the same shape, rather like a shallow rectangular tray with two parallel handles or arms extending from one end to form an open frame. The frame was originally completed by the addition of a wooden crosspiece, to which the strings were attached by means of tuning pegs or levers. At the opposite end of the sound box, a small knob or 'button' has been left sticking out, to serve as the attachment point for the lower ends of the strings. A small bridge would have sat in the middle of the thin wooden sound board, rather like a violin bridge, with notches to hold the strings in place. Neither the bridge nor the board was found, but small fragments of the board appear to survive, attached to the surviving rim of the box.

It's not obvious how many strings it's had, or what they were made from. But already the dimensions of the whole structure lead us to suspect that there were between four and eight of them. Animal gut, horse-tail hair and even silk would all have been available. The sound of the open strings would likely be somewhere between a guitar and a ukelele. But of course, with a lyre's open frame instead of a guitar's neck and fingerboard, it would have seemed more like a harp to play.

As far as I know, the first European music specialist to pick up on Tazhekeev's report (which was published in Kazakh) was Gjermund Kolltveit in Oslo. It was a dramatic moment. It was one of those surprises that you've been half expecting for years, and yet it's still a shock when it comes along. I say *expecting*, because we already suspected that the lyres found in the west and north of Europe were painting less than the whole picture. What stood out from the dots on our maps was that so far, beyond their ostensible heartland of England, France, Germany, the Low Countries and Scandinavia, there was nothing to be seen. Searching through excavation reports had thrown up no hits, even among 'mystery objects'. But could absence of evidence be evidence of absence? It demanded some cool calculation.

The reason seemed unlikely to be environmental: the soils and climates in the territories outside this narrow geographical range weren't obviously unfavourable. Perhaps it was something cultural instead: perhaps their distribution was indicating not the spread of lyres, as such, but a tradition of burying them. Research method might equally have played some part. In Europe, and especially in Britain and Scandinavia, the majority of finds had been in an extremely damaged and fragmented condition. Until we learned to recognise them for what they were they'd been all too easy to miss. Now European archaeologists knew the signs to search for. Could it be that the wider spread of the instrument had so far been overlooked?

Contemplating the maps of ancient Europe for the best places to target, some regions seemed to hold more promise than others, either because they shared cultural traits with Britain and Germany or simply because early medieval archaeologists were particularly active there. Visigothic Spain, Ostrogothic Italy and Vandal North Africa seemed to offer prospects. To the east, we felt that the pagan cemeteries of Central and Eastern Europe might repay further investigation. And in all this, some ancient texts offered a measure of encouragement. The sixth-century Roman author Procopius tells the tale of a Vandal prince, Geilamir, who, when he found himself besieged on a North African hilltop by the Byzantines, appealed to his enemies for some creature comforts. His wish list includes a stringed instrument. In the tenth century the Arab diplomat Ibn Fadlān wrote about a *Rūsiyyah*, or Swedish Viking, funeral that he witnessed near Bulgar, on the banks of the River Volga. He too mentions a stringed instrument being used in the rites; but neither account makes clear what type of instrument it was. Could *they* have been lyres?

Our surprise at seeing the Dzhetyasar object was therefore the surprise of someone finding that a hunch has unexpectedly been vindicated, a prediction verified. It does happen, very occasionally. It simply didn't happen in the way we'd anticipated. Its remoteness from Europe now threatened to upset theories of a broadly European tradition. This was Asia. Had the instrument been traded there from the West? Was the person in the grave a European émigré or traveller? Or was he perhaps a steppe warrior returned from a journey to the West? It teemed with potential solutions of this sort, and with them a disturbing thought began to take shape. Might it be that the *European* instruments were the true outliers – merely the western tip of an *Oriental* tradition? If that was the case, the next question must be: how 'Oriental' exactly? After all, the Silk Road stretches all the way to China.

There's some evidence that the memory of such lyres may have lingered in Kazakhstan through the later Middle Ages. Azilkhan Tazhekeev draws his readers' attention to a traditional Kazakh stringed instrument called a *kossaz*, which like the lyre has two necks. It looks rather like a two-necked lute, and he wonders if it could be descended from an ancient steppe tradition. It could well be. In other parts of the modern world, particularly in north-western Russia and the Baltic region, other lyre-like instruments have survived that we can see may be descended from ancient lyres. There's also some evidence that lyres existed on the steppe in still earlier times. From a thousand years earlier, a picture on a Greek pot in the British Museum shows a similar instrument, perhaps Scythian, that could be the prototype of the Dzhetyasar find.

Meanwhile the puzzle boils down to this. If the Dzhetyasar instrument does prove to be part of another musical iceberg, which way has it been drifting? Towards Europe, or towards China? For the time being we can only guess. In a sense it's the story of music's origins in miniature. The simple, thrilling truth is that, in archaeology, we have to dig to find things, and once we start digging we never quite know what we're going to find – and where chance may lead us next.

CHAPTER THIRTY-TWO

Keystrokes: a Roman organ from Hungary

Aquincum, near Budapest, third century

Whether we're using social media, changing television channels or heating up our food in the microwave, we're all familiar with the humble keypad. Together with its larger cousin, the computer keyboard, it's with us wherever we go. Indeed, it's become so much a part of our daily lives that we tend to take it for granted. If we ever stop to wonder about its origin, we might imagine that the keyboard arrived with the keyed machines of the late nineteenth and early twentieth centuries: early typewriters, mechanical calculators and cash registers. But it has far deeper and – surprising as it may seem – musical origins. In fact, we don't need to look further than the piano keyboard, whose beginnings lie in long-forgotten technologies of ancient music. Together with other traditional keyed instruments – church organs, accordions, button concertinas, hurdy-gurdies – piano keys take us back at least two thousand years, to the keyboards used by musicians in the Greek and Roman world.

Their first physical remains came to light in 1865, at Avenches in the Swiss canton of Vaud. Broken and scattered around the ruins and the grounds of a Roman palace were various pieces of what had once been the internal mechanism of an organ. They weren't much to look at. Staring at them now, you wouldn't instantly guess that they ever belonged together, or that they held any musical significance at all. None of the telltale pipes had survived. There was no trace of the large plinth unit, containing the pump pistons and the water-filled hydraulic regulator that gave the instrument its ancient

Latin name, *hydraulis*. All that remained were the leftovers. To an organ specialist, however, they are parts of the control unit: the brains, or at least the heart, of the instrument. And that's a great stroke of luck, because no other single component could have preserved so much information about the finished instrument and its musical power.

The largest of the pieces is a square of stout bronze sheet, about the size of the page you're reading. Drilled into it are six rows of neat round holes, about the diameter of a pencil, equally spaced. It's reminiscent of the little perforated plate from the Alamo harmonica, except that these are not slots for reeds but holes through which pressurised air would have been allowed to flow to the organ pipes. We can even see how they were opened and closed. At a right angle to each of the six rows are straight guide rails, riveted firmly in place, and between each parallel pair of rails there was once a sliding bar. Three fragments of the sliders were also found, with the same round holes. It seems that by sliding them in or out, the player could open or close the flow of air to each rank of pipes. And that's exactly what the different rows of holes represent: six separate ranks of organ pipes. The slider, presumably oiled, was moved in and out by a mechanical link to a lever on the keyboard. Two of these links also survive. Before the plate was broken, each of the six ranks it supported would have comprised twelve or thirteen pipes, tuned a semitone apart, and that's a lot of pipes – between seventy-two and seventy-eight in all. This was no lightweight instrument like a harmonica or a concertina but a proper organ, made by a professional organ-builder, and no doubt *very* expensive.

We know how the machinery worked because we're lucky enough to have an almost complete specimen to work back from. A hoard of what looked like machine parts came to light in 1931, in the ruins of the Roman city of Aquincum by the banks of the River Danube near Budapest. They were found in a layer made up of the burnt remains of Roman buildings that – ironically – had once been the headquarters of the city fire brigade. They included fifty-two metal pipes, this time in four rows of thirteen, together with all the metalwork needed to drive a thirteen-note keyboard. The moving parts had been protected, or hidden, inside a wooden case. An inscribed metal plate from the outside of the case tells that it was made for the guild of textile workers, and gives the names of the two Roman consuls of the time, Modestus and Probus, enabling us to date the instrument to the year 228.

The burning of the building that contained them wouldn't be the last hazard they'd have to face. While in storage in 1945 they had another narrow escape, during Allied bombing of a nearby gasworks. Again there was much damage to the building, and some of the fragments of organ were never recovered. But about three-quarters of the pieces were salvaged and can now be seen in the restored site museum. At first, spread out in their case, they present a bewildering spectacle. But by cataloguing the details and taking accurate measurements, it's been possible to design and build working replicas. Central to the whole operation is that same perforated control plate.

Since 1931 several attempts have been made to reconstruct the Aquincum organ, both in Hungary and elsewhere, with varying degrees of success. Some tests have suggested that the keyboard would have been stiff and awkward to operate, so that the instrument was probably unsuited to elaborate forms of music. But this conclusion has recently been challenged by Susanne Rühling at the Roman-Germanic Central Museum in Mainz, Germany, working with the organ builders A. Schuke of Potsdam. None of the wood of the keys survives – after eighteen hundred years buried in ordinary humid soil it would be astounding if they had. But by studying and replicating the metal parts that remain, in particular thirteen delicate leaf springs, one for each key, Susanne has discovered that the action could have been light, allowing free and easy movement. Rapid virtuoso fingerwork would not only have been possible but entirely feasible, she believes. And echoing the female lute player of Antinoöpolis, the narrowness of the keys also persuades her that the instrument may have been better suited to a woman's hands than a man's. This is an intriguing thought, because female

musicians seem to feature surprisingly often in Roman artists' portrayals of organs being played.

Another persistent myth that the new experiments dispel has
been the instrument's lack of power. On radio broadcasts and
recordings made between the 1930s and 1950s the first replicas were
not only slow but a little underwhelming, like small and rather
dainty chamber organs. This was a puzzle, given that the Roman
images so often present them being played before large and quite
likely boisterous crowds, at major public ceremonies and sporting
events. Without taking liberties with the evidence, Susanne and
her team were able to produce an instrument that really packs a
punch. When the mechanism is set to allow each key to play its
four pipes at once, or 'coupled', the impact is richly coloured and
full-bodied. When it's combined with the virtuosity allowed by the
new leaf-sprung keyboard, the circus scenes depicted by artists suddenly make sense. As it sprang into life, it must have made a
powerful addition to the entertainments it accompanied.

A compelling insight into the way Romans were able to precision-
engineer tubes for musical pipes came to light in London in 1988.
Archaeologists from the Museum of London were at work on a
construction site along the old waterfront of the River Thames
when they came across something quite extraordinary buried in
the tidal sediment. The location had been within the original City
of London, Roman Londinium, and the discovery called to mind
sophisticated musical lifestyles in the capital's Roman heyday
around seventeen hundred years ago

The object was cylindrical, about sixteen centimetres long, and
about the thickness of your index finger. Three-quarters of its surface was bronze, but protruding from each end were the tips of a
tube of some hard organic material. It was tough enough to be
bone or ivory. The metal looked much the same as other bronze
finds from the Thames waterfront: bright and shiny overall, somewhat pitted but otherwise in sound condition. But a closer look
showed that it wasn't just one piece of tube: it was made up of two

delicate tubes, concentric collars of the same brassy metal: one of them fitted snugly over the bone while the other formed an outer sleeve that was free to rotate and slide. It was part of a musical instrument already known from Roman pictures and a handful of finds from the Continent: the reed-voiced pipe that the Romans knew as a *tibia*. But we'd never come across one in such good condition before.

The Roman *tibia* is related to the earlier Greek *aulos*, as well as to later medieval shawms, bagpipe chanters and the modern orchestral oboe. It's a long, straight instrument, made in several plug-together sections (of which this was one) and voiced with a reed. But whereas the shawm and the oboe are single pipes, the tibia was usually played in pairs, like the deer-bone pipes that we encountered among the eighth-century Anglo-Saxons and Avars. The Romans played them separately, with both reeds placed in the mouth and the further ends held apart, one in each hand. Each pipe had more finger holes than one hand could play, and this explains why sliding collars had been added to the design. It was so that they could be opened and closed in various combinations. In this case we could see the outward forms of two of the finger holes. They were both shut: the last player to handle the instrument had left them in the closed position. But X-ray images showed more of them, hidden inside. They revealed something else too. While the exposed outer surface had become pitted, the inner faces were still in a pristine state, perfectly sealed from the outside world. When the object was eventually disassembled, they were as bright and fresh as the day when the instrument was last played.

It turned out to be more than just another musical instrument. Replicating it on the workbench, it became clear that it was also a wonderful piece of engineering. Just imagine it: a tube of bone or ivory, carefully formed on a lathe, then fitted with a tight-fitting sleeve of paper-thin metal. The tubing is in itself a breathtaking piece of work; but now imagine the bone and sleeve enclosed in a series of tight-fitting outer sleeves. The sleeves need to be exquisitely matched so that each outer one can rotate at the slightest touch of the player's fingers. The whole assembly must be absolutely cylindrical – perfectly circular in cross section and perfectly straight – so that one can slide around the other with a smooth gentle movement while still remaining snug. If there's any slackness, air will escape when the instrument is blown, and the tuning will suffer. The tolerances are extremely fine. And if that doesn't already present the maker with enough of a challenge, now add the delicate task of cutting finger holes into the thin metal. It's very difficult to do without distorting the sleeves and ruining the movement. In short, the object was emerging as a masterpiece of ancient machining; and to this day we still don't quite know how it was made to such precision.

The tibia was a powerful voice in Roman music, much loved by players and audiences alike, and frequently portrayed by Roman artists. There are images of players painted on murals and set in mosaic on the floors of well-to-do Roman homes. The archaeological remains show that, for the most part, these are fair representations, right down to the sleeve mechanisms. Some pictures show the sleeves with little levers attached, like keys. Although the artists often place them in the hands of gods or heroes from Rome's mythical past, they also show contemporary players in the theatre, in religious processions and private entertainments. To music historians, the tunings preserved in the remains tell us how far music theory developed by both Greeks and Romans underpinned practical music-making. But replicas played by imaginative performers also reveal their potential as exceptionally expressive instruments of music, capable of playing in different melodic modes, or scales, and offering a wide range of tone qualities, from wild skirling sounds to softer, sweeter tone colours reminiscent of the soprano sax and the mellow 'chalumeau' register of a modern clarinet.

All these fine Roman instruments show once again how important it is not to be lulled, by mute and delicate fragments, into assuming that they couldn't have been powerful engines of music. And they make us reflect again on music's relationship with technology. There are many simple, home-made instruments, of course; but it's striking how often others appear to push the bounds of possibility. We've often supposed that new music technologies have taken advantage of human ingenuity in other areas of science; but perhaps we should be looking at that relationship from a different angle. From the casting of medieval bells to the acoustic designs of buildings, from the fine iron gongs of Great Zimbabwe to the ceramic panpipes of Cahuachi – and now to Roman tibias and organs, we may question whether musicians and their audiences were not just benefitting from technological innovation but in fact provided much of its inspiration and driving force.

CHAPTER THIRTY-THREE

Lutatia's dance: a Roman lute from ancient Crimea

Kerch, Ukraine, perhaps third or second century

In the archaeological collections of the State Hermitage in St Petersburg, there's a unique group of musical objects from a Roman tomb discovered on the outskirts of modern Kerch in Crimea. The Romans knew the place as Panticapaeum, and by the early 1900s, at the same time as Albert Gayet was digging his way through the necropolis of Antinoë in Egypt, the area had become a focus of intense interest to archaeologists and collectors. Finds from early explorations often lack the context that gives modern finds so much of their scientific value and meaning, but sometimes a musical discovery leaps out from the dusty recesses of archaeology's antiquarian past – and this object is one of them. It consists of sixteen bone tuning pegs and a metal bowl. The bowl has been delicately crafted, beaten out of thin bronze into the likeness of a tortoise shell. It's the only object of its kind that's ever been found. It turns out that it once protected and beautified the wooden sound box of a stringed instrument.

In the ancient Mediterranean world, empty shells of the native tortoise, *Testudo graeca*, were used for many purposes, but their oldest and most conspicuous role was musical. By the end of the nineteenth century, antiquarians and archaeologists had long been aware of ancient images of people playing lyres with tortoise-shell bodies, especially on Greek pottery. So there was no disagreement that the Kerch object must be part of a stringed instrument, most likely a lyre, albeit with an unusually large number of tuning pegs. But what happened next provides another timely lesson in how, and how not, to try to make sense of an unexpected discovery.

I should say that not all early ancient images of lyres show them with tortoises for sound-boxes. They show that the early Greeks and their neighbours had other kinds of lyre besides, most of them made entirely of wood – early relatives of the Trossingen and Prittlewell finds. Only two classical types used tortoises, but they were so picturesque, and gained such iconic status in Greek art, that they came to dominate eighteenth- and nineteenth-century perceptions of Greek music. Inevitably, this familiarity led the archaeologists at Kerch to see or imagine that they had found such a lyre, even though the pieces belonged to the later Roman Empire. It was soon to become an accepted truth. But just how true was it really? A closer look at the original pieces suggests that the reality may have been more complicated, and actually a lot more interesting.

I first saw the metal shell and pegs in 1984 when I paid a visit to Leningrad (as St Petersburg was then known). In their glass case was the caption 'lyra', and to emphasise their identity they'd been mounted in front of a full-size line drawing of the hypothetical instrument, complete with a Greek lyre's three-part frame: its crossbar, its two S-shaped arms and its fan of strings. The arms had even been given the spiral twist that we sometimes see in Roman images of Greek lyres, suggesting a pair of ibex horns.

All this was of course perfectly in line with received wisdom. But that's really all it was. At the time of the Kerch discovery, no such horned lyres had ever been found, as archaeological specimens. And they still haven't. They are known only from pictures and sculptures, where they are typically placed in the hands of what in Roman times were already ancient gods and heroes. This in itself ought to have been ringing an alarm bell. Roman society had an unquenchable thirst for what it believed to have been the old Greek ways of life. Greek culture, or how they imagined it, was admired and venerated immensely. But how well did they understand the reality behind it all? Might the horned lyre be no more than an artist's convention, an idealised form from an idealised ancestral world, inherited not from a physical prototype but through a kind of whispering game?

The search for an archaeological solution took me to museums all over Europe, and soon some rather curious parallels began to emerge. It turned out that the Kerch pegs were not the only pegs to have been found in a cache of sixteen. A second group of sixteen had subsequently been discovered in another grave, this time in a necropolis at Dunaújváros, the site of the ancient Roman city of Intercisa, on the banks of the River Danube, about seventy kilometres downstream from Budapest.

It was at this point that a quite different musical connection began to emerge, and it wasn't to a lyre at all: it was to a kind of lute, a single-necked instrument resembling the Byzantine lute from Antinoöpolis in Egypt, and of course the whole family of modern lutes and guitars. The evidence was preserved in plain sight among the archaeological remains themselves, and supported by a small number of previously overlooked images in a very particular genre of Roman art.

The images were carved in relief on marble sarcophagi and other memorials to the dead. Among all the conventional scenes of Roman gods and goddesses, heroes and tragic heroines, they represent real people, and they offer brief but vivid glimpses into aspects of Roman culture that we rarely see portrayed in mosaics or murals. Some show military officers, clutching implements that symbolise their roles in war, including musical instruments. Others depict civilians with tokens of the accomplishments by which they (or their bereaved families) wished to be remembered. Among them is an instrument in the shape of a lute. It's entirely different from the lyres portrayed on Roman statuary, mosaics, coins, jewellery and pottery. It has a long single neck, broad and straight-sided; it's generally held in the upright position, and attached to the base there's a small oval sound box, the exact shape and roughly the same size as our metal shell in the State Hermitage.

The Kerch shell itself carried some of the evidence. Its

front – which is to say the part that its audience would have seen – consists of two narrow panels, shaped rather like segments of an orange, with a rectangular gap in between. Each panel is decorated in repoussé with a small cherubic head at the top and a larger figure below it. On the left, wearing a diaphanous costume, is a female figure with wings, known as a 'winged Victory'. On the right is a male figure, naked except for a crested helmet and a pair of boots, holding a shield in his right hand and a spear in his left. His appearance and the context suggest that he's Phoebus, the Roman manifestation of the Greek god Apollo, famous among other things for playing the lyre. But the telltale detail is in the structure of the shell. The outer curve of each panel has been fixed to the curved rim of the bowl, but both inner edges remain perfectly straight and parallel, so that they frame a more or less rectangular void. This rectangle is the giveaway: the shell is not the sound box itself but merely a decorative outer casing, enclosing a now-lost wooden box, and the best fit for those parallel inner edges is not a lyre's diverging arms but a lute's straight neck.

A fine depiction of such a lute and its player has been carved on a marble memorial stone from Mérida in central Spain. It's one of a number from different parts of the empire. What's so striking about these players is that they are all women. Some could be mythological figures, perhaps representing the divine Muses mourning the dead, but the Mérida memorial suggests that there may have been real human beings among them. It contains the portrait of a teenage girl, and the accompanying inscription gives both her name and her age when she died. She was called Lutatia, also known as Lutatia Lupata, and she was just sixteen.

Lupata seems a rather odd nickname for a girl. The Latin word *lupa* translates as 'she-wolf', though it's also used (in certain contexts) to imply 'harlot' or 'street-walker'. The identity of the person who's commissioned the monument is also puzzling: she too is called Lutatia, this time Lutatia Severa. Were they mother and daughter perhaps, or teacher and pupil? Or was their relationship a professional one? It's hard to say. But if the extravagance of the gesture is anything to go by, it must have been an affectionate one. The finely carved portrait shows the teenager demurely holding a lute, and we can see her fingering its fingerboard and plucking the strings just as she might a modern guitar or a banjo. What's more, the shape of the instrument's sound box is the very image of the Kerch bronze.

The female connection is repeated at both Kerch and Dunaújváros, where the accompanying grave goods indicate that the dead were both women. It also supplies a fascinating counterpoint to all the male warrior equipment that we've seen buried alongside early medieval lyres, and raises the prospect of a more inclusive human story in which women are seen to play an equally significant role in creating music, poetry and song.

But another mystery of the Kerch and Dunaújváros finds remains to be solved. Sixteen pegs is a lot of pegs for just one lute, and we have to figure out how so many could have been fitted along the instrument's neck and fingerboard. One solution is suggested by the double stringing of a modern mandolin or a twelve-string guitar, where the strings are tuned in pairs. But another is suggested by the modern South Asian *sitar* and *chitra vina* (or *gotuvadhyam*), which allow us to imagine eight strings stretched *underneath* eight playing strings, so as to resonate sympathetically when the playing strings are plucked.

If so, could we be witnessing a South Asian tradition in Roman Europe, nearly two thousand years ago? It's an extraordinary thought. But then again, why not? Perhaps we've become so used to thinking of 'world music' and musical 'fusion' as modern multicultural phenomena, that we're apt to forget just how global and interconnected the ancient world could be at times.

Chapter Thirty-Four

Seeing around corners: towers and trumpeters on Rome's northern frontier

Britain, mid-second century

Nothing much is left today of this once powerful structure up in the hills of Northumberland. It was not a house, as such. No one ever lived here, and today only its foundations and ground courses survive; the rest of the stone was long ago quarried away for nearby farm buildings. But once upon a time it would have had a door, two floors and a high roof, and when it was in daily use nearly nineteen hundred years ago it would have been a vital part of a state-of-the-art military complex at the frontier between Rome and its most northerly 'barbarian' neighbours. At first glance it seems to be just one of many such buildings – small watchtowers or turrets – found along Hadrian's Wall. But there's something odd about this one and its relationship to those nearby; and this irregularity may contain the key to a mysterious gap in our knowledge of the Roman army and the story of Roman music.

The units manning Hadrian's Wall were mostly recruited from the near Continent. For much of the time they were engaged in police and customs work at the edge of the empire, though now and again there were revolts and insurgencies to be put down. It's likely that both roles would have involved some elements of music. However, the evidence for this is elusive. Archaeologists therefore find themselves having to contemplate music's footprint in more oblique ways, drawing inferences when direct observation isn't possible. It's an approach that's familiar to science. Astronomers detect invisible objects like black holes and distant planets obliquely, by studying disturbances to visible features of the space that surrounds them. Neurologists exploring the human brain have been able to determine which parts of it perform exactly which function by studying people who've suffered injuries to specific areas of their brain. It's all about anomalies, and the potential that anomalies have to help us detect unseen things through their visible consequences. Prehistorians call such indirect clues 'proxies', and on Hadrian's Wall, built literally on the border between history, to the south, and prehistory, to the north, they provide a test of a detective technique which will prove its worth later in this journey, when sources of direct evidence become rarer.

Built early in the second century, the Wall ran all the way across England from the North Sea to the Irish Sea, following the crests of the hills wherever possible. Along its hundred-and-twenty-kilometre length was a series of fortified gateways, or 'milecastles', placed at intervals of exactly one Roman mile, which is to say about nine-tenths of a modern mile, or one and a half kilometres. They were supported by an existing series of larger forts along the valley of the River South Tyne, less than an hour's walk to the south. The closest fort to our building was the one at Chesterholm, known to the Romans as Vindolanda, which is famous today for its hoard of delicate wooden writing tablets. With such places to their rear the wall builders began work soon after AD 120, and once they had completed each new milecastle it would become the base for a detachment of about twenty-five men. In between each pair of milecastles they constructed two smaller watchtowers, at intervals of a third of a mile, and our building is one of about a hundred and sixty of these. Today we know it as the 'Peel Gap turret' because it stands in a gap in the hills near to the ruin of a late medieval fortified house or 'peel tower'.

Excavated in 1986, the turret is set within a particularly remote and beautiful stretch of the Wall, in the fortieth Roman mile measured from its eastern terminus and only a short stroll and scramble to the west of Milecastle 39. When we were archaeology students we learned that these turrets might have served a variety of functions, not least to provide shelter for troops manning the battlements in foul weather. Our winter field trips to the Wall left us in little doubt of that. With two of them to each mile they would have meant a welcome respite for anyone on patrol duty. Of course, their main purpose would have been to serve the Wall's security needs, as lookout posts; but the fact that the turrets and the milecastles are so uniformly spaced also suggested links in a chain of communication.

Whether armies are on policing duties, on manoeuvre or at war, it's vital for commanders to maintain oversight of their operations through an effective means of command and control. Today this is generally achieved using radio and satellite communications. The Romans had to rely on more basic methods that included runners and riders. But runners and riders could easily be attacked by the enemy, or delayed by accidents or difficult terrain, so there would have been benefits in also having other systems that avoided dangers of that sort. We know that Roman armies routinely used signals to regulate their daily life in camp and to direct troop movements in the field. Roman writers refer to the raising of standards, such as the famous 'eagles' of the legions, to coordinate units in action or on manoeuvre, and they often mention the use of trumpet calls. The historian Vegetius, for instance, devotes a whole chapter to signals in his book on military practice. Yet the same writers give tantalisingly little information about the actual techniques. No handbook or detailed eyewitness report survives. Archaeologists therefore have had to resort to their imaginations and commonsense reasoning. Simple instructions and warnings seem perfectly feasible, using combinations of flags, mirrors, fire or smoke. But some scholars have begun to wonder whether more complex messages could also have been transmitted, and even relayed from tower to tower.

Could the Romans have used telegraphic messaging along Hadrian's Wall, and could sound have played some part in it? It's an intriguing thought, and not especially fanciful. After all, we know that the army had horns and trumpets. We know that there were professional trumpeters in the Roman army, and that they would have been present in the frontier zones. The evidence for this, slender though it is, is in the form of memorial inscriptions.

One tombstone found at Neuss on the Rhine frontier in Germany records the death of a *cornicen*, a *cornu* player, with the wonderfully alliterative name of Marcus Mellonius Mercator. It reads:

M[ARCVS] MELLON[IVS]

MERCATOR

CORNICEN

LOCO TEST[AMENTO]

DIBV[S] M[ANIBVS] S[ACRUM].

Marcus Mellonius

Mercator,

cornicen,

lies here according to his Will.

To the sacred Shades of the Dead.

The word *cornu* generally describes a type of long, slender trumpet curved in a single spiral loop, like a capital letter G, with a mouthpiece at the inner end and a funnel-like opening projecting overhead. The inscription doesn't reveal whether Marcus had been a military *cornicen* or some civic functionary, but another monument from distant Crimea records a musician who was certainly in the army. The gravestone of one Aurelius Salvianus, a *tubicen* or tuba player, reads:

D M

AVR SALVIANVS

TVB LEG XI CL

QVI MILITAVIT

ANNOS XIIII VI-

XIT ANNOS XXXVI

To the Shades of the Dead.
Aurelius Salvianus
Tubicen of the Legion XI 'Claudia'
Who did his military service
for 14 years, and di-
ed aged 36 years.

Between the D and M of the opening line is the sculpted image of a man standing with a *tuba* in his hands. Could it symbolise Salvianus himself?

His regiment, the Eleventh Legion, never came to Britain, though for a time it was stationed at Mainz on the Rhine frontier. However, there is a British memorial to another military trumpeter and it was found not just in Britain but actually on Hadrian's Wall. Discovered in 1873 in the military bathhouse beside Carrawburgh fort, only thirteen kilometres to the east of Milecastle 39, the inscription again begins with the usual 'D M . . .' ('To the Shades of the Dead') and runs like this:

DM...
LONGI...
BVC C...

Longi in the second line signifies *Longinus* or *Longini*, the man's family name, and other inscriptions suggest that the final *c* in the third line must be the beginning of the word *cohors* or cohort, the unit to which he was attached. The context is self-evidently military, and what's more, scholars agree that the abbreviation *buc* can only mean *bucinus* or *buccinator*. So here was a man, stationed on the Wall itself, who held the status or military rank of trumpeter, and whose instrument was the *buccina*, another type of Roman trumpet, curved like the *cornu*. We may not be certain to which cohort he belonged but we can feel confident that in his day the fort at least would have echoed to the sounds of his *buccina*.

If documents of this kind seem few and brief, actual finds of trumpets are still more elusive. Although their cast bronze mouth-pieces have been found all over Roman Britain, I've yet to see one that's directly associated either with the Wall or with any other signal system. So it's reasonable to ask if the hills of Northumber-land really were alive to the sound of their music, why has so little trace of them been found there? Does their absence not argue against the theory? The simple answer is that it doesn't. As we've seen throughout this book, unless they've been buried deliberately, few portable objects of any intrinsic value ever seem to have ended up where they originally belonged. House floors were routinely swept and debris dumped elsewhere. Refuse was scavenged. And even when damaged, instruments would have been too precious to be discarded. Mouthpieces are usually found cached with other items of scrap bronze, as if waiting to be recycled. That's the trou-ble with metals: they can so easily be turned into something new. But there is another kind of archaeological evidence we can turn to. It's a series of curious anomalies in the architecture of the Wall itself and the still stranger relationship between our turret and its immediate surroundings.

The first thing that strikes most visitors to Peel Gap turret today is its odd position: it's located in a deep hollow between two steep hillsides. If we follow the Wall down the high western bank towards it we're confronted by an even steeper rocky scramble up the east-ern side. It's impossible to see more than a hundred metres in either direction. The second oddity is its position on the map, midway between milecastles 39 and 40. Excavation has shown that it's not one of the two turrets originally planned, 39A and 39B, but a unique third turret, added soon after the wall was finished. It seems to have been put there to correct a deficiency. Up on the hilltops, invisible from the hollow, the foundations of the two original towers still exist, each with the other in clear view. But between them the Wall drops out of sight. It's an obvious blind spot and it seems reasonable to conclude that the new turret was added pre-cisely to remedy the fault. There's only one problem: it can neither see nor be seen from the turrets on either side. So if signals ever had to be sent in the event of an attack, someone would have had to scramble up the hill and wave their arms about. Unless, that is, they had some quicker way of attracting attention.

Could this quicker way have anything to do with Longinus and musicians like him? With trumpeters in the frame, the whole picture changes: there would have been a clear and safe way of communication. And their services could have been useful elsewhere along the wall, since Peel Gap is by no means the only awkward dip. We also need to remember the northern weather. Even towers with perfectly clear views all around could still be unsighted by snowfall, mist and fog. The trumpet's deep, foghorn-like blasts would easily have overcome such obstacles.

In the chapters to come, anomalies of this and similar kinds are going to take on a particular significance in the search for music's fainter footprints. For Arthur Conan Doyle's detective hero Sherlock Holmes, in the original story of the 'curious incident of the dog in the night-time', it was the fact that the guard dog did *not* bark at the time the crime was committed that in the end helped to identify the culprit. We've already glimpsed similar anomalies in previous chapters, from quirks of architectural design to impressions left by long-decayed objects. Not everything needs to be evidenced directly for us to see it. If we're to make sense of still unlit corners of our ancient musical past we have to retune our senses to see and hear what *isn't* in front of us, as well as what is.

PART EIGHT

Age of Iron

The First Century AD to the Fifth Century BC

By around two thousand years ago we're stepping back into a golden age, when what we now call classical civilisations flourished in different parts of Europe, Africa, Asia and America. In Rome it was the age of Virgil's *Aeneid* and the odes of Horace. The Greek world was softened by the lyric and bucolic poetry of Pindar and Theocritus. India was in the formative years of the Tamil Sangam tradition in the south, and the Sanskrit beginnings of what would become the *Mahābhārata* and *Rāmāyana* in the north. From third-century BC China there are the musical chapters of the *Lüshi Chunqiu*, the *Spring and Autumn of Master Lü*, while Plato's *Laws*, Aristotle's *Politics* and Aristoxenus' *Harmonics* give an equally powerful impression of musical thought in fourth-century BC Greece. So, in the strictly technical sense of 'possessing written records', this is still in the realm of history. But if we step outside the narrow circles of the documents, from the Arctic to the southern tips of Asia, Africa and South America, our understanding of the human experience now rests increasingly with the discipline of prehistory and the fossil record of people and things. Fortunately it's a rich resource.

In the Old World we find ourselves entering the heart of the period that Eurasian prehistorians call the Iron Age because it corresponds to the first use of iron in making their tools and weapons. We'll see how a new archaeological discovery in France is transforming our sense of what music meant in the conflict between historical Rome and her prehistoric neighbours. We'll travel on to

Egypt, via the Netherlands, to see how an inscription has shone a new musical light on an old poem and an even older instrument. From there we'll make our way, first to the frozen tombs of Asia's remote Altai mountains, and then on to China where we'll witness one of the great wonders of ancient music: a miraculously preserved state orchestra from the fourth century BC. But first we visit the Meander Valley in Turkey to take a look at a truly remarkable two-thousand-year-old musical score.

CHAPTER THIRTY-FIVE

Mrs Purser's plant stand: deciphering an ancient marble inscription

Western Anatolia, Turkey, probably first century AD

Scribbling notes and reminders to ourselves is part of modern daily life. We do it automatically, without even thinking. Despite all our technology, a note stuck to the fridge door makes sure that we don't forget something important. Ancient people had similar ways of helping them to remember. At the simplest level they made notches on objects to record quantities of things, or the passing of time. Other marks preserved knowledge, such as the ownership of animals or the locations of sown crops. For anthropologists, systems of this kind are forms of tool use, expanding the powers of recollection that nature has given us by utilising the physical world. They are 'prosthetic': they are to memory what a kitchen blender is to a cook or a hammer to a carpenter. Musicians rely on similar tools to record their ideas – fragments of lyrics, tunes, riffs, harmonies – jotting them on a scrap of paper or the back of an envelope. Without them musical ideas can be ephemeral and easy to forget. This particular kind of note-taking uses special codes: our musical notations.

Today we have only a small number of standardised notation systems around the world, but in the more experimental past there were many more. I've mentioned how our modern Western five-line staff notation evolved from medieval four-line staves with square notes; and how they in turn emerged from some of the squiggle-like neumes with which musicians began to capture the shapes of melodic phrases during the early Middle Ages. But we've also encountered, in passing, an alternative scheme in which notes were given names to remember them by. It's called *sol-fa* or *solmisation* after a method devised in the early eleventh century by the Italian monk Guido of Arezzo. Guido's trick was to choose a well-known tune, sung to verses by the earlier Lombard poet Paul the Deacon. In the tune each line of melody began on the next note up the scale. By extracting that one first note and pairing it with its syllable – Ut *queant laxis*, re-*sonare fibris*, mi-*ra gestorum*, fa-*muli tuorum* and so on – he created the familiar series *ut-* (later *do-*) *re- mi- fa- sol- la* still used today.

There were also experiments in what's known as instrumental tablature, where notes of instrumental music were represented not directly according to the way the sounds rang out, but on a square grid that showed the positions the player's fingers would need to occupy in order to play them. We might therefore think of tablatures as foreshadowing the piano roll, in that it's the input action rather than the output sound that's being specified. But early medieval musicians had yet another trick to hand, taking advantage of a form of everyday code that was already in widespread use: the letters of the alphabet.

It's the simplest of ideas. Since most medieval tunes tend to be composed of discrete notes within a seven-note scale, each note was given a Roman letter from A to G. We still do it today. This was an early attempt to render music digital, as it represents the rise and fall of melody not in a graphic, analogue way but in a septimal (base seven) code. One of the earliest medieval melodies to benefit was 'O Roma Nobilis', a song in praise of the holy city and its patron saints. It survives in an eleventh-century manuscript in the Vatican Library in Rome, but the neumes that accompany the words are not precise. There are no neat staff lines, no artificial horizons, and the symbols give only an approximate sense of the tune. However, another manuscript has preserved an parallel record of the tune and this time with both *sol-fa* annotation and alphabetical values. There can be no doubt about how it's meant to sound. Here's the first line, showing both notations:

so so so la so fa la so mi mi re do
d   d   d   e   d   c   e   d   b   b   a   g
O Ro-ma no-bi-lis, orb-is   et do-mi-na

By comparing the rise and fall of the neumes on the Vatican manuscript page with the shape encoded in the alphabetical symbols, it's evident that they are one and the same.

The tune that emerges is pleasant, easily memorised, and well suited to being sung by pilgrims on their journeys. It also happens to suit the tunings of a number of contemporary instruments, notably some four-hole bone flutes like the one from Schleswig, and the six-stringed lyres we saw at Prittlewell and Trossingen. But in writing down the letters, the early medieval writers weren't coming up with something new. They'd inherited it from a Late Roman writer, who'd described the same concept nearly five hundred years earlier.

Anicius Manlius Severinus Boethius lived in Italy between the late fifth and early sixth centuries. It was during the turbulent reign of Theodoric, the Ostrogoth king who held Italy together after Rome's Western provinces fell to the Barbarians. Fluent in both languages, Boethius translated into Latin a number of Greek philosophical works, especially of Plato and Aristotle. He's most famous for the book he wrote while on Death Row in Ravenna: *De Consolatione Philosophiae*, or *On the Consolation of Philosophy*, but he also wrote about music, in his *De Institutione Musica*, *On Music*. By the time that 'O Roma nobilis' was composed, this book had long since become one of the foundations of a proper liberal education. Boethius' words on musical theory became hugely influential, but it's clear that even he was just passing on a method of notation that had been handed down to him over many generations.

The earlier use of alphabetical characters becomes apparent in an object from Aydın, the ancient city of Tralleis, in the valley of the River Meander in western Anatolia. It's a sixty-centimetre piece of a marble column, inscribed with a text in ancient Greek. The lines have been prettily engraved and they include lines of verse. But over some of the words the engraver has inserted something else: small alphabetical characters and graphic symbols. They aren't speech sounds but musical notes, spelling out the melody of an ancient Greek tune. Like the neumes of the Old Saxon *Heliand*, they reveal a poem that's meant not to be spoken but sung to music.

As the column wasn't discovered by archaeologists, we don't know much about its origins. It seems to have turned up around 1866, when construction of the Ottoman Railway was approaching Aydın, and it was handed to the chief engineer, a Mr Edward Purser. At home in Smyrna (today's İzmir), he and his Greek wife Sofia were using it as a plant stand in the garden when in 1883 it was spotted by a sharp-eyed visitor, a young Scottish archaeologist from Oxford called William Ramsay. Ramsay reported that the Pursers had had its broken base sawn off flat, to allow it to stand up straight. In the absence of any context or associated objects, it's not possible to date it directly, but the forms of the carved letters suggest that it was engraved around two thousand years ago. Although at that time the Aegean coast of Asia Minor was already controlled by Rome, the population of the city would have spoken mostly Greek, the lingua franca of the eastern half of the Roman Empire.

I first heard the tune performed in the 1970s, when a colleague gave me an old 78 rpm gramophone record: a recording made for 'His Master's Voice' by the Greek opera singer Arda Mandikian, performing it unaccompanied in about 1954. I later rediscovered it on a 45 rpm vinyl disc that featured a demonstration of the Roman organ from Aquincum. I would eventually record it myself in 1986, when I wove it into an instrumental improvisation for a reconstruction of the Kerch lute. And as interest in Greek and Roman music continues to grow, it's been sung and recorded many times over. The tune isn't at all difficult to sing or play. The lengths of the notes are indicated by little signs above the Greek note-letters; and if I convert the Greek letters into the Roman letters that Guido of Arezzo would have recognised, it looks like this:

    ●   ○   ●   ○   ●   ○

g   d   d bcd   c   b   c   dcb   a   g   af

Ó-son zêis phaí-nou / mē-dèn ó-lōs sỳ ly-poû

              ● ●   ●   ○

g b d c   b cbg af   g b   ac   d   b g g ged

pròs o-lí-gon és-ti tò zên / tò tél-os o chró-nos a-pai-teî

Here I've used ● to represent the Greek symbol for a held note, and ○ for a longer one. The Greek lyrics mean 'While you're alive, be bright, don't be sad: life lasts only a while, and Father Time will soon have his due'. It's what Greek scholars call a *skolion*, a type of poem often associated with drinking and other domestic festivities, celebrating life and friendship.

In the next part of the inscription, the column itself purports to speak to us. 'An image, a stone, am I,' it tells us and explains that it's been set up in an act of remembrance. Unfortunately we don't know to whom or what. The inscription ends abruptly at the now-trimmed end of the marble, but the names of two people have survived the cut. The first is Seikílos, a man's name, and the other a woman's, Eutérpe. Given that the message of the lyric is to 'live for today', or *carpe diem*, has it perhaps served as a grave marker? Is it in fact Seikílos' grieving memorial to a dead Eutérpe? If so, was she his wife, his mother or his daughter? Or could the inscription mean something else entirely? After all, Eutérpe is also the name of one of the Greek Muses, the Muse of lyric poetry.

Viewed from the perspective of our quest, the 'Seikilos inscription' is more than just an individual commemoration; and it's the simplicity of the tune that may provide the first clue. It's hard to see why someone has gone to so much trouble and expense to have it engraved. To our modern ears, once the initial fascination at hearing a two-thousand-year-old melody has worn off, it can sound a little trite, even banal. It seems not to go anywhere. It isn't obviously the kind of tune to get people up on their feet and dancing, or whistling, or humming. Did it hold some personal meaning for the owner of the stone? Or could it be that we're interpreting it – and performing it – too literally? Maybe. There are many examples of songs that look undistinguished on the printed page, until life is breathed into them by a skilled performer. And there is some evidence that this tune may indeed have been very popular.

The evidence is in another version, preserved in a manuscript tradition several hundred kilometres to the West. And this time it's the setting not for a popular Greek poem but a Latin lyric with a distinctly Christian tone. It's the church antiphon for Palm Sunday, *Hosanna filio David*, 'Hosanna to the Son of David'. The resemblance is striking. It uses the same musical mode, or scale, and every single note of the earlier tune is present, in the correct order. One or two extra notes have been added here and there, and a short ten-note phrase has been inserted against the words *in nomine domini*, 'in the name of the Lord'. Otherwise the match is note for note. Here are the two songs, reduced to their modern note values:

Greek skolion: G DD   BCD   CBCD   C   B AG   AF...
Roman antiphon: GGDDDCBCDEDCBCDEDCDCBCAGG AF ACCABABGGG...

skolion (continued):   GBDCBC BGAFGBAC D   B GGGED
antiphon (continued):   GBDCBCCBGAFGBACGDDECABAGGGED

How are we to account for the differences? As a rule, in contrafactum – the age-old practice of using the same melody for two different sets of words – tunes tend to gain extra notes through time. They usually get longer and more elaborate. It may be to do with the new words, or their new meanings, or just a wish to embellish. But in any event, that appears to be what's happened here. And it shows that there must have been people other than Seikilos who appreciated the tune, and shared it with one another.

This naturally brings us back to questions of Tradition, and the robustness (or otherwise) of musical memory. We're often told that, unlike the visual arts, music and dance are transitory art forms, existing only in the experienced moment, which is to say in the process; and up to a point that may be true – at least for many modern Western audiences. But it hasn't been the universal human experience. In the modern traditional ballad-dance repertoires of the Faeroe Islands, for example, ancient words, melodies and steps seem to persist merely through being shared by communities and handed down by example. Of course, the poetic metre, the line of the melody and the vigorous dance rhythm all help to provide the participants with a framework for recollection. But the key may be in the way their memories, however fallible they may be individually, are able to combine in real time to recreate a single performance that's true to the community as a whole. For an unwritten song to survive, it seems, at least part of the magic may be in the act of sharing itself.

So here we have a poem that's a song – and it's a song that's been widely popular and continued to be sung in spite of the passing of time that it laments. It's been part of a tradition. The question now becomes: how ancient might the song have been when the Greek sculptor first set his chisel to the stone: the stone that would eventually become Mrs Purser's plant stand?

Chapter Thirty-Six

Sounding the Last Post: a buried hoard of Celtic trumpets in central France

Tintignac, Corrèze, France, late first century BC

Like lightning, musical fame seldom strikes the same place twice, but the village of Tintignac near Limoges in central France proves to be one of the rare exceptions. In around AD 1150, during the age of chivalry and crusades, of towering castles and Gothic cathedrals, the district had been home to its very own singer-songwriter, Arnaud de Tintinhac. The head of a landowning family with its own castle, he was also a troubadour, which is to say an aristocratic composer of love lyrics. Courtly love was a troubadour's perennial theme, sometimes enlivened with pleasant allusions to the beauty of nature, as we can see in this short excerpt from one of his poems, where he reflects on the sounds of springtime:

lanquan vei los albros floritz
et aug d'auzels grans e petitz
lur chans per vergiers e per plais . . .

when I see the trees in blossom
and hear fowls large and small
[at] their chanting in orchards and hedgerows . . .

So Tintignac was already on the musical map when, in the summer of 2004, archaeologists working close to the village came across something much older and altogether more mysterious than a troubadour's love songs. It would turn out to be one of the most exciting musical finds of the century.

The discovery was made less than a kilometre from the present village, on an archaeological site thought to be a 'ritual complex' from a time two thousand years ago when France, or Gallia as it then was, formed part of the Roman Empire. The aim of the excavation had been to explore the open ground in front of a pair of Gallo-Roman shrines discovered in the late nineteenth century. As evidence mounted that it had been occupied by Iron Age Celts, it became clear that it had also been a major holy place. Around the edges of the sanctuary it appeared that a trench had been dug to receive the timbers of a light wooden palisade, framing a rectangular plot about the size of a tennis court. In the centre the people who lived nearby had put up a stout circular building, with a cobbled yard next to it. It was in the north-western corner of the enclosure that the archaeologists now noticed something that made them sit up. It was the outline of a pit, a hundred and thirty centimetres in diameter, and in the soil that filled it were some corroded iron objects and pieces of bronze.

As they set about cautiously removing the earth they found the remains of swords and spearheads. Like the Cahuachi panpipes, it seemed that they had been deliberately broken. Then when the team dug deeper, more layers of objects appeared, carefully packed into the space. Most were bronze and from their tubular form it soon became apparent that they were pieces of trumpets.

In fact they were parts of several instruments. Some had been cast in molten metal, others hammered from thin sheet, with seams neatly soldered or riveted. Alongside them the archaeologists found an iron-bound cauldron and some extraordinary bronze helmets. One helmet was in the shape of a long-necked bird, perhaps a swan or a crane – both birds traditionally associated with music and dance. The long tubular neck grew out of the front of the helmet to sweep back over the crown like an enormous quiff. Nothing quite like it had been found before: it seemed to come out of the costume department of a fantasy movie. The trumpets, however, made even the helmets seem dull. They had long straight stems and were up to a hundred and eighty centimetres long. At the wider, flared end, instead of expanding into a modern trumpet shape they curved around in the manner of an alphorn or a saxophone, to become animals' heads, complete with savage expressions and gaping jaws. Six were clearly wild boars, strangely stylised – their faces were much more slender than a real animal's – but easily identifiable from their tusks and flat snouts, their manes of bristles and their prominent ears. By contrast, a seventh was shaped in the likeness of a gaping serpent. They seemed a perfect masterclass in Iron Age metalworking. Yet while this find came as a surprise to the press and public, it wasn't wholly unexpected by science. In fact, it was long overdue. Archaeologists had seen something similar many years before – and thereby hangs a rather curious tale.

We now cross the sea to England and forwards in time to the eighteenth century – to the era of the European Enlightenment and the very beginnings of archaeology's modern interest in music. The key player is a young Lincolnshire botanist and antiquary by the name of Joseph Banks. Banks has made his name overseas on Captain James Cook's *Endeavour* expedition to the South Pacific, where (among other things) they've been taking part in international observations of the 1769 Transit of Venus. But while he's been away Banks has had people looking out for antiquities for his collection. One of his many interests as a wealthy Lincolnshire landowner has been the drainage and 'improvement' of the county's low-lying marshes, and among the major projects of the day is the ongoing work of dredging the River Witham. From time to time ancient objects are retrieved from the mud and silt, most of them tools and weapons from various periods, ranging from the Middle Ages to prehistory. But now, in Banks's absence, something quite outstanding has been found: a virtually complete bronze trumpet.

When he returns to England, Banks shows it to various knowledgeable people in London. Among the first to offer his advice is the music historian Charles Burney, who suggests that it resembles an instrument known to the ancient Romans as a *lituus*: a long straight trumpet with a hooked bell. This is actually quite a shrewd guess, given that no one has ever seen one before. However, today we can see that it isn't Roman, as such. It's Celtic – another Celtic boar-headed trumpet. The head itself is missing, somehow detached from the bell, but along the remaining outer curve there's a metal fringe that represents one of the boar's principal features: its bristly mane.

Fortunately, Banks the collector is an archaeologist's dream. He's devoted much energy to organising his collection, to the extent of leaving us a detailed account of where things were found and the condition they are in. He's even commissioned an artist to make an accurate pen-and-watercolour illustration of the trumpet. And still not satisfied, he's invited a fellow scientist, Dr George Pearson, to try to establish the kinds of metal it's been made from. Pearson now performs a range of chemical tests on samples, and in 1796 the two men proudly present their results in a joint lecture to the Royal Society in London. It causes a sensation.

Sadly, the trumpet itself has since disappeared, but our loss is in large measure mitigated by the quality of the records that Banks created. In a manuscript account in his own handwriting, published after his death, he describes all of his objects and the watercolour illustration supplies the rest. It shows the instrument in full colour and fine detail, as found, with a scale alongside it in fractions of an inch. This is a remarkable image for its time, and reveals the state of the metal and the damage that it's suffered. Of these, two aspects seem especially significant. One is the missing boar's head, the other the missing mouthpiece. The mouthpiece looks as if it's been wrenched off on purpose. But why? This question brings us back to the Tintignac story.

Before the discovery in France, if we wanted to know what the missing boar's head and mouthpiece might have looked like, we had to refer to the images left to us by the Romans and the Celts themselves. The Romans knew the instrument as the *carnyx*, from the name applied to it by earlier Greek writers, and saw it as a symbol of Celtic identity and power. This of course made its capture an important point of any Roman military campaign, so it's often pictured on imperial sculptures and coins among the spoils of war. The instruments are also shown in silver repoussé on a large Iron Age vessel found in Denmark, the so-called Gundestrup cauldron, where they are being played in a context that suggests either a religious procession or a scene from mythology. The boars' eyes and ears, their open jaws and bristly manes, are all plain to see. So are the trumpets' joints, which look much like the ones in Joseph Banks' watercolour. Three players stand side by side, and as they blow they point the instruments straight up into the air, so that the boars' mouths project forward.

In 2004 the Tintignac trumpets revealed the very same shapes, and in exquisite 'forensic' detail. The boars' jaws are massive, with long sabre-like tusks; and the ears are enormous, like the leaves of some exotic house plant. One ear is more than forty centimetres long, and its hollow stem connects right through into the instrument. This would have affected the tone, so it must be part of the instrument's acoustic design. But the instruments clearly aren't just for making music. Even when they are silent they possess an aura of power and majesty.

For archaeologists the obvious question has been to ask why people would have placed any of these valuable objects where we've found them: the Lincolnshire remains in a riverbed or along its muddy margins, the Tintignac instruments in a sanctuary. The clue may be not so much in the parts that have survived as in those that haven't. The Lincolnshire *carnyx* lacks its head and its mouthpiece, neither of which could simply have fallen off. They've been wrenched. And nearly all of the Tintignac instruments are missing important parts, even though the deposit was undisturbed. Were they abandoned or, like some other hoards, merely scrap, set aside for melting down later? The nature of both sites and the instruments' emblematic character suggest otherwise: that what we're seeing represents some cultural, even political, act. The timing of the Tintignac deposit appears especially significant. The site stratigraphy places it at the end of the first century BC, the point of transition between the Celts' tribal independence and their new life as subjects of Rome. Have the trumpets been deliberately broken in the way that the Aztecs snapped their flower flutes, or the Nasca broke their panpipes? Or were they perhaps recovered damaged and broken from a field of battle?

Whatever the reason, the eclipse of Celtic civilisation by Rome does seem to coincide with the disappearance of the *carnyx*. Perhaps it vanished in spite of its unique sound, or perhaps it was because of it. Perhaps, like the musical traditions suppressed by the British authorities in Trinidad, it was too closely associated with a cultural identity that was no longer politically acceptable. But even without knowing the causes, such extinctions remain of great interest, as they offer a taste of what may be in store as we delve further back in time. Some instruments are gradually eclipsed by others, in the way that lyres came to be superseded by harps in the Middle Ages and other kinds of instruments arriving from the fashionable East. At other times there have been sudden extinctions. I guess we shouldn't be too surprised if, just as in biological evolution, some musical highways turn into byways, and ultimately into dead ends.

CHAPTER THIRTY-SEVEN

Music & lyrics: the Leiden lyre

Egypt, third century BC

Today we're so used to seeing words printed on things we own and on the buildings around us that we're apt to take them for granted as just another detail of modern life. In our literate age, manufacturers and architects routinely label or embellish their work with text of one kind or another. Some of it may amount to little more than marks and signage, but it can also include elaborate explanations and warnings, proclamations and dedications. Some satisfy commercial needs. Others cater to literary tastes, especially on memorials and architectural facades. It's by no means uncommon to see lines of verse comparable to those on the Aydın column. Wherever there are writing systems it seems there's always been an impulse to put them to decorative use. This was equally true in the ancient world, and one of the surprising benefits that it has brought to archaeology has been the preservation of musical and poetical lyrics.

For a field archaeologist accustomed to the muteness of material finds, the discovery of a written sign of any sort, even a simple craftsman's mark, is always an exciting moment; and when signs begin to resolve themselves into recognisable characters, and then into familiar patterns of words, they are apt to send a shiver down the spine of even the most experienced excavator. There's the echo of human voices in them, naturally, and a breath of fresh air, however prosaic the thoughts they express. Amid all the data and statistics of modern archaeology they evoke the lives of real people

234

and real human emotions. One Roman voice proclaims the names *Catavac[us]* and *Bellicin[a]* on a set of moulded clay panpipes from a Roman farm in Hampshire, perhaps in an assertion of ownership. At Rheinzabern in Germany a mould for mass-producing similar pipes has been marked *Pottalus fe[cit]*: 'Pottalus ma[de (this)]'. When we read such things aloud, even the most trivial announcement speaks to us from the distant past. And sometimes, words hold a hint of something still more engaging, when they touch directly on matters of music, forming, like the Seikilos inscription, a living connection between 'poetry' and song.

A link of just this sort came to light in Egypt in about 1815, some fifty years after the River Witham trumpet was dredged from the Lincolnshire Fen. It's preserved in another wooden lyre, slightly different from the ones seen in earlier chapters but still with all the lyre's essential features. Exhibited today in the Rijksmuseum van Oudheden at Leiden in the Netherlands, it stands about forty-five centimetres tall, with a hollow sound box, curved arms and a sloping crossbar. The wood itself appears to be mulberry, and its surface is polished smooth to reveal a rich golden colour. Its unusually complete condition indicates that it's been preserved by desiccation, like the Antinoöpolis lute. Only the strings and the bridge are missing.

The finder was an Italian treasure hunter from Tuscany by the name of Piccinini. By the time he discovered the instrument it must have been broken, but the parts were sufficiently intact to be reassembled with the aid of some plaster filler painted to match the rest of the wood. It was then put up for sale. The first buyer it attracted was an Armenian merchant called Giovanni Anastasi who doubled as the Swedish-Norwegian consul general in Egypt. He in turn sold it to the Dutch government in 1828, and that's how it comes to be in Leiden. It's not known where Piccinini found the instrument, but another lyre excavated about a century later at Luxor, on the site of ancient Thebes, is so very like it that the two clearly belong to the same tradition of instrument building; they could almost be from the same workshop. On the back of Piccinini's instrument, however, there's something quite extraordinary. Precisely where we saw the complex design of interlaced dragons on the Trossingen lyre, there's a rectangular pattern of marks. It proves to be lines of verse that have been applied using a fine brush dipped in black ink. Although subsequently worn down with handling and cleaning, to a specialist eye they are still legible. The painter has neglected to supply a tune to accompany them, but what they lack in notation they more than make up for by this unique juxtaposition: for the first time poetry is set in close physical proximity to evidence of music-making. The implication seems clear: this ancient verse was meant to be sung.

Written in a late form of the ancient Egyptian script known as Hieratic, originally developed from hieroglyphs, the poem proves to be another love song. It goes something like this:

> O you who are anointed with ointment,
> great and young!
> Be joyful!
>
> Come, let us make this a fortunate day!
> There is no chance of returning,
> And none of living again.
> Kiss often – again, again and again!
>
> Be joyful!
> Kiss often – again, again and again!

It reminds us of the sentiments expressed on the Aydın column: 'live for today', it seems to be saying.

A lyre and a love song: the connection could hardly be more intimate, or more physical. And it doesn't take a poet or a critic to see it as a smoking gun. It's significant because the link between lyres and ancient poets has not always been obvious, or universally accepted by scholars of ancient literature.

Today, thankfully, we are more open to new evidence and fresh ways of thinking. If the tableau scratched on the face of the

Trossingen lyre alludes to the kinds of poetic narrative that survive in heroic poems like *Beowulf* and *Heliand*, in the Leiden lyre the connection to song is equally explicit. The Aydın column appeared to say that Greek poetry and song are different faces of the same coin. The Egyptian text now takes a step further: it shows that for the anonymous scribe, verse and lyre are natural companions.

There's only one catch. The evidence of the text – the forms of the painted characters and the language that it uses – suggests that it was painted in around 250 BC, so the connection clearly existed in the third century. But in a bizarre twist the lyre itself turns out to be much older. Judging by images of lyres in musical scenes painted on the walls of tombs, and by its resemblance to the lyre from Thebes, it seems to belong to the beginning of Egypt's Eighteenth Dynasty. This would place it between about 1550 and 1300 BC, which is more than a thousand years before the lines were painted. How could this have happened? There's general agreement that the lines are unlikely to be the work of a nineteenth-century forger seeking to enhance the lyre's commercial value. They show none of the usual telltale errors. We know too that the song was clearly visible when the museum first acquired the instrument in the 1820s, long before forgers became as skilled as they are today. But there is one possible explanation: that Piccinini or his agents were not the first people to have dug up the instrument. We know that in ancient times tombs were sometimes reopened, either by looters or to serve some official, religious or commemorative purpose. Could someone in the third century BC have extracted the lyre from a fourteenth-century BC tomb – and then buried it again, after refurbishing it and having it suitably inscribed?

We can't say for sure. The lyre is now just another orphan of the antiquities trade, stripped of all the archaeological associations that could have supplied an answer. But it does at least provide one more piece of music's great jigsaw puzzle; and once again it shows how important it is not to jump to easy conclusions, or rush to take everything we find at its face value. The clue, as always, has to be in the science.

CHAPTER THIRTY-EIGHT

Heavy metal: the musical tomb of Zeng Hou Yi at Leigudun

Hubei, China, fifth century BC

When the Chinese city of Wuhan caught the world's attention in the winter of 2019–20, it wasn't its archaeology or its music that made the headlines. But in archaeological circles, the province in which it's situated, Hubei in central China, had long been famous for the wealth of ancient finds discovered there. Among them are some of the most important musical discoveries we've yet seen – and perhaps can ever expect to see. One in particular stands out from the rest. It's nothing less than music's equivalent of the Terracotta Army of Qin Shi Huang: a complete orchestra with, quite literally, all the bells and whistles intact.

By the beginning of the fifth century BC, China had long enjoyed the trappings of a highly developed and refined civilisation. But by the middle of that century it was a civilisation in turmoil. Different realms and their rulers vied with each other and fought wars to gain control over China's vast territorial expanse. This was what today is called the 'Warring States' period, during the declining years of the Eastern Zhou Dynasty. In times of stress, however, states and regimes have a tendency to make extravagant gestures, and few could be more extravagant than the musical showcase uncovered in 1978, on a construction site in 1977 at Leigudun, Suizhou, about a hundred and fifty kilometres north-west of Wuhan.

Leigudun was already known for its antiquities. They include a number of large circular mounds or *tumuli*, with subterranean burial chambers at their centres. But unlike the Anglo-Saxon mound seen at Prittlewell in Essex, which the passing years had levelled to the ground, they were still standing, tall enough to form conspicuous landmarks. When archaeologists began to investigate the largest mound, they found that the burial chamber beneath it had been flooded by rising ground water, just like the Trossingen burial. In fact it was completely waterlogged, and so were all the things that had been buried in it, from lacquered wooden furniture to elaborately cast bronze vessels and ornaments. It turned out to be one of the most lavishly furnished and perfectly preserved burial chambers that archaeology had ever seen, outshining even Tutankhamun's tomb in Egypt's Valley of the Kings. Inscriptions on some of the objects revealed that the man buried here had been the ruler of a region called Zeng. And the profusion of musical instruments in the tomb suggested that he was someone who'd attached particular value to music.

For archaeologists and historians, the odd thing about Zeng Hou Yi is that until the contents of his grave came to light, no one had ever heard of him. And we know almost as little about his realm, Zeng. We don't know its size or its limits: only that it must have had its centre somewhere near Suizhou. Yet here was its ruler, buried in one of the richest tombs ever discovered. And he was surrounded by an entire musical ensemble. Not for him a favourite instrument or two, packed for the journey into the afterworld. There were fourteen stringed instruments of various kinds, mostly zithers (relatives of the modern Chinese *gu-qin* and Japanese *koto*); there were wind instruments, including six bamboo mouth organs, two flutes and two sets of panpipes; and there were several drums. And these are only the portable instruments. In addition, there was an elaborate metal rack of suspended stone chimes and, most breathtaking of all, filling two entire sides of the large central chamber, a vast L-shaped scaffold of heavy timber beams supporting a carillon of sixty-five large cast-bronze bells. Some of the bells are as tall as a family car. This tomb was no hastily dug hole in the ground, but a full luxury apartment of rooms equipped as a state-of-the-art performance studio.

But now the story takes a disturbing twist. Yi was far from the tomb's only occupant. Accompanying him in his chamber were the coffins of eight women, and in an adjacent chamber thirteen more were found. They are believed to be his wives, servants and followers. It doesn't take a sleuth to work out what's happened here. Yi may have died of natural causes, but the same can't be said for these others. So how and why did they die? It's been suggested that they must have taken some kind of drug. If that's true, did they do it voluntarily, or were they somehow tricked or coerced? And were they already dead or still alive when the tomb was sealed? It's a grim thought. Yet however they died, given that musical instruments form the great bulk of the assembled objects it seems reasonable to assume that some, if not all of them, were the court and household musicians.

To say that the instruments that accompanied them are in good condition would be a serious understatement. Locked away in their cool, dark, airless environment, the wooden instruments and the beams supporting the great bells still have their original lacquer coatings, some of them black, others embellished with elaborate multicoloured designs. The bronzes have attracted the same protective coating that we saw covering the brasswork of later instruments uncovered from river sediments; and beneath this film the original metals are so perfectly preserved that, after two and a half thousand years, the bells are still in tune! We know it because on the face of each bell there's a panel of text explaining just how it was meant to sound, and how its tuning related to the other bells in the set: in other words, where it belonged in the musical scheme of the whole carillon. After giving Yi's name and title, it states the name of the note that the bell generates within the Chinese pentatonic scale, and finally the name of the note one third below it. It all sounds eerily familiar. We know that, in the same period, the Greeks sang songs and played instruments using scales of similar sort, which is to say that they are made up, broadly speaking, of intervals resembling our tones and semitones.

By 1978, when the excavations took place, individual bells and small sets were already well known, mostly taken from other tombs of the Zhou era and its Bronze Age predecessor, the Shang. Looted examples had found their way into museums all around the world. It's clear that they'd once played a pivotal part in a highly ritualised musical performance, carrying both religious and political overtones. It was a world where religion and politics were deeply intertwined, and we can be sure that the music the bells served wasn't light entertainment. It was the music of formal occasions – dignified, measured, stately, and increasingly 'classical' in its conservatism and its detachment from the changing currents of everyday life. Like Gregorian chant, or the military band music of modern state occasions, it was meant to present a traditional order: stable and unchanging, a living embodiment of ancestral virtues. Like big bells the world over, they epitomize calm authority, with more than a hint of the divine behind it.

The whole carillon covers a musical range of five full octaves. It would have needed at least two players, wielding long wooden poles like giant snooker cues. And this is where the technological magic really begins. Marked on the face of each bell are not one but three distinct striking panels or targets, one in the centre and two to either side; and by striking the central panel and side panels alternately, the player could elicit two quite distinct tones, rather like a modern Trinidadian steelpan player. This explains the subsidiary tones mentioned in the inscriptions. The scientific explanation lies in the bells' leaf- or almond-shaped cross sections, which allow two quite separate modes of vibration. Typically the two tones are tuned around a minor or a major third apart, and by this means the sixty-four bells of the main series are in theory able to generate a total of a hundred and twenty-eight separate notes. It's a hugely complex, and no doubt extremely costly, piece of musical equipment.

We saw in medieval Schleswig that even the makers of simple bone pipes were working to a plan, aiming to achieve specific tunings. Here, the inscriptions and the bells' observable properties prove that the musicians of the Zeng court had detailed knowledge of an empirical theory of musical pitches and intervals: a theory that was as advanced as anything that was then known in the West.

But sophisticated as the bells' musical properties are, it's the engineering achievement that impresses most: from the three-dimensional concept to the hot metal casting, from the fine-tuning to the sheer drama and majesty of their finished physical presence. Paradoxically, even as they were serving to create an image of a stable, timeless and unchanging government, it was being achieved through enormous feats of engineering innovation and development. The towering achievement must surely be that each bell has emerged from its complex mould in a form that would generate musical pitches close to its intended twin tunings – or close enough to permit fine adjustment to their desired values. The Zhou period is famous for the quality and ambition of its bronze castings, but this is exceptional even by Zhou standards. Not only did the instruments have to ring, they had to ring properly, to extremely fine tolerances. And they had to remain in tune despite being repeatedly struck.

All of which brings us to a rather crucial question. If archaeologists have had a blind-spot, in relation to music, it's that they've tended to view music technology as a creation of technology. No doubt sound and music have struck them as insubstantial, transitory and essentially secondary: something that's merely hitched a ride from technological progress. This has even encouraged some scholars to doubt that it's the 'real' business of archaeology at all. But what if we've been reading the relationship between ancient music and technology the wrong way round? We've seen in previous chapters the prodigious investments of time and wealth that have been swallowed up in the production of instruments and the creation of acoustic structures, to form some of ancient engineering's most remarkable achievements. Could a pattern be emerging? Far from being some casual by-product of human endeavours of a more serious, practical value, could the real legacy of Zeng Hou Yi be that the needs of music have been helping to *drive* scientific and technological change?

CHAPTER THIRTY-NINE

Frozen in time: fragments of harps from Siberia

Altai Republic, Russian Federation, fourth century BC

From the plains of central China to the Gulf Coast of Texas and the hills of southern Germany, it seems there's nothing quite so effective as airless mud and silt for preserving the most fragile evidence of our musical past. It's that smelly black sediment you sometimes find when you're digging for cockles and clams on a sandy beach, or when you tip the earth out of a plant pot that's been standing too long in rainwater. Granted, it may not be quite so good at preserving things as fragile as paper or parchment or papyrus – these need extremely arid conditions, or a nice comfortable library – but it can be a wonderful preserver of wood, leather and textile. There's one natural preservative, however, that can out-preserve even mud. It doesn't come along as often as we would like, but it's played its part in more archaeological discoveries than you might think, and whenever it has, the results have been truly jaw-dropping. It's ice.

Ice has some fascinating musical stories to tell. We know, of course, that extreme cold is a great conserver of perishable things. And refrigeration isn't just a recent habit. Long before the domestic refrigerator was invented, people had access to ice for much of the year if they knew where to look for it and how best to store it. The modern fashion for ice cream, for example, is often said to have begun in Naples, Italy, using dairy cream chilled by adding salt to ice from the northern slopes of Vesuvius. Communities in coastal Peru have for centuries made summer pilgrimages to the high mountain valleys, to bring down blocks of glacier ice for their church rituals. As early as the sixteenth century, workers on European estates would harvest winter ice from specially dug ponds, which they would then stack in underground 'ice houses' for later use in the kitchen. There are records of similar practices in ancient China and Assyria, between three and four thousand years ago.

In the polar regions ice persists all year round, as it does on the world's highest mountains. Such places are the last relics of the great Ice Age, which ended (for most of the planet) around twelve thousand years ago. Among the most persistent are the ice fields that still feed the ancient glaciers in the high Alpine valleys of Switzerland and Austria. They've been shrinking because of climate change, and in the autumn of 1991, above the Ötztal valley on Austria's border with Italy, hill walkers crossing the retreating ice made an alarming discovery. It was a human body, lying face down in the melting snow. At first it was thought that someone had been caught out by the weather and died of cold; and in a sense they had. But it hadn't happened yesterday. Ötzi, as he became known, had met his end while crossing the mountains more than five thousand years ago. His body was preserved by a combination of intense cold and isolation, and because of this we now know quite a lot about him. On and around his body lay his meagre possessions and the tools of his trade. They include an unfinished longbow of yew, a quiver with fourteen arrows, a yew-hafted copper axe, and a pouch containing small stone and bone tools, all safely blanketed under successive falls of snow. Had he been carrying any form of musical instrument, even a simple bark whistle, it would surely have survived. But there was nothing.

Another musical disappointment (tempered with sadness of another sort) came also in the 1990s with the discovery of victims of child sacrifice on frozen peaks in the Andes, high above the Atacama Desert of Peru. These too show breathtaking preservation. Between AD 1450 and 1475, the Children of Mount Llullaillaco had been buried under cairns at a truly astonishing altitude. They were discovered at nearly seven thousand metres above sea level, and their bodies had frozen so quickly and completely that when they were found it looked as if they were merely asleep. They'd been lying there for five hundred years in their brightly coloured clothes, surrounded by the things that had been buried with them. Once again there was no obvious sign of music.

But sometimes things turn out differently, and in fact a series of frozen musical finds had already come to light in the High Altai of southern Siberia. At one group of sites, south of Novosibirsk, ice conditions had created the famous 'frozen tombs of Siberia'. And there, on the high grassland steppe between Russia and China, Kazakhstan and Mongolia, we can see what biting cold can do for music.

In 1947, Soviet archaeologists were investigating a burial chamber at Pazyryk on the Ukok plateau, when they came across a treasure hoard of luxuries from the Iron Age. Locked in ice, this wasn't the usual assortment of bones, pottery, metalwork and stone. A man's body was discovered, frozen in time, complete with his clothing, his flesh, and even his skin tattoos. Around the chamber lay his personal equipment: weapons, objects made of wood and leather, soft furnishings, and at least three musical instruments. There were two small drums made of horn, and broken pieces of a trough-like wooden sound box which appeared to have belonged to a long slender harp, around eighty-three centimetres long. It had been painted red; and over the open face of the box was a skin membrane, also coloured red. Now loose, it had presumably been stretched taut, like the skin on a West African *kora*, a Burmese harp or a banjo.

The survival of all these normally perishable materials was due almost entirely to the way the burial chamber was constructed. It had been dug deep into the ground, and a strong wooden cabin erected inside it. When it was sealed, the excavated spoil has been backfilled and heaped up over the roof, then hidden beneath an even larger pile of rocks. It's a type of mound that's come to be known as a kurgan, which began to appear across the northern plains of Eurasia around five thousand years ago. But it's only in this remote mountain location that their chambers witnessed a peculiarly frigid transformation. The source of the coldness is partly altitude and partly latitude. The burial is close to the forty-ninth parallel north and around sixteen hundred metres above sea level. The winters there are severe, the summers are short, and even at midsummer the earth stays very cold; so when the tomb builders topped out their work with rocks, they were unwittingly setting in train a unique sequence of events. The loose stones now shaded the made-up ground from the heat of the summer sun, while still allowing cold air to flow over it in winter and spring. In this new human-made microclimate, the annual thaw slowed, and a permanent 'ice lens' began to form within the subsoil. It quickly turned the whole burial chamber into a permanent icebox. Any rain, sleet or meltwater that trickled into the chamber from above soon froze solid, encasing everything on the chamber floor.

Only when excavators removed the rocks did the ice melt and lay bare the drama of the stunning funeral tableau. And among all the finery – the gold, the skins and leatherwork, the silks and felted wool, the embroidered hangings and cushions – were the pieces of our wooden harp, already damaged earlier by early grave robbers but luckily abandoned by them in their rush for treasures of a more negotiable kind.

Up to this point, the sound of the harp was not something that most archaeologists had ever associated with prehistoric nomads; but the excavator Sergei Rudenko wasn't most archaeologists. In 1910, on an anthropological expedition to the tribal lands between the Ural Mountains and the River Ob in north-west Siberia, he'd already witnessed the musical traditions of two tribes in particular, the Khants (or Ostyaks) and the Mansi (or Voguls). Among the instruments they used to accompany their songs and dances were a large lyre-like instrument known to them as a *nares-jux*, and a bow-shaped harp that they called a *khutang*. So the discovery of harp remains at Pazyryk didn't puzzle Rudenko at all. The question was simply what kind of harp they represented – and what kind of musical tradition it might reflect.

We can perhaps catch something of the ancient spirit and vigour of steppe music from the traditional 'throat singing' practised today by singers in Tuva and Mongolia, only a short distance to the east. How ancient these traditions are we don't know for sure: those we hear today can't be dated objectively; but people who know them feel them to be very old, and there's little reason to suppose that they are wrong. If you've ever listened to the magical fluting sounds produced by an expert throat singer, you'll know that they are making use of the same harmonics, the same overtones, embodied in several ancient instrument finds and traditions that we've already seen, from trumpets, lyres and mouth harps to simple bark flutes and whistles. The people who built the kurgans clearly belonged to similarly nomadic, horse-riding, tent-dwelling herding folk. To the ancient Greeks beyond the Caspian and the Black Sea, four thousand kilometres to the west, they were known as Scythians, or Sakā. The Greek historian Herodotus provides us with an account of their costumes and their nomadic way of life, and the description he gives fits our man in 'Kurgan 2' exactly, even down to his trousers and his tall pointed hat. He was evidently a person of standing, probably a chief of some kind, like the lyre-playing 'Prittlewell prince' and the Sutton Hoo king.

Sadly there's no other evidence among his furnishings of his musical affiliations or preferences. There are no written materials. But the textiles and decorative metalwork, and the objects in kurgans nearby, paint a picture of tribal mobility, and goods obtained from faraway places: from Qin China and Mauryan India; across the western steppe from Persia and the Middle East; and through Chorasmia from the Black Sea and Eastern Europe. Textile panels and friezes show processions of animals, mythological creatures, humans (including moustachioed horsemen) and part-human, part-animal chimeras. And like the panels of ornament on the Trossingen lyre, there's again something about the designs that suggests that narrative myths and legends are hiding just beneath the surface. The man's weaponry too shows a warlike quality that's reflected not only in the wider reputation of the Sakā but also in their genetics. Genetic evidence connects them to other nomad populations in Asia and Europe, in the Caucasus and the far north – including some around the lower reaches of the River Ob. So we can reasonably imagine the owners of such harps accompanying something like the narrative songs of the Khants and Mansi, to enrich their leisure hours and enliven the hearthsides of their winter encampments.

Some of the character of their music can also be guessed from the kind of harps they played: light, delicate to the touch, but also responsive to strumming. There's some controversy about the true shape of the instrument from the way Rudenko had it reassembled for display. It's difficult to see how it relates to any known harp. So was this a new type of instrument, previously unknown? Or did Rudenko get it wrong? When I inspected the instrument myself in 1985, what I saw offered no reassurance. If anything, the mystery only deepened. It was impossible to examine the individual fragments: they'd been puttied together with a waxy substance, coloured red like the wood to give an impression of completeness. But I could see enough to make me wonder whether they were correctly assembled. There seemed to be too many pieces. Could they be from more than one instrument? There had been two horn drums in the chamber: might there have been a pair of small harps as well? I came away with more questions than answers.

Since then, the nature of the 'Steppe harp' has received further attention. It turns out that it's not nearly so rare as we once supposed, and neither are similar instruments limited to the frozen kurgans. Sergei Rudenko himself found another one at nearby Bashadar. And another was discovered far to the west, in a tomb at Olbia near Odessa on the Ukrainian shore of the Black Sea. More have emerged, desiccated, from kurgans and smaller graves in the Tarim basin of western China, bordering the Taklamakan Desert. Some excavations have turned up several at a time. At Zaghunluk there were three harps; at Yanghai, five. At Aisikexiaer they've found no fewer than eleven. All of them follow the same familiar formula: the long, hollow sound box with one end solid and the neck mortised into it. The form of Rudenko's restoration remains anomalous.

There's clearly more work to be done on the Pazyryk remains. But they and the subsequent finds are at least safe from further deterioration. The same can't be said for musical treasures that have not yet been excavated. And there may be many of them. Siberia is an enormous and sparsely populated place. Look for Novosibirsk in an atlas or in satellite imagery and then work southwards to the mountains where Russia and Kazakhstan meet China and Mongolia. You'll see just how remote it really is. But remoteness is no protection from climate change, and the future of the permafrost is already worrying researchers. To complicate matters, the rights of indigenous populations need also to be borne in mind. Archaeology can be controversial, especially when it's imposed from afar. Not all indigenous people are in favour of further excavation, particularly where cemeteries and human remains are likely to be involved; and reviewing archaeology's chequered history across the world, this is hardly surprising. Still, if anything can focus minds, it's surely the possibility of rediscovering these fascinating ancestral voices. After all, the alternative might be to lose them forever.

PART NINE

Age of Bronze

The Sixth to the Fourteenth Century BC

In our journey through the Iron Age in search of music's late prehistoric roots, we've so far travelled from Turkey to Egypt by way of France, and from China into Central Asia, looking for pointers to the origins of some of the things that define music for us today. In the next chapters we're going to delve deep into archaeology's next layer, to explore the music of the Bronze Age, the second great period of Old World technology. We'll return to Europe's western seaboard, to see how music was depicted in its late prehistoric 'rock art'. From a peat bog in Denmark we'll extricate a series of magnificent cast bronze horns, before heading east again to Egypt, to inspect two delicate trumpets from probably the most famous Bronze Age tomb anywhere in the world. But first we leave behind our Chinese bell-ringers and nomad harpers, and exchange the preserving power of their airless sediments and intense cold for an entirely different kind of medium: fire.

When we think about our ancestors' use of fire, we're apt to focus on their domestic lives: their ways of preparing food, and their need for light, warmth and personal safety. But fire and heat also played a vital role in their technological progress. We've already come across several instances of iron smithing and bronze casting in the manufacture of Iron Age musical instruments. Now our focus shifts to the age of the oldest metals, when furnaces and forges first enabled mineral ores to be transformed into useful objects. It's also the age of the earliest Greek poets and the tombs of pharaonic Egypt.

But paradoxically, our first foray is going to transport us not to the cities and palaces of the Mediterranean world or the Near East: not yet. Instead it's going to spirit us away to a remote island in the Atlantic Ocean, and an unexpected discovery that shows how, even here, life could be softened by song and by the sweet, seductive sounds of the lyre. If we were expecting our ancestors to show a certain roughness and lack of musical subtlety at that time, then we're in for a surprise. From the complexity and sophistication of their music technologies, we'll see that already they display a degree of inventiveness, energy and ambition that may strike us as thoroughly modern.

Chapter Forty

Fire and flame: the Skye lyre bridge

Scotland, sixth century BC

We've all been there. We've lost something and are searching for it everywhere, but without success, until days, weeks, even months later, we stumble across it in a place where we'd never thought to look. Something similar happened recently in archaeology, in the hunt for the final piece of a particularly intriguing puzzle: how exactly the ancient Greeks played the lyre. The missing item turned up not in Greece or the Mediterranean, where we'd been looking, but far away, on an island on Europe's remote Celtic coast.

It wasn't only the Greeks of the classical period who were in awe of lyres. We know that the Celts too celebrated them in their visual arts. And like modern guitars – classical and folk, jazz and rock, flamenco and Hawaiian – they seem to have existed in several distinct versions. Yet they've all had something in common: they were the songsmiths' musical accompaniment, the backing to their lyrics. What's more, it's clear that their song traditions weren't just about entertainment or even religious ceremony. It was one of the ways in which people preserved their pasts, and defined and expressed their identities.

Happily, Greek civilisation has left us with a large body of evidence, containing most of the details we need to recreate the instruments they played. From their sculptures and the beautiful musical scenes portrayed on their luxury ceramics, we can guess how they must have been shaped and assembled, and can observe the way they were handled and played. The hand gestures and finger movements, the plucking and the strumming, are often shown in exquisite detail. But for the finest points of the instruments' construction nothing quite beats archaeological finds, in particular the scraps of wood, bone and metal that emerge from time to time among the furnishings of tombs.

The material evidence for what we've come to think of as 'Greek lyres' comes mainly from the Mediterranean and Black Sea basins, from modern Turkey and Ukraine as well as the Greek colonies in what's now Italy. Ordinarily, remains of this sort would give music's archaeologists enough to build accurate replicas. But until very recently there's been one last piece missing from the puzzle. It's a crucial piece too: it's the bridge. And we know from experience with later lyres that this is the most important single element in the whole elaborate structure. No matter how accurately you've been able to recreate your ancient lyre, when it comes to playing the finished reconstruction the key to how it's going to sound, and how you're going to play it, will rest with the bridge.

The bridge normally sits on the centre of the sound board, the resonating deck, where it's held down firmly by the tension of the strings stretched across it. Later in the lyre's long history, whenever we've been lucky enough to find a bridge still attached to its instrument – as it was on the Trossingen lyre – it's been able to tell us more than any other part about the way the instrument worked, and the kinds of sounds it made. Partly, that's because its function is to conduct the energy from each vibrating string onto the sound board, which will then convert it into sound. Bridges made of contrasting materials, such as wood and bronze, give different tones. Being necessarily thin, sound boards seldom survive intact, and even when they do, they rarely keep their shape; but a bridge has two little feet, so to speak, and the shapes of its soles reveal the kind of surface they've been designed to stand on. They can even indicate the kind of material: the firm flatness of a wooden board or the gentle sag of a drum skin. A bridge's principal musical influence, however, comes from the notches spread along its upper edge to hold the strings in place.

Their shapes and configurations preserve valuable information. Under the microscope we can sometimes make out and measure the impressions left inside them by the pressure of long-vanished strings. Their alignment and spacing show precisely how the strings were stretched across the face of the instrument: how far apart they were set, whether they ran parallel to one another or whether they spread out in a fan. We know from world music today that such shapes vary greatly from one lyre tradition to another, reflecting the contrasting techniques that different cultures use in trying to get the best out of their instruments. In lyres, like lutes, much of the dexterity is in the player's right hand: the plucking and strumming hand which agitates the strings just above the bridge. So whenever we came to that thrilling moment when we first fitted strings to a new replica of an ancient lyre, there was an uncomfortable feeling. It was the feeling of not knowing what a vital component should look like, or even how large or small it should be. How can any reconstruction claim to make 'authentic' sounds when such a critical piece of the puzzle is missing? Fortunately, archaeology has a way of throwing up unexpected answers.

The breakthrough came one day in 2008, when archaeologists in Scotland were investigating early Iron Age deposits of wood ash on a hillside on the Isle of Skye. From one of the layers they picked out a small piece of charred oak. It was only one of many fragments of charred wooden objects, but it had a very particular shape which matched the bridges of later lyres. It's a neat little thing – very delicately made, and small enough to fit inside a matchbox. One end has been snapped off, but enough of it remains to show that the complete object would have formed a symmetrical arch. The underside of the arch is smoothly curved, while the top edge is straight like the parapet above an arched gateway. The complete end develops into a flat foot, showing that it was meant to stand upright on a flat surface. But what puts its musical identity beyond doubt is the row of small notches that have been cut into the ridge at precise, measured intervals. We can see that there must originally have been seven of them. With the initial study concluded, the obvious thing to do was to make copies and fit them to modern replicas of different kinds of lyres.

On the workbench two things quickly became apparent. The first was that the close spacing of the notches presents the strings in a way that makes them easy to strum, just as they were on the Trossingen lyre. But there's an anomaly. The sole of the surviving foot isn't quite perpendicular. It's been carved at such an angle that the bridge tilts very slightly when it's placed on a level wooden soundboard. It will stand up, but only just, and with anything more vigorous than gentle strumming the pressure of the strings tends to flip it over with a loud bang. This is inconvenient, but there's no denying its authenticity: it's obviously what the original maker intended. The search for an answer then highlighted a second anomaly, this time in the notched ridge. The ridge line has been filed flat before notching, but here too the angle isn't quite a right angle. It has a distinct tilt of its own, and in quite the opposite direction. Minute examination shows that it can't be due to damage or shrinkage. There's only one possible explanation: the bridge has been made to serve an instrument in which the sound board and strings were not parallel: they must have diverged by at least fifteen degrees. This angle is significant. We moved the bridge to a different kind of lyre, using a replica I'd made some years earlier. It was a copy of the remains of an ancient Greek instrument in the British Museum. To our astonishment, it offered a perfect match.

The remains of the Greek lyre consisted of the usual three-piece superstructure – two arms and a crossbar or 'yoke' – and part of its sound box. But crucially, the remains showed one very distinctive structural feature: the frame and sound box weren't parallel but subtend a shallow angle, and it's an angle that suits the Scottish bridge perfectly. How can this possibly be? Is it just a lucky coincidence, or might there be some connection? What cultural phenomenon of European prehistory could possibly explain it? While the two finds are from around the same time, they are separated by more than three thousand kilometres. We know that the Greeks knew quite a lot about the *Keltoi* of mainland Europe, but how much could the Atlantic Celts have known of the Greeks? It turns out that the site itself held some clues.

It's known as *Uamh an Ard Achadh*, or High Pasture Cave. Exploration began in 1972, when cavers from the University of London set out to map an underground watercourse. As they worked their way up its bed in the dark, something in their torch beams attracted their attention. It was a side passage rising steeply up a series of rough rocky steps, and when they followed it upwards they found that it had been blocked from above. It wasn't an accidental collapse. On the rock steps and in the blocking earth there were signs of human activity. They noticed several pieces of polished bone, apparently placed there deliberately. They made a careful note of the location, and a subsequent survey of the grassy hillside above located the exact spot. It was in a dried-up stream bed.

Excavation showed that no one had actually lived in the space above the cave; there had never been a house. But late Bronze Age and Iron Age people had been performing all kinds of craft activities there, including state-of-the-art bronze- and iron-working. And much of what they did seems to have had a ritual dimension. They'd also done a lot of feasting, and to define the space above ground, they'd built a stone wall around it, enclosing a circle about nine metres in diameter. Within that charmed space sat the entrance to the mysterious pothole, with its steps down into darkness. It was clearly at the very heart of whatever rites were being performed.

Reopening the stairway, the team now revealed how and when it had been blocked. It turns out that in around 50 BC, all the metalsmithing, feasting and celebrating suddenly came to an end. And as if to emphasise the finality of the moment, someone blocked it up. But they didn't just block it. Like the panpipes we saw deposited during the closure of the Nasca temple at Cahuachi in Peru, they'd placed something else in the blocking earth. It was the body of a woman.

As far as we can tell she hasn't been the victim of sacrifice: her remains show no telltale wounds. Looking at her skull, it seems she may have died of septicaemia; she had a very large dental abscess that was evidently still infected when she died. But there's also a hint of sacrifice about her, because she'd been buried with two strange companions. Next to her were the bodies of a newborn baby and a newborn pig. This has a bearing on how we read the evidence for the presence of a lyre, or lyres.

The bridge was discovered in one of two hearths that occupied either side of the entrance to the stairway. Digging down through the ash, layer by layer, the archaeologists noted that these weren't simple bonfires or domestic hearths. The hearths had seen many repeated burning events, spread over several hundred years. At the end of each burning, the fire had been extinguished rather than left to burn itself out. And that's how the small bridge had been able to survive, quenched just before its charcoal could turn to ash. Radiocarbon dating has placed the ash layer in the sixth century BC, roughly midway through the sequence of fires, which is to say roughly contemporary with the rise of classical Greek civilisation.

All this makes the site a rather remarkable place. It's distinguished by its close proximity to the mysterious underground space, with water flowing through its deep recesses. The cave itself can only be entered through a narrow stairway that's set between two fires. And strange things seem to have been going on there for at least seven hundred years. Along with the sounds of fire and water, and countless noisy craft activities, we now have evidence that lyre music was some part of the visitor experience. It's a combination that has more than a hint of the Underworld about it; indeed, if the cave had been found anywhere in Greece, one name would immediately have sprung to mind. Orpheus: hero, god, poet and lyre player. It might, even here. Could the cave have been connected in any way to his cult, or one like it? And if so, could our little bridge have indeed belonged to a Greek lyre? Well, yes – and no. How we read the riddle boils down partly to a question of viewpoint.

Orpheus was probably the greatest musician of Greek legend. The Greeks credited his singing and playing with magical powers:

not only could he tame wild animals, he could charm the very rocks of his native mountainsides. He therefore became the subject of veneration, and Orphism became one of the great mystery religions of the ancient world. It attached great importance to oracles, divination and prophecy, and its associations with underground spaces reflect Orpheus' most famous exploit: his daring descent into the Underworld to rescue his dead wife Eurydice.

Of course Greeks were not the only Bronze and Iron Age people who were attracted by the numinous character of deep underground spaces. And today, in archaeology's post-colonial, post-binary era, rather than imagining cultures interacting through individual human and material exchanges, we prefer to see congruences in terms of zeitgeists, in which shared ideas and practices grow out of shared, many-stranded networks. We're no longer as convinced as we once were by hierarchical notions of centres and peripheries. The Isle of Skye may appear to us to be on the farthest margin of Iron Age Europe, but really it's true only in the topographical way that, for example, the United States and Canada are peripheral to modern Europe. It does *not* mean that the place and its people were culturally backward. Indeed, Greece's musical development could have owed far more to the musical achievements of its Barbarian neighbours and forebears than ancient Greek writers – and some later historians – have liked to believe. Certainly at High Pasture Cave the Atlantic Celts have shown that they may still have something important to say in the matter.

CHAPTER FORTY-ONE

From image to icon: lyres and memorial stones from Bronze Age Spain

Luna-Valpalmas, Zaragoza, eighth century BC

The media flurry that followed the announcement of the High Pasture Cave find in October 2010 was a consequence partly of its prehistoric date and partly of the way we've tended previously to visualise prehistoric life in the far Atlantic regions of Europe. We may now be familiar with the glories of 'La Tène' Celtic art and 'Hallstatt' Celtic technology, yet when we think of the daily lives of ordinary Iron Age communities, we somehow revert to imagining a lack of style and colour, and a certain coarseness of being: driven by harsh necessity, and subject to poverty and violence. This has had the effect of lowering our expectations of their musical sophistication. It doesn't help that many of the places where Celts lived now appear wild, remote and depopulated. It doesn't help that excavations of Iron Age domestic sites often paint a picture of life stripped of its vitality and comfort and colour. It's especially unfortunate that textile and leather remains are so very rare, fragmentary and stained to a uniform brown by tannins in peaty ground water. And in the Bronze Age this impression gets worse.

It's a paradox. Elsewhere, even on Europe's wild Atlantic seaboard, finds and monuments of the late Bronze Age show that at least some communities enjoyed prestige, power and a measure of luxury. But to accept that indigenous Bronze Age people in the far west could have had fine musical traditions, including songs with lyre accompaniment, demands a different view of the prehistoric world and raises a raft of new questions – and expectations. Nowadays the plucked string, with its ability to underscore poetical expressions of heartfelt emotion, seems inseparable from civilised thinking. The Romans, and the Greeks before them, began the myth, believing that the fineness of their music was one of the things that separated them from their 'uncivilised' neighbours. In particular their writers seem reluctant to attribute northern 'Barbarians' with finer musical feelings. They might show a taste for epic – for heroic tales of ancestors and gods and cataclysmic events of former times, and certainly an enthusiasm for the raucous music of battle – but not for lyricism.

Early Chinese regimes entertained much of the same disdain for the cultures beyond their borders, and even for each other, while the Spanish conquistadors would later (with one or two notable exceptions) take a similar view of the musics and instruments that they encountered in Mexico and Peru. Fortunately, modern archaeological methods, coupled with some lucky breaks in the field, make such impressions hard to sustain, and one area of research where musical questions are being asked is in the study of Bronze Age art.

The pictures that are being talked about are preserved in what's known as 'rock art', by which we mean primitive geometrical designs and pictorial motifs, scratched, chipped, hammered and otherwise etched into smooth stone surfaces. Beyond the earliest written records, designs of this sort are as close as we get to eyewitness perceptions of the past, and one of the most impressive pieces of musical rock art was found at a place called Tiñica del Royo, near Luna-Valpalmas, sixty-five kilometres from Zaragoza in the Ebro Valley of north-east Spain. Raquel Jiménez is one of the people who've recently brought it to the attention of music historians. In fact it might be the key to one of the central mysteries of Bronze Age music.

Over the years, the Iberian peninsula has produced more than a hundred and forty prehistoric memorial slabs, several of which include musical elements. They are generally supposed to date from the late Bronze Age and the so-called Orientalising period, because their images share features with imagery in eastern Mediterranean art. If you want to form a mental picture of a typical stone, imagine a smooth slab of rock about the height of a ten-year-old child, roughly rectangular or square in outline, with faint designs on one face. Pecked or chipped into the surface, most likely with a hard stone tool, even now the marks appear quite fresh against their darker, more polished backgrounds.

Some designs show stick people with elaborate headgear that are believed to be women; but others have a distinctly masculine and warrior-like look. These 'warrior stones' sometimes have a figure standing with a sword hanging from his belt and sometimes horns on his head. They often show spears, and what looks like a shield: a large, circular disc with a nick in the edge. There may be a two-wheeled chariot, drawn by a pair of animals. But on several slabs there's something else, something that looks very like a lyre. It has almost all the necessary attributes: the sound box, the arms and the crossbar; and parallel lines have been drawn from top to bottom, where we'd expect strings to be. The quality of execution varies a great deal, as do the numbers of strings; but viewed as a whole the identification seems credible enough. Their only odd feature is that the lyres are shown floating in empty space. There's no musician to show us how they were played. In fact there's no one there at all. What can the artists have been trying to say?

This is where the stone from Luna-Valpalmas has something to say. Now on display in the museum in Zaragoza, it stands about a hundred and thirty centimetres tall, and it's been shaped from a single piece of smooth, fine-grained sandstone, light cream in colour. On it the engraver has scratched two designs. The upper one is another circular shield, embellished with concentric bands and zigzags. Below it is something that looks so very lyre-like that it can't possibly be anything else; and it turns out to be a eureka moment in the search for Bronze Age music.

It immediately resolves the ambiguity of the lyre-like motifs on the other stones. Precisely delineated, we can see the features that their coarser execution hasn't been able to show. It's the same type of instrument, with a round bottom to its sound box, and gently diverging arms. Where the arms meet the crossbar, their tips project through it for a short distance, just as they do in later Greek lyres. The strings are likewise spread out in a fan. It's as pretty a portrait as we could hope to find, given its setting and allowing for the fact that it's been scratched on sandstone. The question, for Raquel and her colleagues, is whether the images indicate a contemporary lyre tradition, native to Iberia, or whether the instrument was known to the artists only at one remove: through imported artworks or by word of mouth.

It's a problem that's long troubled archaeologists, because it isn't only in Spain that enigmatic, detached, musical motifs have been found hammered, pecked and scratched onto stone surfaces. We've seen several scratched triangular graffiti in a medieval church at Howell in Lincolnshire, not far from where I'm writing: obviously harps, or children's ideas of what harps look like. But there's no supporting context; again, they merely float in space. Another floating motif was noticed many years ago in western Sweden, among ancient images that can be seen carpeting outcrops of bedrock smoothed by the glaciers of the last Ice Age. Known locally as slab carvings, or *hällristningar*, they included animals, warriors with swords – sometimes with their axes raised as if fighting or dancing – and a selection of waggons, boats and even fully-manned longships. Spread out in what seems to be a random order, some of the figures hold up objects that to the eye of faith might even be horns or trumpets, and one looks eerily like another lyre. It has a round body with a frame above it and a mark down the centre of the frame that could signify strings. Even by the standards of the Spanish lyres it's crude, and for a long time there was some controversy as to whether it really was a musical instrument. But today the Luna lyre draws it back into the frame; and there may be a further clue on the same stone. Seven small waisted shapes near the top of the design look suspiciously like pottery drums.

This phenomenon of detached motifs is common to a number of cultures and periods. In the north and east of Scotland, in the territory of the ancient Picts, they are carved on so-called 'symbol stones', early medieval monuments that are not so different from the Spanish ones. Among them are several large triangular harps. Back across the North Sea, the Baltic island of Gotland is famous for its 'picture stones' of broadly similar date, known as *bildstenar*. They are assumed to represent the things they portray: 'ocean voyage', 'homecoming' and so on. But to what end? One example from the parish of Lärbro shows a detached shape closely similar to a lyre. Since two actual lyre bridges have now been found on Gotland, in graves of the same early medieval period (in Swedish terminology, the 'Younger Iron Age'), it's maybe not as wild a suggestion as we once thought.

Some scholars have suggested that images of this sort are connected in some way with narratives, perhaps from the mythic past, perhaps from remembered history. One famous image of a man seated on an eight-legged horse is undoubtedly narrative. It's the Old Norse god Odin, Oðinn, the one-eyed patron of poets, and his horse Sleipnir, returning home to Ásgarðr, the dwelling-place of the Æsir gods. The Picts' inclusion of Christian symbols hint at the same process. In previous chapters we've already wondered about the serpents, warriors and birds that decorate the Trossingen and Sutton Hoo lyres. Greek and Roman artists routinely place particular instruments in the hands of gods and heroes from their own mythical past, to help identify them: Orpheus, Marsyas, Mercury, Apollo, even Mithras. None of these is an abstract figure, but a character in a story. Indeed in a whole web of stories.

So this tale of Bronze Age lyres has been about much more than just another instrument from another stage in the ancient history of music and storytelling. We're now at a point so deep in the past that our focus is shifting to their ultimate origins, and archaeology's ability to evidence them, in whatever form. As a body of proof it still feels painfully light on detail, but in the search for origins sometimes it isn't weight of evidence that's the key. Sometimes the

Lutatia and her lute. Memorial to a teenage girl, Mérida, Spain, perhaps 2nd century.
(Chapter 33)

Hidden depths. Milecastle 37 ('Castle Nick') on Hadrian's Wall, England, early 2nd century.
(Chapter 34)

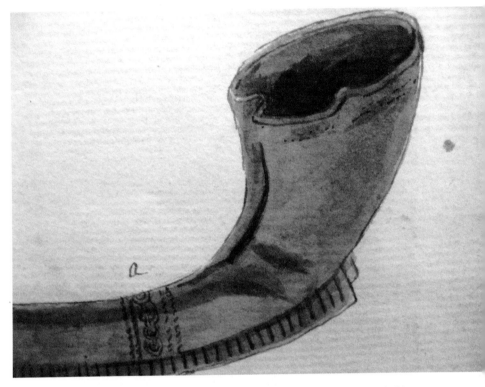

Celtic twilight. Detail of a *carnyx* from the River Welland, England, probably 1st century. (Chapter 36)

Standing on ceremony. *Carnyx* hoard from Tintignac, central France, 1st century BC. (Chapter 36)

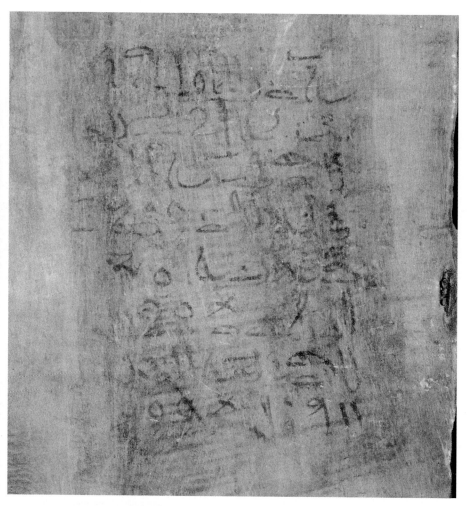

Music and letters. Lyrics added *c*.250 BC to the back of an Egyptian lyre. (Chapter 37)

Suspended music. *Niuzhong* bells uncovered in a Chinese tomb, 6th–5th century BC. (Chapter 38)

Hymn tune. Clay tablet (facsimile) with musical notes, from Syria, 14th century BC. (Chapter 44)

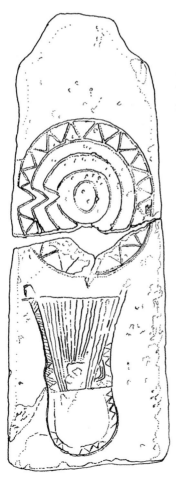

Symbol stone. Memorial with detached images from Zaragoza, Spain, 7th century BC. (Chapter 41)

Musical mystery. Waterlogged tubes buried in a wooden water tank, Charlesland, Ireland, c.2000 BC. (Chapter 45)

Background music. Sumerian lyre player pictured on the 'Standard of Ur', Iraq, *c.*3000 BC. (Chapter 46)

Triumph of ingenuity. Leonard Woolley, holding up his latest plaster cast, Iraq, 1927–8. (Chapter 46)

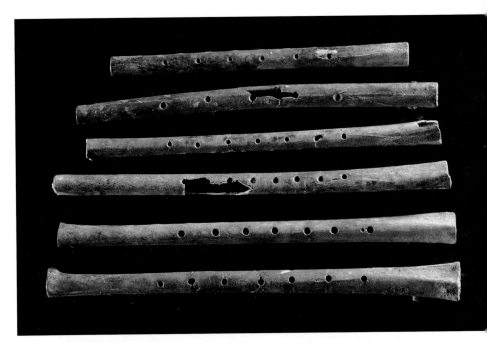

Tuning the world. Crane-bone flutes from Jiǎhúcun, China, *c.*7000 BC. (Chapter 46)

Music from nature. Ringing stone with percussion marks, Brittany, France, traditional.
(Chapter 48)

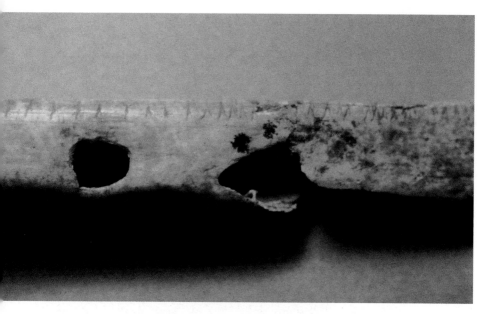

No simple matter. Vulture bone pipe from Isturitz, southern France, *c.*27,000 years ago. (Chapter 49)

The author, made up by the costumes department, prepares to play a replica Isturitz pipe for a BBC television documentary. (Chapter 49)

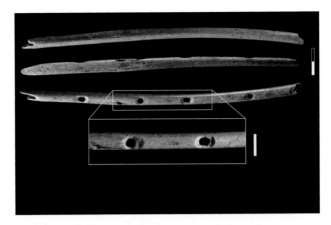

Oldest remains. Swan bone pipe from Hohle Fels,
Germany, *c*.38,000 years ago. (Chapter 49)

Moments in time.
Three australopiths
walking in step, the
smallest in the tracks
of the largest,
Laetoli, Tanzania,
c.4 million years ago.
(Chapter 51)

breakthrough comes when the smallest thing helps to establish an existence in principle. If the High Pasture Cave bridge has carried the story of the lyre back to the earliest Iron Age, these images now carry it beyond into the Bronze Age. The question is: do they bring us any closer to its origins? The forms we're seeing are unexpectedly sophisticated. Clearly we still have some distance to travel.

In the next chapter we're going to meet another Bronze Age discovery, but this time a piece of hard physical evidence of such startling ingenuity, magnificence and power that we may need to need to throw away the rulebook and start all over again.

CHAPTER FORTY-TWO

Tales of the unexpected: the six bronze horns of Brudevælte Mose

Nordsjælland, Denmark, c.800 BC

One summer's day in 1797, Ole Pedersen was cutting peat in a bog to the south of his farm near Allerød on the Danish island of Zealand. It was a small bog, known to generations of his family as Brudevælte Mose. There's little sign of it today: there are just arable fields of plough soil, dotted here and there with prehistoric burial mounds. But as he worked his cutting tool he felt the blade strike something hard. When he started to dig, two long slender tubes of bronze emerged, then two more, and then another two. Conical in shape and curved, they were evidently trumpets; and before long he also uncovered a corresponding bundle of six trumpet mouthpieces close by. It was barely a year since the discovery of the River Witham trumpet had been announced to the Royal Society of London.

The medieval harp neck from Carncoagh in County Antrim has shown us the power of peat to preserve fine wooden objects, but it's equally effective at preserving metal. In the eighteenth century, peat cutters working in raised bogs in Ireland began to find substantial deposits of ancient metalwork, including large horns of cast bronze. One beautiful curved horn had already been discovered in 1639, at a place called Gallehus on Denmark's Jutland peninsula, made of pure beaten gold and embellished with human and animal figures. Almost a century later, in 1734, a similar one was found in the same place. A runic inscription showed them to be comparatively recent, dating from around the fifth century AD. But the horns that Ole Pedersen had discovered were far larger, far heavier and very much older.

Of course, living in Denmark, farmer Pedersen wouldn't have known anything about the Lincolnshire find. But he realised that he'd found something important, and no doubt quite valuable, because he wrote to inform the Danish Royal Treasury. He would almost certainly have heard of the Gallehus instruments, and maybe the pyrites on the surface of his bronzes had lent them an appearance of gold. At any rate the bronze 'lurs' (as they became known) were soon on their way to the national collections in Copenhagen, where all but one of them can still be seen.

Each of the instruments consists of a curved tube more than two metres in length, and even when we see them surrounded by the treasures of the Copenhagen collections they make a breathtaking sight. But just how old might they be? In 1837 the Danish antiquary C. J. Thomsen compared them with other early artefacts, especially tools and weapons, and attributed them to the second of his proposed three ages of ancient technology: *Bronzealderen*, the Bronze Age.

At that time there was no way of determining prehistoric dates even approximately. It would be another hundred years before the American physicist Willard Libby would trigger the Radiocarbon Revolution that has so transformed our sense of archaeological time. Until then all dates would remain strictly relative. But Thomsen knew that the Bronze Age represented an older period than the Iron Age, and that these Danish horns didn't look like any Iron Age find. An Iron Age horn would be shaped in more or less the modern manner, and hammered from thin bronze sheet, whereas the instruments from the Brudevælte Mose had clearly been cast in molten bronze. It seemed that they were not only *very old*, they were also *very odd*.

The first thing that's strange about them is the thinness of their metal. It's easy enough to imagine how Bronze Age foundry workers could have cast solid shapes like axes, swords and daggers using simple two-part moulds. But what sort of casting technology could possibly have generated metal so thin and light in such a complicated shape? Just how clever it must have been has only recently become apparent – and it turns out that 'odd' doesn't begin to do it justice. Replicating them has proved extremely difficult, and as time has gone by and failed experiment has followed failed experiment, the mystery has only deepened. If modern engineers can barely reproduce even small portions of the instruments in their well-equipped laboratories, how could they have been made in an era of prehistory when – so everyone assumed – most people were living a primitive, mainly agricultural lifestyle?

My colleague Peter Holmes has done most to reveal the secrets of their creation. Studying their surfaces closely, he was able to see the telltale signs – the traces of the various phases of their making. He began to realise how the clay core and the outer moulds must have been made, and was able to visualise how they might have been assembled keeping the intervening air space – the shape of the horn – open by inserting 'sacrificial' metal spacers that would become absorbed into the castings. He had no problem imagining how the mould might have been heated and the bronze melted. These are things that are familiar to modern foundrymen, and they are known to music historians from the cast bells of medieval Europe and ancient China. But there were some crucial differences. In the Brudevælte instruments, the spaces were much, much thinner than any bell casting, and yet the molten metal must still have flowed freely through them. It meant that the core needed to be preheated to a precise temperature, and that the molten bronze had to have a consistency that would allow it to flow without congealing. For all this there's no handy set of rules, no handbook, no seeking advice from old-timers. To this day their creation remains a mystery.

Nevertheless, they still hold some important clues. The first is that, however challenging the processes might be to recreate today, there can be no doubt that someone in the remote past has indeed mastered them. What does this tell us about the people who made the horns and about the conditions in which they worked? What does it say about the facilities at their disposal? What does it reveal about the patronage of technological innovation within their society? What does it say about their cultural priorities, and about the value they attached to music? Imagine the investment, the resources that would have been needed, the skills that had to be learned and maintained, the materials that had to be sourced and brought together: the fuel, the clays, the metals, the tools and equipment.

But perhaps the greatest investment the instruments showcase is of an intellectual kind. It's in the knowledge that they reveal, not just of materials and techniques, but of three-dimensional spaces and shapes. If the castings are astonishing, the geometry is of a very special order indeed. Many Danish Bronze Age horns are notable for their carefully tapered cones and perfectly circular cross sections. This is all the more remarkable when we consider the way they curve. But the Brudevælte horns take it one step further. Peter's measurements show that throughout their lengths they deviate from a perfect cone by just two and a half millimetres. And that's not even setting a record. In another pair of instruments from a *mose* called Fuglrisdam in Jutland, the individual 'yards' or sections of tube deviate by less than one millimetre.

Farmer Pedersen's discovery presents us with an additional challenge. It challenges the way we imagine the origins of musical behaviours. The Irish and Danish horns are the earliest 'brass' instruments found so far in Northern Europe: they provide a 'first appearance datum' for their types. But their complexity is troubling. What if they hadn't been found? What if all we had to work with were medieval and Roman horns, or Iron Age instruments like the Tintignac and Witham finds? How might we have imagined their Bronze Age precursors? I've no doubt that we'd instinctively have expected something a lot less advanced. It would surely be common sense that, the further we go back in time, the more likely we are to see at least some diminution of ambition and expertise with each backward step. At some point, eventually, we should reasonably expect to find trumpets hollowed out of wood instead, or even natural cow horns. Yet here in the Bronze Age, more than two thousand years before the Bekan and River Erne horns, we find ourselves confronted with more, not less, complexity. We've witnessed prodigies of investment at Leigudun in China. We've noticed an unexpectedly high level of ambition in the High Pasture Cave lyre bridge. We've seen extreme complexity and delicacy in the mechanism of the Roman organ from Aquincum. Could it be that as we go further back in time, the complexity of things might not diminish but might sometimes increase as well?

CHAPTER FORTY-THREE

Manipulating the past: the tale of Tutankhamun's trumpets

Luxor, Egypt, *c.*1320 BC

When the British archaeologist Howard Carter began to break into what he hoped would be the undisturbed tomb of an Egyptian pharaoh, his patron Lord Carnarvon asked impatiently, 'Can you see anything?' The year was 1922 and they were at the far end of a rock-cut passageway, deep underground in Egypt's Valley of the Kings. Carter was at this point balanced up a stepladder, with his head through the hole he'd just knocked in the top of the sealed doorway, trying not to scorch himself on his naked candle flame. 'Wonderful things!' he called down to Carnarvon. He wasn't exaggerating.

Archaeologists are no strangers to disappointment. We can often find ourselves enthusing about the merest scraps of bone or pottery, so it's not hard to imagine the tension filling the air, followed by rising euphoria as Carter began to relay descriptions of the furnishings he glimpsed in the gloom. Already they glinted with gold and ebony and other precious materials. For both men it was to be a life-changing moment: the pinnacle of their archaeological careers. Secure behind the sealed door, shielded from insect attack and protected from fluctuating atmospheres, lay a whole inventory of things: hundreds of objects, large and small, of polished wood, metal and textile. They'd been waiting there in the silent darkness for more than three thousand years. Furniture was stacked around the walls like the props room of an old theatre, and tucked away among the objects were musical instruments. To start with they seemed the least of the treasures, but two of them were going to make newspaper headlines all over the world.

When Carter and Carnarvon finally entered that first chamber, they must have felt overwhelmed by the sheer enormity of what they were seeing. Almost from the beginning there were signs of the musical treasure to come. In the immediate foreground was a couch in the form of a cow, and resting on it was a pair of frame rattles, or *sistra*. On the floor of an annexe at the back of the chamber they would later find a pair of elegant ivory clappers. And to their right lay a box containing a beautiful bronze trumpet, close to another sealed door. The instrument's flared bell was emblazoned with the images of four figures: it was the boy-king Tutankhamun, accompanied by the gods Amun, Ptah and Re-Harakhte.

Carter soon had his hands full, cataloguing and removing all the objects to safe storage, under the watchful eye of officials from the Egyptian Archaeology Service. It took him months. But then, on 16 February 1923, with the antechamber finally cleared, the sealed north doorway beckoned. Opening it the archaeologists found a second and larger chamber, housing the king's tomb. It too was furnished, and dominating the space was his massive wooden shrine. Its casework would later prove to be just the outer shell of several sealed cabinets, nested one inside the other like Russian dolls. Already Carter knew that the king's mummy case must still be intact. But just inside the doorway he came across another trumpet. It was very like the first except that this time it was made from silver. On its exquisitely ornamented and gilded bell were images of the same three gods, together with the king's cartouches – his personal devices that spelled out his name in hieroglyphs. Inserted into its tube, to prevent it from getting bent, was a tight-fitting wooden core of exactly the same trumpet shape. Decorated with colourful painted designs, it was as beautiful as the trumpet itself.

My first close encounter with the trumpets came in 1976, when I was a graduate student. Peter Holmes, who we heard about in the previous chapter, had already made an accurate copy of the bronze instrument. It was a beautiful piece of work. I particularly remember marvelling at the soldered seam that zigzagged delicately down the length of the gleaming tube, like some ancient zip fastener. And it was with Peter playing it that I first heard the tremendous blast of sound that it could make.

Back in 1976 it seemed to most specialists that the instruments had been selected for burial arbitrarily, and occupied no special place in the boy-king's funeral tableau. But more recently the German Egyptologist Alexandra von Lieven has identified some evidence of purpose. To start with, she notes, they were all deposited in pairs, or at least in twos. And she finds it odd that of all the wonderful instruments that had been in circulation since the Middle Kingdom, a royal burial of this magnitude should contain only these six relatively simple pieces. There are no harps, no lutes, no flutes or drums, of the kinds we'd normally associate with the Egyptian pursuit of royal pleasure. But on the other hand, each instrument carries certain symbolic associations. When we see trumpets in Egyptian pictures or mentioned in papyrus texts, they are clearly connected with military signals and ceremony, and express royal authority. This seems to be reflected in their location in the tomb complex: they've been placed near doorways, with other symbols of authority and status stacked close by. Next to the bronze trumpet were bows and arrows, while concealed within the outer shrine case were some staves, more bows and arrows, and ostrich-feather fans. These are all ceremonial items which Alexandra is inclined to see as an echo of how things had been ordered in the king's audience chamber in his palace, or in his camp during military expeditions.

The clappers are long and curved, like a pair of boomerangs, rounded on one side and flattened on the other so that the flat sides can be brought together with a satisfying clack. One end of each clapper is shaped in the form of a human hand. Alexandra writes that instruments like them were used in a cult festival commemorating the birth of the sky goddess Hathor 'the Hand of Horus', which in Tutankhamun's time was celebrated at the beginning of

March. Coincidentally or not, this also seems to have been when Tutankhamun's funeral took place: scattered throughout the tomb chamber and around the mummy Carter found garlands of spring flowers, and fruits that are usually in season between mid-March and late April. Interestingly, the clappers are inscribed with the names of two female relatives of the pharaoh: a queen called Tiye and a princess named Meritaton.

The frame rattles too have religious associations. They are often depicted in ritual scenes where their pleasing tinkling sounds might serve to mollify an angry god or goddess, such as the aptly named Dangerous Goddess. But it seems they were also used when people petitioned the king at court, and that their sound was believed to create a favourable impression and achieve a more propitious atmosphere. Their placement in the antechamber, as though left there by the last person to leave, may well have been motivated by protocols of that sort. In short, none of these beautiful things is 'just' a musical instrument. None is there to represent entertainment.

When we try to imagine Tutankhamun's funeral rites, it's hard to say what would have happened in the tomb, or in what order they might have happened, before the door was finally sealed shut. But it seems reasonable to guess that the enclosed space would have reverberated at least to the sounds of murmuring voices and shuffling feet, maybe even of prayers, incantations and hymns. What role might the trumpets have played? Were they there just to dress the set, so to speak, just to be parts of the tableau? Or were they meant to be played? The evidence is equivocal, but it's not impossible that they were used. The bells in the tomb of Zeng Hou Yi were set up for performance, and so was the lyre in the Prittlewell burial, fully strung and quite possibly still in tune. If they were, Peter's replica suggests that, the impact would have been instant and extremely powerful. It wouldn't have been particularly 'musical', however, or at least not in our modern tuneful or harmonious sense of the word. It's the South African *vuvuzela* that springs to mind rather than the Reydon flugelhorn.

*

Replicas like Peter's are without doubt the best way to experiment with ancient instruments of this or any sort, for two reasons. First, the trumpets were not ancient relics in Tutankhamun's day: they were modern instruments in perfect condition. So to explore their properties we need perfect modern copies. Second, it's simply a matter of conservation. Once you've had time to explore the effects of deep time on ancient instruments through a microscope, you begin to appreciate just how fragile they really are, no matter how strong they may seem to the naked eye. It's not just their structural and acoustical properties that have been affected, but also their sur-. faces, and the traces of original use that their surfaces may preserve. Play them and you're compromising their evidence.

Oddly enough, Carter and Carnarvon seem to have appreciated the fragility of their finds (as no doubt did the Inspector of Antiquities who was keeping an eye on them) and as far as I'm aware neither tried to take musical advantage of them. It's possible that Carnarvon might have succumbed to temptation, as a man with an eye to a headline; but tragically he was bitten by an insect only a few days after the discovery, and died soon afterwards. Carter seems not to have tried at all. He may have been opposed to the idea. But alas, the story doesn't end there. Sixteen years later, on 2 March 1939, he too died. By this time wireless radio was well advanced, and in Cairo someone at the Egyptian State Broadcasting Service thought they knew the perfect way to mark the great man's passing.

That someone was called Rex Keating, and he opened negotiations with the museum authorities, who agreed. The instruments were taken off display and readied for action. Rehearsals followed in Cairo, with a volunteer bandsman from the British Army. The noises he made were somehow less musical than he or Keating hoped they would be, so he did what any enterprising bandsman would do and inserted his own military mouthpiece. The result was catastrophic. With the first loud blast, the instrument fell apart.

Some days later, with the pieces glued back together, a second attempt was made, this time in a live broadcast. The player was another army volunteer, Bandsman James Tappern of the Royal Hussars. Like his predecessor, he'd brought his own mouthpiece, and with it wedged into place with paper, he played a haunting phrase that echoed around the museum gallery. It was a global sensation. It seemed the authentic voice of ancient Egypt was being heard again after three thousand years, enchanting millions of listeners worldwide. James Tappern's innocent sleight of hand went for the time being unnoticed, and its musical significance was glossed over by the BBC. It seems the public's thirst for entertainment already trumped the public's right to the truth.

Nowadays the deception is common knowledge among the experts, and merely part of ancient music's chequered history. It's widely understood that the sounds we hear James Tappern making in the recording were largely the outcome of his modern mouthpiece. Without it the instrument's tone and musical range would have been altogether different. So the moral of the tale is obvious enough. If we truly wish to discover how a very ancient instrument may have worked and sounded, we simply can't be massaging the evidence to serve our own twenty-first-century expectations. We must first do the science, and then listen to what each and every new discovery has to say to us.

PART TEN

Dawn of Civilisation

1400 to 5000 BC

Civilisation, we're told, began in the ancient Near East, with the emergence of humankind's first towns and cities; and digging through into that deeper, darker layer of our civilised past between around three and a half and seven thousand years ago, you might think we should be approaching the beginnings of music's story at last. Archaeology, however, has still more surprises in store.

The era is marked by innovations and 'first appearances' of many kinds: advances in farming and seafaring, in ceramics and building and other industrial crafts. In the palaces, cities and empires of the ancient Near East and South Asia, it also witnesses the invention of writing for practical record-keeping and accounting; and as the ambitions of the record-keepers increased, they soon moved on from merely counting and listing things to creating permanent records of their thoughts, emotions and experiences. Poetry makes its first clear physical appearance at around this time, in Near Eastern cuneiform and Egyptian texts between about 2500 and 2000 BC. And wherever there are poems, songs can't be far away. They include hymns, laments, love lyrics and heroic epics. The question is: were these things truly new to humankind, or was it just the act of writing them that was new?

In the next chapters, this question is answered by yet more amazing survivals. We'll return to Ireland to sound out one of the strangest discoveries from all of music's prehistory, before travelling east to Mesopotamia to marvel at the magnificent gold and silver lyres from the royal tombs of Ur. But first we must pay a visit to the Mediterranean coast of Syria, and an ancient ruin on a headland. Its name today is Ras Shamra, and there archaeologists unearthed something quite spellbinding. Among the ruins of an ancient library they came upon the oldest evidence yet of people writing down tunes, and annotating them in such a way that we can still read and try to perform them.

CHAPTER FORTY-FOUR

Oldest song: musical notes from Bronze Age Ugarit

Ras Shamra, Syria, *c.*1400 BC

Around three and a half thousand years ago, a scribe in the palace archives of a city on the coast of Syria picked up a blank writing tablet, and with the tip of a freshly cut cane stylus began to impress the words of a hymn into the soft, leathery clay. The scribe's name was Ammurabi and the religious poem he was copying invokes the name of the goddess Nikkal or Ningal, the wife of the ancient Sumerian moon god, Nanna. Out of the darkness of the past we can almost hear his voice intoning the words. Translated into English they might look something like this:

   i: For the One to whom ye sacrifice:
  ii: Let two sacred loaves be prepared in Her bowl
     when I bring unto Her my sacrifice.
     Up to Heaven offerings have been raised
     for health and happiness.
 iii: By the silver sword-symbol at the right foot
     I have offered them up.
     I beseech Thee to do away with my transgressions.
     Without concealment or denial I bring them to Thee,
     that I may be found pleasing in Thine eyes,
 iv: Thou who lovest them that come to be reconciled.
     I am come to lay them before Thee,
     to have them set aside with rites of reconciliation,
     and at Thine footstool not to . . . [*here a word or phrase is lost*]

If like me you're keen to know how they would have sounded originally, here are the same lines transliterated from the original tablet into modern Roman script:

i: *aš-ḫa-aš-ta-ni-ya-ša:*
ii: *zi-ú-e ši-nu-te zu-tu-ri-ya ú-pu-ga-ra-at*
   ḫu-ur-ni ta-ša-al ki-il-la mu-li ši-ip-ri
iii: *ḫu-ma-ru-ḫa-at ú-ua-ri ua-an-da-ni-ta ú-ku-ri ku-ur-ku-ur-ta*
   i-ša-al-la ú-la-li kab-gi ú-li-ú-gi ši-ri-it ú-nu-šu
iv: *ue-ša-al ta-ti-ib ti-ši-ya ú-nu-ul kab-ši-li*
   ú-nu-ul-at ak-li ša-am-ša-am-me-ni ta-li-il uk-la-al tu-nu-ni-ta
   sa- . . . [here four syllables have been lost] . . . *-ka*

The words are written in Hurrian, the ancient language of the Mitanni Empire that once stretched from south-east Turkey to northern Syria and northern Iraq. But the words are only the beginning. Immediately below the text, Ammurabi has also inscribed what look like lines of code, made up of words and numbers – and below them he's inserted a short explanatory footnote in Akkadian, the Semitic lingua franca of the region. It's a tantalising combination – but can we make sense of the code?

This fourteenth century BC tablet is a wonderfully compact little object, formed from smooth, cream-coloured clay. It's about twenty-five centimetres long, with a rounded shape that lends it the appearance of a miniature pillow or an elongated bar of soap. The writing consists of little wedge-shaped indentations, formed by the tip of Ammurabi's cane stylus. It's what we call a cuneiform script, meaning that the writing tip itself has been wedge-shaped. The lines of code turn out to be a kind of musical notation, and they open a window not only into ancient musical performance but also into how humans may have begun to visualise ways of making permanent records of their musical thoughts.

In the fourteenth century BC, people all over the Near East were writing on tablets like this one. They were robust when other portable materials like wood, parchment and papyrus tended to disintegrate, and clay was cheap and plentiful, so the tablets survive in prodigious quantities. It seems that at first they were mainly used for making lists and records of transactions, and for correspondence. But their most engaging application was to record works of a scientific and philosophical nature, and for writing down stories in verse form. When they are found they are often buried among the ruins of archives and libraries, so this small musical tablet is just one of hundreds of thousands that have now found their way into museum collections. However, its musical content puts it in a very special category. And it does seem to have been a category – almost a library classmark – because pieces of more than thirty more hymns were unearthed from just one patch of ground. The momentous discovery was made at a place known as Ras Shamra, a headland overlooking the Syrian sea about ten kilometres north of Latakia. Today it's an impressive archaeological site: a large tell, or mound, about a kilometre from the ocean and close to the modern village of Burj al-Qasab.

Tells are accumulations of building materials left by the repeated collapse and rebuilding of human habitations over long periods of time, with each new house floor laid on top of the levelled remains of its predecessors. Their archaeological layers can therefore be very deep and broad. In the case of Ras Shamra they cover an area around five hundred metres across, in places reaching a height of nearly twenty metres above the original ground surface. For thousands of years the city had been an important trading centre, at the western end of major overland trade routes. Its name is preserved in the Bible and the Quran, where it's called Ugarit.

By the time of Ammurabi, Ugarit displayed some astonishing architecture. Archaeologists have found the foundations of two temples, alongside some substantial private residences. Most impressive of all are the remains of a massive stone-built palace. There were several separate libraries within the city, too, and over the course of several excavations since 1926, hundreds of tablets have been recovered intact or in fragments. Our tablet is from the palace library, where it was scattered with other musical records around the rooms, perhaps when the city was sacked sometime between 1200 and 1180 BC. One section of the library was evidently concerned with religious texts, including hymns and cult songs. It's safe to assume that the thirty or more surviving musical tablets and fragments are only a small sample of what's been lost, but they are probably representative.

When this hymn tablet was found it was broken in three pieces, but apart from the loss of a few small flakes it's complete, and now reassembled. The code consists of alternating words and numbers. Although the words alternate regularly with the numbers, the numbers seem to jump about in a quite irregular way. There seems to be no arithmetical logic or pattern to them. Here's a sample from the first two lines of code:

Line a: *qáb-li-te 3 ir-bu-te 1 qáb-li-te 3 ša-aḫ-ri 1 i-šar-te 10 uš-ta-ma-a-ri*
Line b: *ti-ti-mi-šar-te 2 zi-ir-te 1 ša-[a]ḫ-ri 2 ša-aš-ša-te 2 ir-bu-te 2.*

To us the numbers within the code seem to lack meaning, but here the code words come to the rescue. The same words feature on other cuneiform tablets, including mathematical texts, and there it's evident that they've been borrowed from the names of the strings of a particular musical instrument.

It's actually quite an ingenious way of encoding a tune. We've already seen something like it in Europe in the early Middle Ages, where the note names *ut, re, mi, fa, sol* and *la* were borrowed from the first syllables of the lines of a well-known song. Mesopotamian tablets from Nippur and Ur, in present-day Iraq, show that there too people were thinking of musical notes in terms of names of strings, and that they used similar names to those used by Ammurabi. The instrument they refer to evidently had nine strings, and it's widely believed to have been some kind of lyre. We even know the name of the tuning scheme that Ammurabi uses. It's a song, he says, in the tuning called *nidkibli,* and the piece belongs to the genre of song that's called *zaluzi.* Of course this doesn't help us much, because we don't know how Near Eastern lyres of Ammurabi's time were tuned. Naturally enough, no lyre survives that's still in tune. Should we imagine an instrument tuned to a descending scale, from left to right like a modern Irish harp, or ascending like an upright piano? Or might it be something more convoluted, like the re-entrant tuning of a Zimbabwean *mbira* thumb-piano?

Performers approaching the hymn have therefore had to start by making a number of assumptions. The first has been to assume that the lyre has been tuned to a straightforward scale, based around a 'heptatonic' octave of seven notes. The second is that it's also diatonic, meaning that, like the white keys on the piano, it's made up of tones and semitones. As it happens, the octave principle does appear to be confirmed by the way Mesopotamian theoretical tablets arrange their notes in cycles of seven. However, the numbers remain controversial, to the extent that while some experts argue that they indicate the number of times that a particular note should be repeated, others think that it might relate instead to some aspect of finger technique, perhaps the position at which the string is to be touched.

It's hard in these circumstances to arrive at a single reading of the melody that everyone can agree to. But at least the various competing interpretations mark a beginning, a start from which we can begin to explore. And while we conduct our experiments, there are some distinct crumbs of archaeological comfort. Because, from an archaeologist's point of view, some important facts are *not* in doubt.

Crucially, there can be no doubt that Ammurabi's lines of code do represent a method of notation. And it's perfectly possible to make them work as music, even if (at present at least) the different assumptions that we have to make lead to quite different outcomes. At a separation of three and a half thousand years, none of this should really come as a surprise; after all, it's the oldest example of musical writing that's *ever* been discovered. The bigger question for archaeologists today is this: how new – or ancient – was the system when Ammurabi himself was using it? And, more fundamentally, why were he and other scribes of his time finding it necessary to write music down in the first place? What might have been their motivation?

The fact that they decided to inscribe religious hymns, and not (as far as we know) songs of a more entertaining sort, may suggest that they needed to establish a kind of 'authorized' or at least agreed version for performance in religious rites, as Christian monks would later codify early medieval liturgical chant. As for how long it may have been in development prior to Ammurabi's time, the clue may be in the conspicuous lack of any evidence that it's still work in progress: the system seems precise and confident. It's clearly rooted in widely shared musical practices. And in this respect, to an archaeologist at least, the tablet's most striking feature is what the scribe does *not* say. When he specifies *nidkibli* as the mode in which the music is to be performed, he states it as though it's perfectly obvious what this means. He evidently sees no reason to offer any further explanation. We can only suppose that it's because, in the words of Leonard Cohen, 'everybody knows'.

CHAPTER FORTY-FIVE

Pipe dreams: early Bronze Age wooden pipes from Charlesland

County Wicklow, Ireland, *c.*2000 BC

Sometimes in music's archaeology, things come bouncing at us out of left field. A surprise of this sort came along one day in 2003, on a building site at Charlesland near Greystones, a seaside town on Ireland's east coast. As the team of field archaeologists turned up to dig that morning, they probably thought they were going to be recording just one more prehistoric 'burnt mound'. Ahead lay another day's work of survey and excavation. We can picture them on the hillside, with patches of sunlight drifting slowly across the green countryside and glittering on the distant sea. Only yesterday, they'd cleared away the thirty centimetres or so of topsoil to lay bare an oval patch of fire-cracked and shattered cobbles. It was about twelve metres across, and there was nothing to suggest that something unique was going to happen. But we now know that they were about to make a discovery that would change the way we think about music's prehistoric past.

We've reached the Early Bronze Age, around four thousand years ago and more than five centuries before the destruction of the libraries of Ugarit, in Syria. There are no written records here to help us in our quest; but in the northern and western parts of Britain and Ireland these 'burnt mounds', shallow heaps of burnt and cracked stones, are a common feature of the prehistoric landscape. In Ireland they are known by their traditional name of *fulacht fiadh* (pronounced fullah fee) and ninety-nine times out of a hundred you can safely predict what you're going to find. Hidden somewhere beneath the cobble layer will be a rectangular pit, dug down into the subsoil and covered with some sort of lid. There may be more than one pit to each mound. Each will be typically about the size of a generous aquarium tank or a large bathtub, and filled up with earth. But it's the stones that offer the first pointer to their original function. Like the hearths that preserved the scorched lyre bridge from High Pasture Cave in Early Iron Age Scotland, this kind of place was all about heat.

Usually the pit has been lined with stone slabs and sealed with clay, so 'tank' might indeed be the best description. It's then been filled with water, while somewhere close by someone has been heating cobbles in the glowing embers of a fire. Known to archaeologists as 'pot-boilers', one by one they've been lifted out of the flames and dropped into the water, no doubt with a satisfying splash and a roar of steam. We don't know for sure whether it's been done as part of some industrial process, or for cooking, or even for bathing; but experiments have shown that it's a perfectly good way to heat a large volume of water out of doors. With time and persistence you can even bring it to the boil. After a time the repeated shock of heating and cooling causes the cobbles to crack and shatter. They have to be replaced; and this explains the presence of the so-called 'burnt mound'.

Once the archaeologists have carefully plotted the last of the stones on their site plan and moved them to one side, trowelling usually reveals the squared outline of the top of the pit, and the earth inside it. And normally that's more or less all there is to it: just earth, right down to the bottom. This day in Charlesland, however, there's going to be more.

The archaeologist in charge of this particular excavation is Bernice Molloy. It's a hands-and-knees kind of job. Of the four pits under the mound, this one is lined with wood. As her painstaking work proceeds, the first things to emerge are some fragments of woven wattles, perhaps the remains of the cover, preserved by waterlogging in the saturated ground. It's a good start. Next into view are the upper edges of the wooden side panels. They too are thoroughly waterlogged, soft and sponge-like, though they still maintain their original shape. This also is promising. But now, as more of the wet soil is removed, fragments of something else begin to appear. It's the first hint of the musical treasure to come. They seem to be short lengths of wooden tubing. Down on the floor of the tank, resting directly on the intact wooden base board, there are six more. And they are no casual jumble: they form a compact group, arranged side by side in order of length. It's as if they've been tied together. Lying flat against the bottom board they look very much like a set of panpipes, or even the pipes of an organ. They've each been carefully shaped and hollowed from a piece of solid wood, and they aren't small. The longest is fifty-eight centimetres long. What can they possibly be? What can such an elaborate structure be doing buried in a *fulacht fiadh*? And just how long has it been there?

The date is the least difficult to guess. Burnt mounds have been known to range from the late Neolithic to the Iron Age, which means they were created between about five and two thousand years ago. And whatever people were doing with them, they evidently continued to do it for a very long time. But could such a delicate and complicated piece of equipment really have been made so long ago? Radiocarbon analysis of wood from one of the planks shows that it's one of the oldest of the Irish *fulachta fiadh*, and a sample from one of the tubes confirms that they date from around 2000 BC.

No wooden tubes of such length and technical ambition have ever been seen at such an early time in our history. And this presents us with another challenge. There are no other finds from the Late Neolithic or Early Bronze Age to compare them with, anywhere in the world. Yet their resemblance to a musical instrument is striking. They have features that we'd normally associate with musical technology.

Each of the pipes from the floor of the tank is completely

preserved, or very nearly so. They all have the same external diameter – about twenty-nine millimetres – and their lengths range between thirty-six and sixty-two centimetres. They've been hollowed out with consummate skill and ingenuity. We've seen from the River Erne horn that ancient instrument-makers would often choose to make long wooden tubes by splitting a solid pole into two, and hollowing out the halves before binding them back together. Not so here. These tubes have each been drilled, bored right through from one end to the other, in the modern manner. Their makers must have had a lathe of some sort, because at each end the bore and the outer diameter appear exactly concentric. The thinness of the tube walls is impressive too: just three to six millimetres thick. It's the sort of precision that we might expect to get from a modern musical craft workshop.

But the clue that confirms these objects were meant to serve a musical purpose is preserved in their internal diameters. Not only are the lengths of the tubes graduated, stepped like a set of organ pipes or panpipes, but the bores show a corresponding gradation: from twenty-two millimetres in the longest pipes down to sixteen millimetres in the shortest. It may seem like a small technicality, but subtle as the differences are, they represent a distinctly musical signature: proof that the pipes really have been the work of musical minds drawing on a tradition of accumulated musical knowledge. We can see the same concern for proportion in a modern recorder consort and we've seen it in the Nasca panpipes of Peru. Now here it is in Early Bronze Age Ireland. Which brings us to the burning question: what kind of instrument might we be looking at? What kinds of musical knowledge could have been circulating in Ireland four thousand years ago?

One of the most interesting features of the Charlesland tubes is the fact that each pipe has been made from yew – a tree species we've already seen exploited in several early Irish musical instruments. And while there are no finger holes of the kind that we'd expect to see on individual flutes, close inspection has revealed that on the surfaces of some pipes there are bruises left by tight cords. Others have traces of the fibrous organic material still adhering to them. It looks as if they might be from some kind of binding. It's therefore likely that the tubes (or at least the seven that were found lying together on the floor of the pit) were parts of one single complex object. There's no indication of how they've been voiced – mysteriously, the voicing ends have all been cut off before burial – but otherwise their resemblance to a set of panpipes is undeniable.

Might their dimensions have anything to say about their melodic potential? Again it seems they do. One relationship immediately stands out: the longest pipe is exactly double the length of the shortest. And by measuring the rest we can calculate the frequencies of the tones that they might originally have made in the hands of a musician. What we discover comes as bit of a shock.

When we blow into them like a trumpet, or with a reed, the pattern that emerges is an unexpectedly tuneful one. The longest pipe gives a note close to C-sharp on a modern piano, with the shortest pipe sounding one octave higher. And in between, in ascending order, there's a slightly lowered E, then an F-sharp, then a slightly lowered G-sharp and a slightly raised A-sharp. To all intents and purposes they form a pentatonic scale: a tone – a minor third – a tone – another tone – and another minor third. It sounds weirdly familiar. But could it just be coincidence?

Fascinating as such relationships are, in some ways the most compelling proof is preserved in the object's structural complexity: the sophistication it represents as a design concept, and the remarkable quality of its execution. We might surely be forgiven for expecting to find at least *some* primitive traits in their construction and appearance: some hint, some acknowledgement, that we're getting closer at last to their ancient point of origin. But that's clearly not the case here.

Like the musical annotation on the Ugarit tablet, there's no evidence that we're witnessing a 'primitive' technology, a technology still in a state of youthful simplicity or experiment. They leap into view fully formed. Does this mean that, contrary to received archaeological wisdom, musical traditions may begin in an explosion of creativity? Or could it be simply that their true origins, their moments of invention, are still hidden from us? As it happens, it's a dilemma that we're going to encounter again in the very next chapter, when we come to explore the musical treasures of ancient Mesopotamia.

CHAPTER FORTY-SIX

Sounds of silver and gold: the magnificent lyres of Ur

Tell el-Muqayyar, Iraq, *c*.3000 BC

In the archives of the British Museum there's a black-and-white photograph that captures a magical moment in the history of archaeology. It shows a middle-aged man in knee-length shorts, holding up a strange, fragile-looking object to the camera. He's the archaeologist Leonard Woolley and the object he's holding is a Sumerian lyre.

The image was captured sometime around 1929 on the site of his latest excavation. In Arabic the name of the place, Tell el-Muqayyar, means 'Mound of the Poor Man', and it lies in the desert near Nasiriyah in what's now southern Iraq, close to a dried-up channel of the River Euphrates. When excavations began, the highest point on the mound was a good twenty metres above the level of the plain, and covered an area of around twenty hectares. But this is no ordinary village perched on a natural hilltop. Like the mound we saw at Ras Shamra in Syria, it's the remains of a whole city. Begun around five and a half thousand years ago, its mass is mostly an accident of history. It seems that whenever a building collapsed, its mud bricks were simply spread out to form the platform for a new one, and so as generation succeeded generation the ground level slowly rose. It's a 'tell', and there are tells like it all over the Near East. Perhaps the most famous is Hisarlik at Çanakkale in western Turkey, which Heinrich Schliemann believed to be the Troy of Homer's *Iliad*. But Tell el-Muqayyar comes a very close second. Woolley identified it with the biblical city of Ur, 'Ur of the Chaldees', which the Book of Genesis tells us was the birthplace of Abraham. And within its ruins he and his team discovered the remains not just of a lost civilisation but also of its music. The evidence takes the form of the oldest stringed musical instruments ever found.

Around four-and-a-half thousand years ago the inhabitants were Sumerians, a people with a developed agricultural economy, an elaborate social order and a political system based on city states. Their art has preserved images of gods and mortals and scenes from mythical events and adventures, but we also know some of their poetic literature, preserved in cuneiform tablets and rock inscriptions, from hymns and gnomic verses to songs celebrating famous rulers of their past. They've also left some of their narrative tales, among them the cycle of stories about the hero Gilgamesh, king of Uruk, and his doomed quest for happiness and eternal life in the world after the Flood.

How the instruments came to light makes an equally compelling tale, of archaeological persistence and ingenuity. Remains of lyres had emerged from two 'pits' forming the entrances to tombs which Woolley dug in his seventh season at the site, during the winter of 1928–9: the so-called 'King's Grave', PG 789, and the adjacent 'Queen's Grave', PG 800. Both complexes represent the same phase of the city's Sumerian history, known as the Early Dynastic Period IIIa, which is to say almost five thousand years ago. The remains in the pit guarding the King's Grave were fitments from a lyre, with a gilded sculpture of a bull's head mounted on the end of its sound box like the figurehead of a sailing ship. It's now in the Penn Museum in Philadelphia. In the antechamber to the Queen's tomb they found more fitments, which would later prove to be from two instruments crushed together by falling debris. One includes another bull's head and indicates a lyre. (Ox heads seem to be a common feature of Sumerian lyres, or at least of lyres in royal circles, and may represent the god Shamash.) The other is a harp. Both are now in the British Museum. In all three instruments the wooden frames and sound boxes had long since disappeared, consumed by organisms in the humid soil, and it was merely their inorganic ornaments that saved them: their gilded details and their decorative panels of blue lapis lazuli and white shell, held together with bitumen.

But the moment of extraordinary drama came during 1929–30, Woolley's eighth season at the site, when he and his archaeologist wife Katharine were exploring another deep feature, about ten metres to the south of the Queen's Grave. They called it the 'Great Death Pit', PG 1237. Larger than the entrance pits to either the King's Grave or the Queen's Grave, it had been an open, roofless rectangular space dug down into the same made-up ground. They'd already found several of these 'death pits' associated with tombs, and I'm sorry to say that that's more or less exactly what they were. This one contained more than seventy dead people, buried in serried ranks, sixty-eight of them women. They seem to have been servants and attendants, and quite possibly wives – anyone who'd had the misfortune to belong to the royal household when the king or queen died. And here, towards the eastern corner, close to the entrance ramp, the Woolleys found probably the finest musical treasure that the world had yet seen.

Describing the discovery, Woolley tells us that in one place his assistants were carefully paring away the earth when they came across a small void in the ground, like an animal's burrow. It was about the thickness of his wrist and led down into a cavity. Shortly afterwards they found a second hole close to the first. He cautiously felt inside them with his fingertips. 'Something unusual about their shape seemed to call for special treatment,' he recalls. What happened next was his stroke of genius. Realising that they might once have held parts of a wooden structure, now turned to dust, he made up a liquid mix of plaster of Paris that he'd had the foresight to include in his toolkit, and poured it in. Then he waited. Once he was sure that it was set hard he carefully swept away the surrounding earth – and gasped. 'The result,' he says, 'was a complete plaster cast of a harp, whose substance had long since vanished (except for the copper bull's head and the shell plaque which decorated the front end of it), and thus the first hint that we had of a grave's presence also enabled us to preserve the best object in it before we knew what it was.'

It was a moment of revelation. In fact it wasn't a *harp*, in the technical sense: it was another lyre; and there were signs that it had once been entirely coated with burnished silver foil. And that was just the start. Buried with the lyre were two more instruments: an even larger bull-headed lyre, richly ornamented with gold and lapis lazuli, and an equally impressive harp-like instrument with the standing figure of a stag at the base of its forepillar. The photograph in the British Museum shows Woolley with the smaller lyre. The camera has captured him revelling in his prize, with an impish twinkle in his eye. If he looks pleased with himself, it's not surprising. So he should be. His quick thinking and imagination have given substance and form to something which would otherwise have become just another jumble of decorative fitments.

But the instruments are only part of the story. The Woolleys also found a number of images of lyres being played. One was in a mosaic panel mounted on a box-like wooden object known as 'The Standard of Ur'. Covering both the front and back of the box are elaborate scenes from Sumerian life, scenes of warfare on one side and of peace and prosperity on the other. One of the latter shows a large banquet, and in the background stands a man playing a lyre. This lyre too has an ox head, and behind him someone appears to be clapping. The second depiction once graced the front of the lyre in the King's Grave, PG 789. A lyre pictured *on* a lyre: it's remarkable. But the scene it shows is altogether stranger. It shows a group of animals making music. The lyre is being played by a seated calf, while a fearsome-looking bear grapples with the other end of the instrument. Sitting comfortably on the bear's right foot is a dog brandishing a sistrum rattle. All the animals have human hands. The fingers of the dog's left hand touch something rectangular resting across its knees. It looks remarkably like a clay writing tablet.

In spite of all the unexplained allusions, and thanks in part to the animals' human hands, both of these lyre scenes contain useful indications of how a Sumerian lyre was customarily played. In the scene with the calf, bear and dog it's even possible to see fine details of its tuning mechanisms; all of which helps when it comes to building and playing experimental replicas. And build them we have. A few years ago, I based some experiments around one of the three instruments from the Great Death Pit, the so-called 'Silver Lyre' now in the British Museum.

One of the pleasures a job like that offers, by way of compensation for long hours spent at the workbench, is the smell of fresh timber as you work it. I'd chosen boxwood and Lebanon cedar to build a replica, and cedar is among the finest of the aromatic timbers. But the greater reward is in the sense of anticipation as you work. Both smell and anticipation came together for me in the Silver Lyre. It's partly a question of size. In music's archaeology, most of the finds that we deal with day to day are relatively small things: pocket-sized for the most part, or at least easily portable – bone flutes, rattles, pan-pipes, trumpets, small harps. And however elegant they may be, and however attractive their sounds – at times surprisingly loud and strident, at others beguilingly sweet – they have a tendency to be light, bright, and even shrill. We can't help sometimes craving some deeper tone. Even stringed instruments like the Antinoë lute and the Trossingen lyre are closer to the sound of a mandolin or a ukelele than they are to the rich lower notes of a guitar or a concert harp. The Sumerian lyres are in a different category altogether.

They are big. I calculated that my finished replica of the Silver Lyre would only just fit into the space behind the front seats of my car. And this size immediately carried certain implications for the sounds it was likely to make. So it was with bated breath that I started fitting and tensioning the strings. There were eleven of them, each with its own tuning lever. I'd chosen sheep gut as a likely material, and the sounds that now began to sing out from the sound box were every bit as rich and powerful as I'd imagined they would be. They had a depth and mellowness to them that wouldn't be possible on smaller lyres from a later period.

Of course, the shape of the lost internal wooden structure could only be an educated guess, so its acoustical character would only be approximate. But its exterior form made it a delight to play. For a start, the strings, being long, had a correspondingly long reverberation time. They rang beautifully. But their greater length had another musical advantage. The large open frame meant that almost the whole of each string was accessible from both sides – that's to say, accessible equally to both hands – and it was a delight to discover what a variety of tone colours could be produced by fingering and strumming them in different places. Most glorious of all were the harmonics, the series of subtle overtones that could be sounded with careful fingerwork. We've seen how playing and singing harmonics has formed an integral part of several ancient musical traditions. On my Silver Lyre, these harmonics were even richer and far easier to play. With eleven strings, and efficient lever mechanisms to tune and retune them, they offered an almost unlimited palette of sounds for improvisation. They were a delight to play, and magical to listen to.

Yet lurking behind the sounds were some familiar ghosts: the ghosts of a lost music – in this case, of a whole civilisation. What kinds of musical repertoire had the early Sumerians developed for the lyre, and what songs should we imagine the instrument supporting? They've left us just the barest bones. Even the tablet from Ugarit preserves just the uncertain outline of the melody that accompanied the Hurrian hymn, and the Sumerian lyres of Ur are more than a thousand years older. So we're left to draw what musical inferences we may from the forms of the instruments themselves, as they reveal some of the musical needs that they were adapted to serve.

Once again, what puzzles us about these lyres and harps is the level of musical sophistication that they evidence. Not only are they among the oldest and largest stringed instruments to have survived from ancient times but, like the Brudevælte horns and the Charlesland pipes, they are at the same time elaborate and elegant. Their designs show a consistency that suggests that even four-and-a-half to five thousand years ago they belonged to a thoroughly established musical and technological tradition.

Like most archaeological success stories, Leonard and Katharine Woolley's musical success was due to a combination of things. In archaeology you need a plan, and of course preparation. You need energy and stamina, and you need patience, and hope. You need to be in it for the long term. But you also need a measure of luck along the way; and most of all you need the imagination to know what to do when your luck turns and the unexpected happens. Just how energetic, how lucky, and how imaginative, *we* will need to become, in order to trace our musical roots still further back in time, will shortly be revealed.

PART ELEVEN

Journey's End

7,000 to 38,000 years ago

As we begin the final descent in our epic musical journey, we begin to notice time passing at a faster pace. Thus far we've been travelling comfortably through epochs measured in years and centuries, but already we've seen them broadening – and the rate of expansion is about to become exponential. Changes that we've been accustomed to track across centuries will take place over millennia. Periods of human history that might once have spanned ten or twenty generations – the Aztec Empire, ancient Rome, the Zhou Dynasty – now give way to cultures and 'technological complexes' that endured for several hundreds. We're about to enter the Stone Age. And yet the musical discoveries still keep coming.

When we explore finds of flutes from the earliest Neolithic, the New Stone age, between seven and nine thousand years ago, our world of farmed landscapes and focused settlements is still just about recognisable. But by around twelve thousand years ago, we find ourselves entering a much cooler, drier world, marked by lower sea levels, deserts, dense ice sheets and vast plains of grassland and forest. We're now entering the Palaeolithic, the world of the Ice Age hunters and the vast migrating herds of animals on which they depended for their survival.

The search for their music will eventually draw us into ancient rock shelters and caves in France and Germany, where it's left its mark alongside the better-known glories of palaeolithic art.

But first we travel east to the plains of central China around nine thousand years ago, to discover the most ancient instruments that Chinese archaeologists have yet found, and see how important tuning was, even then, to the melodies they played and sang.

CHAPTER FORTY-SEVEN

Dances with cranes: bird-bone flutes from the Stone Age burials of Jiǎhúcun

Henan, China, c.7,000 BC

If ever there was a moment when a student dig struck musical gold, it was in May 1986. The place was a village called Jiǎhúcun in rural north-central China, and the excavation involved students and professors from the universities of Zhengzhou and Hefei.

Jiǎhúcun is a small, well-ordered waterside settlement, sitting in a flat landscape that's part of China's vast central floodplain south of the Yellow River. Since 1983 the project had been exploring the remains of a recently discovered prehistoric site. Archaeologists had already worked out that it dated from the earliest phase of the Farming Neolithic, which in China was around nine thousand years ago. But what they found that spring, buried in the earth, would send a shock wave through the scientific community and shine a piercing new light into one of the most perplexing black holes of music's prehistory.

Whether we're aware of it or not, we're all children of the Farming Neolithic. These days fewer and fewer of us make a living out in the ploughlands and pastures, but we still depend on the farmed landscape for most of the things we eat. It was during the Neolithic period, the 'New Stone Age' between four and nine thousand years ago, that hunting and fishing finally gave way to growing crops and keeping livestock, and our ancestors began to change the natural world they lived in. It's also the era of the first permanent villages and towns. The rapid expansion of ceramic industries, producing bowls and plates not very different from some of the wares we still use today, became one of the defining features of the 'Neolithic revolution'. Indeed, the Neolithic marks the first appearance and development of so many of the material things and ideas that make us feel modern and civilised that it's tempting to ask: could this period also hold the keys to the origin of music as we know it today?

It might; but due to the passage of time archaeologists have had to work hard to find the evidence. Even in Western Europe, where the farming revolution arrived relatively late – around six thousand years ago – it would be optimistic to hope to find a fine wooden instrument that's survived uncorrupted in the ground for so long. The Prittlewell lyre revealed the state of fragmentation that a delicate wooden structure can suffer after only fourteen hundred years, despite being protected in clean sandy soil. So any evidence that does remain tends to be laden with ambiguity: 'mystery objects' that might (with the eye of faith) be simple rattles and scrapers, and large pots whose waisted shapes lend them the appearance of some modern tribal pottery drums. And of course Neolithic technology was strictly limited to the materials that came naturally to hand. Without some miracle like the waterlogging that preserved the wood of the Bekan and River Erne horns, without the desert conditions that preserved the Antinoöpolis lute, or the freezing cold that preserved the contents of the Pazyryk tomb, we're dependent on instruments having been made from harder, more robust materials – from stone or shell, pottery or bone – and in the Neolithic, instruments made from these materials have tended to be limited to devices of the simpler sort. However, there are happy exceptions to any rule, and one of the happiest of all came to light that day on the edge of Jiǎhúcun.

The Chinese name of the site, 賈湖村, means Jiǎ Lake Village, and it's an apt one. Around fourteen kilometres north of the city of Wuyang, the lake today is little more than a horseshoe-shaped pool of water and wetland, curving around the western half of the village. In former times it must have been a bend in the course of a meandering river, which silted up to become an oxbow, one of many isolated pools scattered over the central Chinese plains. Disastrous floods once plagued these flatlands of the Huai River and the Yellow River, and it seems that around eight thousand years ago, rising flood waters forced the settlement's inhabitants out of their houses once too often. They took themselves off to higher ground, never to return. As the centuries went by, flood deposits built up over what was left of their abandoned homes, so that their floors and foundations were preserved under a thick layer of sand and gravel. Only the horseshoe lake remained to mark the spot, cut off from the main river. When farmers eventually returned, they were cultivating new soils that had formed a metre above Neolithic ground level. It wasn't until the early 1960s that people became aware that there might be something unusual and important hidden deep below.

From 1983 onward, investigations showed that the settlement once occupied about five and a half hectares of land, enclosed on its west side by the lake and on its eastern side by a moat-like defensive ditch. The first radiocarbon dates indicated that it began to prosper around nine thousand years ago. The structures within its perimeter included the footings and cellars of dwelling houses, and a number of kilns where clay pots were fired. But here and there among the houses were small cemeteries and it's here that the musical finds began to appear. People's bodies had been laid to rest with things that mattered to them, which for some had included beautiful musical pipes. They were made from the long bones – the leg and wing bones – of that most graceful and musical of birds, the trumpeting, dancing, red-crowned crane.

Amazingly, even after thousands of years buried in open ground, the instruments were so well preserved that they seemed no worse for wear than the bone flutes from medieval Schleswig, or the double pipes from Anglo-Saxon Ipswich. It's also surprising how many of them there were. Although by the time the first phase of work ended in 1987 only part of the site was excavated, there were already more than twenty, and since then still more have come to light. Their surfaces are glossy, as if they've been deliberately polished or repeatedly handled, and they show the usual coloration of worked bone or ivory that's been buried for a long time: once ivory white, now a creamy beige stippled with gold and brown.

It's clear how cleverly and delicately they've been worked. The solid ends of each bone have been trimmed off to open up the cavity, and the bones have been given their melodic range by the addition of a line of small round finger holes, between five and eight to each instrument. Instruments were also found buried in pairs, or at least in twos because the pairs aren't necessarily identical. One of two seven-hole flutes from Grave 282 has been described as 'precisely made . . . the finest of all the bone flutes from the excavation', while the other is less so. In Grave 341 one instrument has been given six finger holes while the other has only five. What's even more striking about Grave 341 is that it's dated between eight and a half and nine thousand years ago. This places the flutes among the oldest of all the Jiǎhú flutes, and incidentally the oldest example of a pair of instruments found anywhere on earth.

So how might they have sounded, and were they tuned to suit musical scales that might give us a sense of the melodies of the songs that people were singing at the time? There are two ways to approach these questions, and they go hand-in-hand: the first is by experimenting with replicas, and the second is through minute cross-examination of the objects themselves.

Most experts believe that they were meant to be played as end-blown flutes – like blowing across the neck of a bottle – and when they are played like this, replicas of the instruments from Grave 282 make sounds that resemble those made by some of the flutes of medieval Europe: flutes which were also made from the long bones of large birds, including cranes. The Jiǎhú sound may have been a little more 'breathy' perhaps, and more variable, but otherwise it would have compared well in tone and range. Even the tunings bear comparison. The placement and sizes of the finger holes generate musical intervals that come close to the ones we might expect to hear today.

It's been suggested that this shows that around eight thousand years ago Neolithic musicians in China were already using tones and semitones in the way that we do today, and the idea draws some support from a bone flute found at another site, at a place called Ruzhou in Henan Province. The notes that the Ruzhou instrument was engineered to play form a scale of intervals that are almost identical to modern semitones. The scheme may not be very practical for playing tunes, and indeed it may be no more than a pitch pipe – a handy reference for a singer. But it proves the point. It's also been suggested that there's an overall progression from the five- and six-hole flutes in one of the earliest graves, Grave 341, to the eight-hole instruments in one of the latest graves, Grave 253. It's hard to be certain with such a small sample, but it's not impossible. However, from the examination of the physical objects themselves there's one additional detail to conjure with, and it's a significant clue hiding in plain sight. It's the kind of fine detail that might easily have gone unnoticed.

The clue is not in the shaping of the flutes, as such: it's preserved on their surfaces. In Europe's Middle Ages, we saw finger holes of flutes and pipes being positioned in ways that generated scales of notes which, to our unaccustomed ears, seemed at first to be out of tune. It was as if tuning hadn't been a particular concern of their makers, and that any notes sufficed. But closer examination revealed that this was far from the truth. Although indistinct to the naked eye, fine scratch marks showed that even before the holes were drilled, the bones had been marked out with the medieval makers' predictions of where drilling ought to achieve a particular pitch – however odd that pitch might seem to us now. And having bored the holes they'd gone on to fine-tune them by making some of them slightly oval, or undercutting the upper edges of others. Now, to our surprise, a full seven thousand years earlier, we see the selfsame markings in Neolithic China. Several flutes show little cut marks across the holes or transverse scratches dividing the spaces between them. They are so exactly like their European medieval equivalents that it's almost uncanny. There seems to be only one satisfactory explanation: that even back in

China's New Stone Age, flutes were being deliberately and systematically tuned.

Several questions now clamour for answers – just as they did with the Brudevælte horns, the wooden pipes from Charlesland and the lyres of Ur. What of their wider musical context? Are these flutes the *only* instruments that were known to the people living in Jiǎhú, or are they just the ones that earth and burial rites have favoured? Were they unique to the Chinese Neolithic, as they seem at present? Could they mark Neolithic China as one of the places where humans first invented complex, finger-hole flutes, and with them our modern sense of tonality? Fortunately, we can enlist some help from other finds from the Chinese Neolithic.

In another of the Jiǎhú burials, Grave 344, two more flutes were discovered. But they weren't the only instruments buried there. There were also tortoise shells; partly filled with small stones, they appear to have served as rattles. It's a first intimation that there was more to Neolithic music-making than flutes alone. And elsewhere in China excavations have produced evidence of another instrument we've seen before: the mouth harp. We've already looked into the strange case of the Eurasian mouth harp, which, at its abrupt first appearance in the archaeology of medieval Europe, seemed already to be fully formed. For many years, claims of earlier dates remained controversial. But a recent archaeological discovery in China now reveals mouth harps so ancient, so deeply prehistoric, as to leave us almost speechless.

These ancient mouth harps have been made not from metal like their European counterparts – this was after all the Stone Age, when metals were still unknown – but from animal bone. Yet they still function on the same principle. Shaped from a single strip of bone, about ten centimetres long, each instrument has a slender vibrating tongue. The whole thing looks rather like a hair clip, and indeed that's what some of them were first thought to be. But they aren't. They are true mouth harps.

If you place an exact replica between your teeth, and if you flick the free end with your thumb, the vibration agitates the air in your mouth and makes it ring. One site in the ancient city of Shimao in Shaanxi Province has produced more than twenty of them, all Neolithic. And in a separate excavation, at Taosi in Shanxi Province, a similar instrument was found inside a well with a radiocarbon date that places it around four thousand years ago. This is a game-changer not only for the origins of mouth harps but also for the beginnings of music itself. Because once again it gives us a clue to the mystery of ancient tuning and melody.

Mouth harps are melodic instruments that allow the player to articulate sequences of musical pitches. But what's so fascinating about them is that, whereas in theory the tunings that Jiǎhú makers were giving to their flutes were infinitely adjustable, according to preference or even to whim, in the mouth harp they express a universal physical property of matter. The notes and intervals that they produce are those of the harmonic series. Octaves, fifths and fourths, major and minor thirds, tones and semitones: all of them are present in mouth harps of any age, just as they are in trumpets, in simple tree-bark flutes, and in the overtones that can be played on stringed instruments like lyres. They show that for musicians even as long ago as the Neolithic, not all of the shapes of music were the outcome of human invention: some were defined by the very fabric of their material world – and by the very air they were breathing.

CHAPTER FORTY-EIGHT

Echoes of creation: Ice Age hunters, artists and music

Grotte d'Isturitz, France, c.12,000 to 15,000 years ago

If the elegant crane-bone flutes and tortoise rattles played by the farmers of Jiǎhú have given us a glimpse of the unexpected complexity and ambition of music-making in the early Neolithic era, it's only natural to wonder about the hunters and who preceded them around twelve thousand years ago. As they followed their wild prey across the vast northern 'mammoth steppe' of Siberia, Late Upper Palaeolithic pioneer communities drifted southwards and westwards into Europe, while in the north-east low sea levels and retreating ice sheets enabled them to cross the land bridge of Beringia from East Asia into Alaska and the Americas. What kinds of music did they carry with them?

In western Europe we call these Late Palaeolithic people Magdalenians, after the rock shelter site in France where their characteristic stone tools were first discovered: the Abri de la Madeleine, in the pleasant valley of the River Vézère, a tributary of the Dordogne. A delightful spot today, it may not have been so delightful twelve thousand years ago, to our tastes at any rate. But here the sheltered gorges of the Dordogne system would have offered refuge from the bitter winters, both for the people and their prey; and it's here that we can imagine them playing music on bird-bone pipes of their own, sheltering at the foot of the cliffs and in the mouths of caves. One place in particular has preserved surprising evidence of their creative talents. It's known as the Grotte d'Isturitz, the Caverns of

Isturitz, and like High Pasture Cave in Iron Age Scotland, it's an underground river system with a fascinating musical story to tell.

The Isturitz caves cut through one of the limestone foothills of the Pyrenees, the high mountain range that separates France from Spain. The name of this particular hill is Gaztelu. Like Isturitz it's a Basque name, because historically this was Basque-speaking country. Long before humans came on the scene, the nearby Erberua, the Arbéroue river, had found a weakness in the limestone that offered it a shortcut through Gaztelu, carving and dissolving a chain of subterranean channels and chambers on its way through to the other side. It created quite a large space, forming two major chambers, but then in due course a further weakness in its bed allowed the water to drain through to a deeper level, known as the Oxocelhaya system, and this left the upper chambers empty and (more or less) dry. Enclosed dry spaces were much sought-after in the Age of Ice, when humble tents and turf-and-brushwood shacks would have offered the only form of shelter out on the open plains, so they wouldn't have remained empty for long.

The Magdalenians would have been glad to get out of the cold and wet, and to have found a place to offer them some personal safety – after all, they were not the only hungry predators roaming the landscape. Here they could make their fires and cook the meat they brought back from their hunting. From the bone fragments they left behind at various sites, it seems they had a taste for fish, ox, bison, reindeer, wild horse and mammoth. And although it seems less pleasant to us, there's some evidence that they may also have been cooking and eating one another, or at least consuming their dead. Perhaps cannibalism was connected with religious belief, making it a ritual rather than a dietary requirement. But at any rate it was in the deep spaces within such hillsides that the Magdalenians also left a vivid record of their artistic impulses. They expressed them with great energy, style and accomplishment – and nowhere more so than in the images they painted on their cave walls.

The chambers of the Isturitz system were first explored by a man called Emmanuel Passemard. In 1912, six years after his countryman Albert Gayet found the Byzantine lute in the necropolis of Antinoë in Egypt, he began to dig test pits inside the cave. Deep underground he found himself walking across surfaces that were covered in a pale crust of crystalline calcite, rather like the limescale inside a kettle but built up slowly over many thousands of years. We can form some impression of the scene from more recent discoveries, like the Grotte de Chauvet, which features in Werner Herzog's wonderful feature-length film *Cave of Forgotten Dreams* (2010). At Chauvet we can see the floor of the cave littered with objects left behind when the last prehistoric person left, never to return. It seems that the only entrance had been shut by a massive rockslide from the hillside above, locking them out. Humidity and occasional drips from the roof had then fixed everything in place under a thin crystalline coating, like garden furniture after a hoar frost. And that's exactly what had happened at Isturitz, when it too was closed by a landslide.

When Passemard broke through the calcite crust he discovered that in some places the earth beneath it was filled with layered evidence of human occupation. Among the first signs of domestic activity that he came across were shallow, saucer-shaped hearths, filled up with bits of animal bone, the remains of meals. But mixed in with the meat bones were pieces of worked stone, bone and deer antler, which hadn't simply been cut up or broken into pieces: they'd been worked and made into things. He was startled both by their great number and the quality of the workmanship that had gone into creating them. Among them were broken pieces of bone tube with holes bored in them, which looked like parts of musical instruments. They were made from the ulnas of birds: the bones from the part of the bird's wing that's equivalent to our human forearm. But the birds they'd been taken from weren't gentle cranes. As if to symbolise the harsher world in which the Magdalenians lived, and died, they came from large raptors – from eagles and carrion vultures.

To pick up one of these ancient pieces today and to hold it in the palm of your gloved hand is to feel something quite extraordinary.

Between twelve and sixteen thousand years old, they are now light and delicate, and time has left the pale bone picturesquely mottled and blotched. Like the Jiăhú flutes, they've been shaved smooth with a sharp blade so that little trace of the bone's natural outward form can be seen. There are also clear areas of wear, polished smooth either deliberately for effect or simply from being handled. They're utterly enchanting. The immediate question of course is: what would they have sounded like, and what kind of music could Magdalenian people have made with them?

By the late 1990s music historians asking these questions tended to focus on reconstructing the objects' overall shapes, but they seemed to be paying little attention to their surfaces and none at all to the kinds of microscopic analysis that – by then – we were routinely applying to medieval bone flutes. I therefore realised that I had to go and investigate for myself. At the National Museum of Antiquities in St-Germain-en-Laye I met the objects' curator Marie-Hélène Thiault and my colleague Francesco d'Errico from Bordeaux, and together we began a detailed examination that would last several days. In a back room of the museum we began with simple magnifying glasses and the museum's binocular microscopes. At that time we still had some doubts as to whether they really were musical – medieval and later traditions warned us that not every perforated tube has to be musical. But what we now saw only reinforced our sense of the objects' special character.

There were two pieces, from different bones. They'd each been broken at both ends, and sadly none of the original ends was anywhere to be seen. But the holes had clearly been made with great deliberation and, it seemed, ingenuity. Unlike the Jiăhú makers, who'd employed a rotary action similar to the techniques used by their Roman and medieval successors, each hole had been gouged with parallel strokes of a chisel-like blade until the cavity was reached. Given the coarseness of the technique, the resulting shapes were surprisingly circular. The blade would of course have been stone at this very early date – probably a kind of flint; and although flint, like broken glass, can be given an extremely sharp cutting edge, the edges tend to be brittle. This explained why the end result was less neat than the Chinese holes. But they still seemed perfectly functional, and the individual strokes well controlled. It must have taken a lot of work. And judging by the extent to which subsequent handling had imparted a gloss to the surfaces, they must also have gone on to see quite a lot of action.

The fact that they were incomplete was naturally a disappointment. The broken-off pieces had never been found, and this had robbed us not only of any way of knowing how many holes they'd had originally, but also of how they might have been tuned. And the loss of the blowing ends meant that we could never know how they were meant to be voiced. We couldn't even be sure of the kind of instrument they'd been. Emmanuel Passemard had chosen to label them *flûtes*, which was a reasonable enough choice for an archaeologist writing in French, but it now proved to be a mixed blessing because in other languages it imposes a particular meaning on the finds. 'Fluting' and 'whistling' are by no means the only ways that ancient people could elicit sounds from tubes. They could sing into them, as a kazoo player might; they could make buzzing noises with their lips, as horn, trumpet and didjeridoo players do; and they could use a split reed to achieve the kinds of sound that an oboist or saxophone player or bagpiper does today. And none of these methods is beyond the bounds of possibility in the Palaeolithic.

Of course their broken state meant that there would be little point in trying to produce working replicas: there were just too many unknowns to make it worthwhile. And yet, there was one tremendous upside to the problem. Because they were incomplete, it was unlikely that either the excavators or subsequent curators and students would have been tempted to play them. So we could now be confident that the patterns of finger wear we could see were left by ancient music-making. Just imagine: finger wear on instruments that were broadly comparable with the pipes of Jiăhú, but left by Magdalenian musicians – cave-dwelling hunters towards the end of what used to be called the Last Ice Age. And this brought with it another tantalising question. Their pipes seem at last to be cruder in their manufacture, and simpler in their concept, than anything seen in Neolithic China. Might it be that we're finally witnessing some of humankind's first essays in the art and science of instrument-making? Are we at last drawing close to the limits of music's physical, material footprint, and of archaeology's ability to recover it?

It might seem so. But if you've followed music's story this far you'll already know that in music's archaeological past, appearances can so easily deceive. We've now reached what's known as the Last Glacial Maximum. We're surrounded by ice sheets and mammoth steppes. And yet the truth we're about to discover is that we're not even half-way to our goal. What we're going to see next is surely the most breathtaking sequence of musical discoveries that archaeologists have ever made.

CHAPTER FORTY-NINE

Lights out of darkness: the world's most ancient musical pipes

France and Germany, *c*.27,000 to 40,000 years ago

Hidden away in the foothills of the Atlantic Pyrenees, in the Basque country of south-western France, the Grotte d'Isturitz isn't one of those caves that we remember for their murals. Its walls don't have the painted tableaux of Lascaux or Altamira, Niaux or Chauvet. There's little sign of all those glorious phalanxes of horses, deer, wild ox, bison and mammoth. If there are any marks on the walls, they are merely dots and lines, daubed in a reddish ochre. But what Isturitz seems to lack in visual splendour it more than makes up for in other ways. Its sheer size renders it an unusually resonant space in which to shout and clap and sing. And it turns out that the two bird-bone 'flutes' from the Magdalenian, the latest period of its Stone Age occupation, were only the most recent in a long line of musical artefacts that its ancient inhabitants left behind.

In 1928 Emmanuel Passemard was succeeded in his explorations of the site by Louis-René and Suzanne de Saint-Périer, and by the time their investigations ended thirty years later, the number of instruments recovered had risen to more than twenty. And they weren't just more of the same. They extended music's timeline back into two previous phases of human endeavour: the Solutrean and the Gravettian. Their respective assemblages of stone and bone tools showed evolutions in design from one cultural layer to the next, and helped to establish their relative chronology, so that even before the advent of modern radiometric dating techniques it was clear that the oldest must be very old indeed. We now know that it meant older by another ten thousand years, or more. Within their respective layers, the earlier instruments were accompanied by decorated bones and ivory, as well as over twenty scratched pebbles, small plaques and cobbles. The scratched designs resemble the graffiti we've seen on the walls of medieval churches – except that here they show the bison, mammoths, horses and deer that we'd normally expect to see drawn and painted on cave walls. Some stones have been repeatedly used, superimposing one image over another until the individual motifs can seem difficult to disentangle. Some even show traces of ochre, while others carry impact marks that suggest that they may have been used for hammering something. Could the ochre and the percussion have had a musical dimension?

Hammering and other percussive forms of sound-making have recently become a hot topic in the archaeology of caves and other ancient spaces. From the finely built courts where the Aztecs played their ritual ball games to medieval European church architectures, from Greek and Roman theatres to the megalithic monuments of Europe's Bronze and Neolithic ages, music historians and archaeologists have begun to debate whether there may have been more to them than meets the eye. In underground spaces, sound effects are particularly noticeable, and atmospheric. We can hear echoes, reverberations and sometimes the build-up of 'standing waves' – sustained resonances on particular musical frequencies – whose strength and impact have inspired scientists, especially acousticians, to devote a great deal of time and energy to measuring, processing and mapping them. And it just so happens that one place that's attracted particular interest has been Isturitz itself.

Entering the cave system from the northern end, modern visitors to Isturitz have often noticed the way their voices and footsteps resonate, and some years ago these observations were taken a stage further. French acousticians discovered what they believed to be a correlation between areas of the cave where resonance was especially pronounced and the ancient placement of small round red dots, each about two centimetres in diameter. Through the 1980s and 90s measurements were taken that seemed to bear this out. They also noticed that some of the limestone features of the nearby Oxocelhaya cave system – stalactites, stalagmites and folded calcite 'draperies' – had resonances of their own when struck, and found evidence that these properties may have been appreciated in the distant past. At Arcy-sur-Cure, to the south-east of Auxerre in Bourgogne-Franche-Comté, similar limestone structures had been repeatedly struck and the percussion marks overlaid with ochre. Sealed under ancient calcite, they couldn't be modern. It seemed that ancient people may have been exploiting them as natural 'stone chimes'.

This question of resonance has recently benefitted from a survey of caves in northern Spain, using the latest analytical and scanning techniques. One of the holy grails of archaeoacousticians is to find links between the sound effects that we notice in ancient places and signs that they were actually noticed and exploited in their day. There is of course no guarantee that acoustical phenomena that seem remarkable to us were intended or appreciated by our ancient ancestors. To presuppose that they must would only lead us into circular arguments. But analysis of the distributions of visual motifs on the Spanish cave walls, including lines and dots, has revealed that they often occur in places with enhanced low-frequency-resonance responses. The association is perhaps weaker than it was at Isturitz, but it still seems statistically significant.

But of course we already knew that sound must have been significant for people at Isturitz. The presence of the two bone pipes in its Magdalenian layers had already given that game away. Clearly its inhabitants were not just aware of sounds; they were engineering them, and putting them to creative uses. And the Magdalenians were not alone in doing so.

One of the most dazzling aspects of the Magdalenian instruments is their age. At the time of the Passemard and Saint-Périer investigations, it wasn't possible to estimate the antiquity of the different phases of the site's prehistory in years. Archaeology could only place them in a sequence relative to one another, according to the changing types of stone and bone tools that they left behind. But with the advent of radiometry in the 1970s, the true vastness of the timescales they represent began to emerge, and the figures were astonishing. The Magdalenian proved to have started around seventeen thousand years ago and only declined with the Last Glacial Maximum and the melting of the ice some five thousand years later. And deeper than the Magdalenians, their predecessors could be traced back through the earlier Gravettian to what the Saint-Périers called the Final Aurignacian, around thirty-three thousand years ago. And they found evidence of music there too.

These earlier instruments achieve their finest expression in the Gravettian, a phase of technological development that stretches from twenty-two back to thirty-three thousand years ago. And one of the thrilling realisations that the Gravettian finds bring with them is that they are once again complicated pipes, delicately made, with multiple precisely formed finger holes. Gone is the roughness of the Magdalenian fragments. They are in better condition too. One pipe is to all intents and purposes complete. At a first glance it might even be mistaken for a medieval bone pipe, or one of the crane-bone flutes of the Chinese Neolithic. But closer inspection reveals that it's neither of those things. It's something much, much older. In fact, many thousands of years older.

I have an accurate copy in front of me as I write, produced in synthetic bone from our careful study of the original. It's twenty-one and a half centimetres long and for most of its length it's about a centimetre in diameter. It's hollow and almost straight, though at one end the tube expands where it approaches what was once the bird's elbow joint. The joint itself has been neatly trimmed off, together with the wrist joint at the other end – and it's at this end that we find the turning-point in the plot of this particular tale. We have a museum curator called Dominique Buisson to thank for it. In the late 1980s he was reviewing all the prehistoric bones from Isturitz when he made a discovery. He'd already been able to reassemble several bone fragments that had become separated, and now he realised that one of the lengths of worked tube from Emma-nuel Passemard's 1914 season was the missing end of a near-complete instrument found in the same chamber by the Saint-Périers in 1939. The surfaces of the break fitted back together perfectly. It was a heart-stopping moment. Up to this point we'd been flying almost blind. We'd almost given up hope of ever seeing what a complete Palaeolithic pipe might look like. Now we had one in full view, and it was a revelation.

With both ends preserved, it was now possible to see exactly how its finger holes had been placed in relation to the whole instru-ment. Like the Jiǎhú flutes, there seemed to be nothing remotely tentative or experimental about it. There were four neat holes and around the margin of each hole the bone had been shaved flat to form a shallow oval platform. It was the sort of platform recognis-able from later flutes and pipes the world over, designed so that the player's fingertips can feel for and then close the hole effectively. The holes themselves were clearly laid out in two pairs, with a slightly larger gap between the second hole and the third. And the whole row was positioned towards the broader end of the bone. The platforms too were asymmetrical, set at a slight angle so that they naturally invited our fingers to touch them obliquely. It seemed to imply that the instrument was meant to be played from one corner of the mouth: the right corner.

Asymmetries of this sort are always of interest when interpret-ing past designs, because by deviating from the most obvious, simple form, they suggest a degree of specialisation. After all, it was a deviation from perfect symmetry that helped establish the musical purpose of the medieval choristers' windows on the west fronts of Lichfield and Wells cathedrals. Now here it was in the Palaeolithic. Yet one new fact stood out from all the others. Having both ends intact and complete meant that for the first time it was possible to see how the instrument was meant to be voiced.

What we saw under the microscope was remarkable. There was no visible adaptation that could have served a flute-like blowing technique. There was no sharp or angled edge. Whether by design or through long use, both ends showed perfectly smooth, rounded rims.

It's true that the replica I have in front of me *can* be voiced as a flute – but only just and if I don't mind getting the same fuzzy sound we hear when we blow across the top of an empty bottle. Could it have been played with an inserted reed, like a modern oboe or a bagpipe chanter, or blown through pursed lips like a trumpet? The original shows only the polished smoothness of the rim. But it's an important point and it carries an important implication. Each way of voicing it creates quite different sounds, differences not just to the 'tone' or 'colour' of the sounds, but also to the pitches of the notes. Played as a reed pipe or a trumpet the sound is more strident, more assertive, and because in this mode the air column behaves as if it's closed at one end – the mouth end – it plays a much lower and richer series of notes. Just how rich, and how neat a series, I discovered one evening when I tested my first replica in the stairwell outside my third-floor laboratory. As a flute it only whiffled and hissed. But played in the manner of a Renaissance cornett, it suddenly roared into life. The whole stairwell began to vibrate. There was nothing remotely flute-like about the sound. And what's more, it was now playing a recognisably tuneful scale: first *do-re-mi*, then *fa* and then a sharp *sol*. This was unexpected, to say the least.

We've had such surprises before, of course. We've seen them especially in the paired deer-bone reed-pipes from Anglo-Saxon England and among the Avars in early medieval Hungary; and the way we make sense of them is, or should be, the same. Unfortunately they haven't always been, and it's taken the older instruments into some strange interpretive backwaters. Often when an excavator has found a pipe that's suspected of being musical, they've begun by applying the generic label 'flute', and then asked around for advice about flutes. This is all well and good when we're certain that that's what it is, but not when we're not. It's quite the wrong question to ask. The beauty and the importance of Dominique Buisson's discovery was not that it *proved* that bone pipes were played as trumpets. It doesn't. But it makes trumpeting more likely, and once again the different musical implications reveal the perils of jumping to assumptions. It's why today the very first thing we do when we're confronted with something outside our archaeological experience is to put aside preconceptions and *interrogate the object*. We need first to discover what *it* may be trying to tell *us*.

Dominique Buisson's completed Gravettian pipe isn't the only substantial specimen from the caves. Another refitted Gravettian pipe is very nearly complete; and although it can't be fully replicated, at least with the same degree of confidence, the obvious similarity between the two provides eloquent confirmation that we're looking at evidence of a musical *tradition*. Both instruments use the same bone, and they both have their finger holes arranged with a larger space between the second and third. In the second instrument someone has drawn attention to this larger space by marking it with three parallel scratches. In other words, the spacing has been part of a plan. The marks look eerily like the parallel lines painted between holes on some of the clay flutes from Aztec Mexico. A third find establishes another key fact: that the tradition reaches back still further in time, into the Late Aurignacian. Now, it's possible that elements of late Aurignacian technology and culture persisted alongside the Gravettian; but even at a conservative estimate the association could push this third instrument to between twenty-six and thirty-seven thousand years ago. And this is confirmed by some finds from more recent excavations. In caves in southern Germany, investigators have brought to light specimens of pipes that can be dated to the Early Aurignacian.

If fire was ever to break out in the virtual museum of this book, and only one of the objects described could be snatched from the flames, our next and final object would probably not be every archaeologist's first choice, or even every music lover's. It's a small and rather dull-looking piece of a bone-like material, and it seems altogether insignificant alongside the fine instruments from Gravettian and Aurignacian Isturitz. But in a way it has a still higher claim to be saved: because few such fragments can ever have shone such a penetrating light onto ancient music-making. It's all about the way technical toolkits and musical skill sets were inherited and shared.

Again it's from an Aurignacian layer. What remains of it is less than two centimetres long. It's cream in colour with the usual dark speckling, and it seems no more than a worked and polished sliver of bone. But despite its diminutive size it has a unique story to tell about Palaeolithic life and music's place in it. It's a tale that, as it happens, also has something to say about the ingenuity and persistence of archaeologists: the theorists, the analysts and the excavators in the field who labour in all weathers in the hope of that next great breakthrough.

For some years now, Susanne Münzel and Nicholas Conard from the University of Tübingen in southern Germany have been discovering musical bone pipes from further and further back in time. The first discovery was made in a cave known locally as the Geissenklösterle Höhle, in the valley of the River Ach at Blaubeuren in the Swabian Jura. It was identified from its carefully worked finger holes, and the layer that it came from was Aurignacian. But this was only the start. In 2004 they found something still more surprising. This time the material wasn't bone: it was mammoth ivory.

Why anyone would try to fashion a slender, hollow pipe out of solid mammoth ivory, when they had plenty of naturally hollow bird bones to work with, is a puzzle. But at the Geissenklösterle cave someone evidently did, and they've done it extremely well. Carefully reassembled, the fragments form a neat tube a centimetre across, of which nineteen centimetres remain. It has a shallow curve, and evidence of four perforations. The hollowing technique that's been used is oddly familiar – we've already seen it in the medieval wooden horn from the River Erne in Ireland. The Palaeolithic makers have first split their tusk into strips, and from one of the strips they've shaped a solid rod of the right size. They've then split the rod in half lengthways, hollowed out the two pieces and bound them back together. It's a work of skill and, most of all, imagination. When the find was announced in 2004, it excited not just prehistorians but especially music's archaeologists. It was the ultimate challenge to the old, tired idea that there's something intrinsically 'simple' about prehistoric pipes. It pointed to a whole new level of ambition and investment in music, as long ago as the Aurignacian, around thirty-eight thousand years ago. But there was that one nagging question: why? Why had they invested all that effort in making an instrument that was virtually a replica of a natural bone?

The answer was partly provided by that innocent-seeming fragment of ivory that was rescued from our hypothetical bonfire. In 1931 the archaeologist Gustav Riek had been excavating at another cave, the Vogelherdhöhle in the Lone Valley near Niederstotzingen. But although he'd found a number of interesting things, he seemed to have found nothing to compare with the smaller fragments of bone and ivory from Geissenklösterle. This naturally troubled the Tübingen team, and in a moment of inspiration they decided to revisit Vogelherd and investigate. In 2005 they began to sieve through Riek's old spoil heaps, and they were rewarded. Among the small fragments they picked out were two little pieces of tube. One was our fragment. It proved to be part of another split ivory tube. And it shares another distinguishing feature with the Geissenklösterle ivory pipe: along the line of the split is a neat series of grooves that may have provided a grip or key for some kind of binding material.

The details are undoubtedly important, but the real story is in the similarities and in the geographical distance that separates Geissenklösterle from Vogelherd. Even as the crow flies, they are around thirty-five kilometres apart. So not only is it now known that the Geissenklösterle ivory pipe belongs to a distinct type of instrument but it seems that the type wasn't limited to just one place. Still more instances have recently come to light.

The icing on the musical cake emerged at another cave investigated by the same team, at the foot of the Hohle Fels, a limestone crag near Schelklingen. There they found what now ranks as the earliest bird-bone pipe and indeed the earliest musical instrument in the world. Radiocarbon analyses of the strata in which it was found show it to be a staggering *forty* thousand years old. Again it's a bird bone, this time from the wing of a vulture. It was only one of a number of remarkable finds, the most famous of which is the ivory statuette known as the 'Venus of Hohle Fels', which was unearthed just seventy centimetres from it. But there in the same layer were two more fragments of split ivory tube.

With the Hohle Fels bones and ivories we finally come to the limit of the fossil evidence – and sadly to the end of this present journey: a journey that began with pianos and amplifiers and all the paraphernalia of twentieth and twenty-first century music technology. We're now at a point that's no more than two thousand years, maybe even less, from the arrival of the first modern humans in Europe. Outside the cradle of Africa, where they began their journey, the Old World is still populated with older species of our human and hominin family, and there's no one at all in America, South or North. Or at least not yet.

But while it may be the end of one journey it's by no means the end of the road. Because, ancient as the Hohle Fels finds are, even at this early date they are still fine and elaborate instruments. For the time being, their wider material background still eludes us. We've yet to discover any of the musical technologies they may have been expressing in softer materials like wood and skin, sinew and twine; and so far there's no obvious sign of more ephemeral, transitory musical behaviours such as dance, song and poetry. What we do have is really no more than a glimpse through a keyhole. But it's a powerful beginning. The question is, where next? To answer *that* puzzle, we're going to have to step outside the box, to see what oblique musical inferences might be drawn from traces that earlier human lives have left us.

PART TWELVE

Beyond the Horizon

40,000 to 4 million years ago

All good tales should have a beginning, a middle and an end, or so we're told, and if this were a conventional history of music we ought by now to have reached some point of origin that could bring our journey to a satisfying close. So far, however, there's been little sign of one. As millennium has preceded millennium, we've noticed how, ravaged by time and environment, the evidence has been gradually thinning out; but nothing that we've yet seen has suggested the crudeness of execution or the lack of ingenuity that we might have expected from truly 'primitive' ancestors. At the first appearance of instruments around forty thousand years ago, their forms are if anything *more* elaborate and *more* coherent than those that succeeded them. Wherever there's sufficient evidence we see complexity and pattern. Wherever there isn't, the gaps in our musical knowledge seem increasingly like the blank unexplored spaces on old maps of the world. In short, what we've been seeing has been First Appearances—and that's not quite the same as Beginnings.

So if this isn't yet the moment to set aside our quest, how much further back should we be looking? And what surprises may future archaeologies have in store for us there? In the pages that follow we're going to be peering into a crystal ball to try to sense what, with luck and persistence, we might yet be able learn. To do this we'll meditate on some ancient human behaviours: behaviours that may not be *directly* related to musical actions, so far as we know, but may still afford us indirect glimpses through some of the musical potential that ancient human bodies and behaviours really do display. We'll see their breath control revealed in hand stencils sprayed by mouth onto the walls of painted caves between forty and forty-five thousand years ago. We'll see how, around a hundred thousand years ago, they rehearsed patterns and symmetries in visual ways that, if they'd ever chosen to express them in sound, would have constituted another of the defining features of musics we know today. We'll discover how around a quarter of a million years ago the anatomies of human hands and fingers were capable of delicately manipulating objects and materials, and around a third of a million years ago we'll see minds wrestling complex problems of time and movement, in the remains of elegant javelins. Between half a million and a million years ago we'll see hints that they found meaning or amusement in the ringing sounds of the rocks they were quarrying to make their stone tools. And from there we'll venture deeper still. We'll explore the architectures of their evolving brains, revealed as imprints in the bony linings of their skulls, and we'll look at the role that molecular genetics may some day play in unpicking the finer processes of their musical and linguistic development.

From these very different stories out of our remotest past, we'll hazard some guesses as to what may or may not have been going on in our ancestors' musical minds, drawing hope and encouragement from the proven capacity of the material world – aided by modern archaeological science – to delight and surprise us at almost every turn.

CHAPTER FIFTY

In search of lost music

c.40,000 to 900,000 years ago

Much of what we humans do as we engage with our world, and with each other, we do with our hands. We make things by hand, and we use hand gestures to communicate our feelings and emphasise our meanings. We've already seen how between thirty and forty thousand years ago the creators of the Isturitz and Hohle Fels pipes used stone tools to make elaborate tubes with acoustical properties that they could then manipulate, turning sounds into music. We can also see that the hands and fingers that did the work held powerful symbolic meaning for many Palaeolithic people, because they often left images of them adorning the walls of caves. In some cases they've simply daubed their palms with a coloured paste and pressed them directly onto the stone – a primitive form of printing still known to schoolchildren the world over. But they also used another, more sophisticated method that gives us access to an otherwise invisible ingredient of speech and song. It's the way they've used their lungs and lips in order to project and direct a stream of air.

Some of the earliest instances have been found in Indonesia. Paintings discovered in a cave on the tropical island of Sulawesi provide evidence of an extraordinary complexity of mind. They show not only how our ancestors expressed their views of the world but how they coordinated hands and eyes in making expressive movements and gestures.

The Maros-Pangkep caves of Sulawesi lie in the wild limestone karst hills of the inland part of the island's southern peninsula.

Around forty thousand years ago, the people who lived there were already performers skilled in the art of rock painting The murals they painted using powdered charcoals and ochres show mostly portraits of animals, such as wild pigs and buffalo; and once again there are painted silhouettes of human hands. But investigators had a major surprise in store for them. At first the paintings were assumed to have been created between ten and twenty thousand years ago. But in one cave a thin coating of calcite that had formed over them could be dated using the Uranium-Thorium method, and it showed that it had begun to form more than thirty thousand years ago. More surprises were to follow. Near the stencilled hands was a painting of a large wild pig which was at least thirty-five thousand years old. And then, at the end of 2019, results came in for some hunting scenes in a third cave. The hunted animals were pig and buffalo, and analysis showed that they were created at least *forty-four* thousand years ago. In January 2021, an image of an adult male 'Celebes warty pig' was reported from a fourth cave, painted in dark red ochre in a scene that included traces of two other animals. Once again there were hand stencils close by, and the earliest of them was at least *forty-five and a half* thousand years old.

Archaeologists believe that the hand stencils were sprayed in some form, but are divided on exactly how that was achieved. It might have been done by flicking liquid ochre pigment with the fingers or with a stiff bristle brush, but the nature of the spatter suggests to most experts that it was blown as a mouthful of powder and saliva directly from the artist's lips, or mixed with water and blown through some kind of container. A traditional view of ancient humanity favours the saliva mixture; but either way, the power was probably from the lungs, and it must have involved a very particular set of sensations, and sounds, as well as lip gestures of the kind that we'd associate with the fluting and trumpeting we've inferred from the Palaeolithic pipes in France and Germany.

We've already imagined Palaeolithic people singing and whistling in their caves. Were they also raspberry blowers? The thought would seem to conjure up a whole new world – not just harsh and utilitarian, but also creative, even comedic.

We may never be able to say whether they were speaking to each other with words, or singing tunes, or blowing raspberries. But in these silhouettes we do at least have evidence that they used their lungs to do something other than just breathe.

The images from Sulawesi may be the oldest surviving intact expressions (so far) of our human urge to represent things, but the ochre and charcoal backstory doesn't end in the caves of Maros-Pangkep. We next travel around the world to southern Africa, and back across an even greater gulf of time, to glimpse the lives of some of the very earliest members of our species. They are the so-called 'archaic *Homo sapiens*' who lived around a hundred thousand years ago, fully fifty thousand years before their northern descendants began to migrate out of Africa and populate Asia and Europe.

Blombos Cave is situated around three hundred kilometres east of Cape Town, at the foot of a cliff that looks out over the South Atlantic and Indian Oceans. It's one of many caves in South Africa and Namibia that have produced evidence of the earliest modern humans. Chris Henshilwood began excavating there in the southern summer of 1991–2, initially to chart the cave's occasional occupation during the last two thousand years, but beneath those deposits he found something much, much older. Stone tools and residues of earlier human activity have since been shown to cover a period stretching from seventy to a hundred thousand years ago; and besides stone and bone implements they include pierced shells of sea snails, thought to have been used as beads.

Chris and his colleague Francesco d'Errico, whom we met in Chapter 48 researching the finds from Isturitz, suspect that the beads may have had a musical or quasi-musical dimension, perhaps like the shell 'jingles' from the Natchez 'Fatherland Site'. Strung together they would have made a pleasing sound and formed an attractive accompaniment to movement and dance. In the entrance to the cave, the archaeologists found further signs of human activity, and among them were pieces of solid ochre, deposited alongside the shells. There's evidence that the ochre was being ground up to make coloured powders and pastes, which were then stored in abalone shells. But two pieces of ochre are most unusual. Found in 2002, they are still in their natural solid state, but someone has squared them off, and then added fine designs in the form of engraved lines. The lines are straight, and they criss-cross to form neat geometrical lattices. Several more examples have since been found, dating from between seventy and a hundred thousand years ago.

The obvious question to ask is why ochre powders and pastes should have been so important to people. Some ingenious solutions have been put forward, citing preservative and even medical applications. But most experts think the colours were the most likely attraction, and although no figurative paintings survive from such a long time ago, painting of some kind seems the most plausible explanation, on walls or on objects, perhaps also on their bodies. This is supported by other finds. On one small fragment of stone someone has drawn nine parallel red lines using a sharpened piece of ochre as a crayon; and a piece of animal bone has been engraved with eight parallel lines. None of the designs is depicting anything in particular, at least not as far as we can tell, but it's hard to deny their decorative qualities, or the regular manner in which the lines have been spaced. Their regularity also reminds us of a musical phenomenon that has been particularly difficult to evidence in music's fossil record: the patterns of sound that we recognise as rhythm and cadence – components that are as important to music as melody and tone colour.

It's not the first time that we've seen such patterns. We've noted fine parallel lines engraved between the finger holes of bone pipes from the Grotte d'Isturitz; in fact, some of the Isturitz pipes carry whole sequences of scratched, evenly spaced marks along their backs and sides. Here at Blombos the spacing is no less uniform and precise. It suggests that, around a hundred thousand years ago, there was already a taste for regulation and spatial measurement. Dare we imagine a similar appetite for regularity in other areas of people's lives, such as in the sounds they were making?

The Maros-Pangkep and Blombos cave finds show that when we saw modern humans first expressing their artistic talents on their arrival in Europe, we were right not to imagine them discovering them in just that moment. They were surely abilities that had travelled with them on their epic journey out of Africa; so it's hard to believe that when our still earlier African ancestors began to display their graphic skills, music (or something very like music) wasn't also part of their lifestyle. This doesn't make its existence any easier to detect or prove. But just occasionally the fossil record comes up with another oblique physical clue that gives us food for thought, and one of them came to light in 2013, in another South African cave.

It seems that in a series of separate events between a quarter and a third of a million years ago, people found their way down into what's now known as the Rising Star cave system, near Pretoria. And having got there, deep underground, for some reason several of them never left. Only their skeletons remain to tell their strange tale. There's no direct evidence of any music-making there; in fact, they seem to have had no possessions with them at all. But their well-preserved hands and feet reveal something rather interesting. We're now looking into humanity's past in terms not just of our cultural origins but of the development of our human anatomy. The people in Rising Star Cave are not our direct ancestors; known today as *Homo naledi*, they appear to represent a distinct, and now extinct, lineage that had diverged from ours some time before. Yet their skeletal remains have preserved an unexpected glimpse of our common ancestors.

The remains were discovered by Lee Berger and his team from the University of the Witwatersrand. Amateur cavers had already been visiting some of the site's darkest recesses since the 1990s. It's not one of those grand, wide-open seaside caves, filled with light, where pirates might hide their loot or smugglers stash their contraband. Here, above ground, there are only three narrow ways in or out, and unless you know where they are you might never guess that there was anything down there. But below the surface there's a labyrinth of galleries and connecting passages extending more than two hundred and fifty metres from north to south and nearly a hundred and seventy-five metres west to east. Some of the passages are too narrow for people to squeeze through, while others climb steeply up or tilt dangerously downwards, sometimes complicated by rock falls. Nevertheless much of the system had already been explored and mapped by the time two cavers first caught sight of the bones and showed photos to Lee Berger. He was already excavating nearby, and keen to investigate, but there was one major obstacle. The approach to the deep chamber where the bones were lying was only eighteen centimetres wide: far too tight for a grown man to squirm through. Nevertheless, after advertising for suitable archaeological volunteers, he was able to assemble a team of strong but slender young women, and during the southern summer of 2013–14 they excavated a small area of the cave floor. What they found there astonished the archaeological world.

They recovered the bones of a number of individuals, including one virtually complete skeleton. The skulls were small and showed that these people's brains had been nearer in size to those of apes than they are to our species, or even to the brains of the 'archaic humans' at Blombos. But there was something oddly modern about their hands and feet. The bones of their feet were definitely human, and with their well-articulated ankles and straight leg bones, they would have been able to stand fully upright and to walk with long, efficient movements. Indeed, if they'd wished to, they could have skipped and jumped, kicked and even danced. But the hand bones were even more intriguing. One of the hands was found intact, lying palm upwards with all the bones of the wrist and palm, the fingers and thumb, still in their correct positions. The fingers and thumb were surprisingly mobile and elegant. This wasn't a fumbling, gripping paw for snatching fruit or prey, or solely for hanging from the branches of trees. They seem almost like artists' or pianists' hands: mechanically at least, they could have typed this page – or played the blues.

This has been a puzzle for anthropologists, because most of the other body parts found in the cave – ribcages and shoulders – suggest that they were derived from a far more primitive, ape-like ancestor. Why would such small-brained, primitive people have needed such 'gracile' limbs and delicate grips? No doubt they were useful to get around and help them manipulate their material world to their advantage. But was that all they did with them?

The manipulative skills that the delicate hands of *Homo naledi* afforded their owners would have given them a survival advantage, and perhaps a creative potential, that was limited only by their powers of mind and imagination: their ability to connect cause and effect, to conceive and invent things, and to communicate, learn and teach. Anthropologists like Lee Berger are delving deeper and deeper into the past to see how human aptitudes and ambition grew, exploring the evolving architectures of their brains and the genetic evidence of their heredity. But before we look into some of those final materialities, it's time to pause and consider one particular case in which we're able to see just how far early humans were able to translate some of these aptitudes into action.

The narrowness of our view of deep prehistory was exposed suddenly and vividly one day in 1994, on the outskirts of a small town called Schöningen, not far from Hannover in northern Germany. The discovery was made on the edge of an opencast mine where an inferior coal called lignite, or 'brown coal', was being mined. Like true black coal, lignite is a compacted swamp deposit of vegetable matter, but much younger. At Schöningen it dates from around fifty million years ago, and to get to it, miners don't have to sink shafts – they can simply dig down through soft earth. Some of the intervening strata have been waterlogged, however, and contain not only the bones of prehistoric mammals but traces of the lives of people who were hunting them. What archaeologists found there completely changed our ideas of prehistoric technology.

Exploration began in 1983, directed by archaeologist Hartmut Thieme. He had earlier excavated Neolithic structures at the northern end of the site, dating from seven-and-a-half thousand years ago, but the layers he now exposed held far earlier and wholly unexpected riches. They were around *three hundred* thousand years old. There were butchered animal bones and stone tools, and sealed beneath some of the sediments were bones and ivory that had survived not as dry, partly mineralised fossils but in their original form, soft and damp to the touch. More exciting still were remains of waterlogged wooden objects. Some of them appeared to be handles for stone tools. One looked like a throwing stick, for launching missiles. Others included several long, slender wooden poles, made round in cross section and sharpened to a point at one end. They were obviously weapons. But it was almost impossible to credit that they could have survived for so long.

The people who made them could have been Neanderthals, but they might just as easily be the work of the earlier and smaller-brained *Homo heidelbergensis*. They've cut and shaped them with stone tools; but their purpose in doing so was unexpectedly advanced. They clearly weren't planning just to skewer trapped prey at close quarters. At the opposite end from the point where a prodding spear would require a secure grip, they've been carefully thinned to create a tapering tail like a modern sports javelin. Their makers were exploring aerodynamics and ballistics, creating the first human-made projectiles that we know to have been actually *designed* for flight.

To prehistorians the finds gave a new sense of ancient humans' cognitive powers and survival strategies. But there are wider implications too. It's opened our eyes to new opportunities for the recovery of ancient 'green' technologies: technologies that might in theory have included music technologies like the tree-bark flutes we saw at the very beginning of our journey. Could there be a musical dividend to this waterlogged wood from such a remote time?

The very first dividend may be in the way a javelin works, in real time. To launch a javelin or indeed any missile successfully at prey requires cognitive power. It requires a thorough sense of space and time, of animal behaviour, and an ability to envision the projectile's likely trajectory under different atmospheric conditions. It demands split-second timing and, in all likelihood, synchronisation with other people. All these components have their musical equivalents of course: in the control of voices and instruments; in composing and executing melodic lines with phrasing and cadence; and perhaps most important of all, in that most socially adaptive of all human activities – singing and playing together. While we haven't yet found any musical instruments among those waterlogged deposits at Schöningen or anywhere else, these tools and weapons show that such things could survive. They also show that whoever was crafting them already had the skills and tools needed to make fine instruments – if they'd wanted to.

Around four hundred thousand years ago, the forerunners of the people who devised, shaped and deployed the javelins at Schöningen belonged to a still more ancient kind of human. Today we know them as the 'Upright People': *Homo erectus* in Europe and Asia, and *Homo ergaster* in Africa. They roamed and hunted, gathered and scavenged, across much of the Old World, and every last one of us alive today is descended from them. They inhabited a world that was on average drier and cooler than it is today. Measurements of their skulls show that their brains were quite small, but archaeological finds imply that they were far from dull-witted. From their limb bones we can see that they walked as we do, completely upright with a good long stride, and they could be as light and agile on their toes as we are today. They were also skilled with their arms, hands and fingers, and they've left us a wealth of evidence of their creative powers, preserved in the stone tools they used. Butchery was no doubt their prime purpose, but if they were able to butcher meat, as their hunting sites show, they could have cut and shaped other stuff besides. Microscopic traces on some of their tools reveal use-wear likely to result from cutting and preparing wood. But it's the making of the tools themselves that may hold the strongest musical clue.

Stone tools of this period come in several shapes. Some are quite rough and ready: mere cobbles, broken to create a sharp edge. In archaeology, these broken stones are usually described as 'Oldowan choppers and scrapers', referring to their use by an earlier people living at Olduvai Gorge in Tanzania. But another design, the so-called hand-axe, has gone on to become Upright People's archaeological trademark. They are technically known as 'Acheulean bifaces': Acheulean because they were first discovered at Saint-Acheul, near Amiens in Picardy; and biface because their flatter, more leaf-like shapes have been worked from both sides. If you ever get the chance to handle one, you'll notice that it may ring a little when you tap it.

To produce such elegant forms in stone, with only other stones as tools, demands a good deal of work and dexterity. It also entails acute observation and planning. It involves selecting a suitable piece of rock and striking bits off the outside using a hammer, usually another rock. Archaeologists call the technique 'reduction': like a sculptor, you chip away at your chosen stone until you've reduced it to the shape you want. Experiments show that some rocks are more suitable than others. A fresh lump of flint is perfect, if you can find one; but whatever type of stone you use, the important thing is that it should be hard and brittle, so that when the hammer strikes obliquely onto an exposed angle or ridge, instead of merely crushing it to powder the shock will cause a thin flake to pop neatly off. And if the knapping works well, the finished effect can be rather beautiful.

The analogy with sculpture is apt for other reasons too. Bifaces are often notable for their symmetry and proportion. Some are even stylish. An example in the Museum of Archaeology and Anthropology in Cambridge still has a fossil seashell naturally embedded in its glassy matrix. Today any self-respecting flint worker (and they do still exist) might regard it as a structural weakness, to be rejected. But this ancient maker has gone on to create an object around it. Tool and fossil even share the same axis of symmetry. And it's not unique: another find from Kent has a sea urchin at its centre. There's clearly been some visual aesthetic at work here, and in it we can already sense something of our own way of thinking. We detect a curious mind and a creative imagination. They were attaching importance to what they saw with their eyes and felt with their hands. So why wouldn't they also have found significance in what they heard with their ears?

It isn't entirely a rhetorical question. Percussion of the sort needed to convert raw stone into fine tools naturally draws archaeologists into the realm of sound. You simply can't strike flakes off a stone without making noise, and quite a lot of noise: from the necessary banging and cracking of the hammer to the incidental tinkling and clattering of newly detached flakes falling to the ground. And as you thin and lighten your stone, so the sound of the emerging object changes with each impact. Intentionally or otherwise, you're not just shaping it: you're also in effect *tuning* it. Did these changes affect the way Upright People imagined their creations? Did it help them in a practical way, just as we use tapping and listening to our advantage in many modern crafts? Might resonance have added to the character of the process and even to the 'personality' of the finished tool? We can only wonder. And yet it's not sensible to exclude from our speculations the perceptual dimension, or indeed the social potential of groups of people performing the same craft process at the same time. At the very least, the noises they made would have formed the background soundscapes of early Stone Age life. They would have offered endless scope for rhythmic synchronisation, provided that people had acquired the subtlety and plasticity of mind to be able to engage in such things. And that's the big 'if'. Had they yet acquired that subtlety and plasticity?

What we need is some hard material evidence to test the theory. In previous chapters we've seen the dangers of wishful thinking: the circular arguments that inevitably follow when we impose our own cultural values and expectations on the remote past. So it comes as a relief to find a possible clue among objects recovered from the famous Lower Palaeolithic sites of Africa's Great Rift Valley. Around half a million years ago the inhabitants of what's now Olduvai Gorge in Tanzania, East Africa, chose to make their cobble tools and bifaces from two local rock types: from water-worn rocks of basalt, formed from solidified volcanic magma; and from another hard igneous rock with a tendency to form slabs. Ancient people evidently took the trouble to source this second rock directly from outcrops, and careful examination shows it to be a fine-grained mineral called trachyte. It has a slightly oily feel, but it has a more fundamental property too: it emits a powerful ringing sound when you hit it.

In 1791, the German geologist Abraham Gottlob Werner was so captivated by the sounds he obtained from some of his German trachytes that he named them *Klingsteine*, literally 'klinking stones', but in 1801 the chemist Martin Klaproth gave them a new label: phonolite. The name stuck, and the Olduvai trachytes remain pho-nolite to this day. It seems somehow significant that Upright People should have found themselves drawn to such a material. So was it just its usefulness that attracted them, or could its unusual sonority have been a source of fascination for them too?

CHAPTER FIFTY-ONE

Brains, genes and synchronisation

*c.*2 to 4 million years ago

Not far from Rising Star Cave, the final resting place of *Homo naledi*, are the equally breathtaking caves of Sterkfontein. It was here, before the Second World War, that the anthropologist Raymond Dart first identified the remains of an upright, ape-like people that we now call *Australopithecus*, or 'southern ape'; and it was here too that in 1947 further excavation revealed a complete skull of the species *Australopithecus africanus*. Radiometric and palaeomagnetic analysis has dated these remains – today numbering several hundred individuals – to between two and two-and-a-half million years ago; but recent results suggest that some could be as much as 3.5 million years old. Can they tell us anything about how the earliest human and hominin brains and bodies were changing?

In addition to the increasing sizes of ancient fossil brains through archaeological time, there's also something to be learned from their internal forms. The inside surface of a hominin cranium preserves an impression of the brain's external shape. This is fortunate because brain tissue is among the first to be lost when a body is left exposed to natural forces, but from the curious way that these inner surfaces undulate, we can reconstruct something of the lost brain's outward 'architecture'; and by comparing it to both older and younger examples, we can begin to see how brain structures were changing. From a musical point of view the areas that are of particular interest are those known to be implicated in the way that we make and decode speech, language and musical sounds.

The brains of the Australopithecines are a lot smaller than ours – typically around four to five hundred cubic centimetres compared to our eleven to thirteen hundred – but they also reveal that some regions became privileged through time. In a skull of *Australopithecus sediba* from nearby Malapa, another of Lee Berger's discoveries, it seems that the shape of the frontal region behind and above the eyes preserves details of the neural reorganisation that would eventually lead to our own genus, *Homo*.

One of the scientists who've done most to explore the potential relationship between the finer details of Australopithecine brains and the origins of language and music is Dean Falk at the University of Florida in Tallahassee. She's detected evidence for changes to three regions of their cerebral cortex: the 'dorsolateral pre-frontal association' cortex, the 'parieto-temporo-occipital' cortex, and the part of the frontal lobe of the brain's left hemisphere that's known as 'Broca's speech area'. In later humans all three are implicated in the performance and reception of language, speech and music, and significantly, all three appear to be already undergoing change in *Australopithecus africanus*. This evidence can be seen in 3-D models derived from laser scans, and forms the basis of her theory that mother–baby communications, known as 'Motherese', may have played a role in the early emergence of language.

But however promising the evidence may be, inevitably there are technical obstacles to further understanding. So far, most really ancient skulls survive only in fragments, and even among the complete specimens the finer details are not always as crisp as we would like. Some of the blurring is caused by the cushion of fluid and the meningeal membrane that surround the brain, and it's particularly noticeable in young and old individuals. Equally frustrating, even the clearest scan can never show more than the outermost surfaces of the brain, and it's hard to imagine ever being able to access the deeper neural connections and networks in this way, except by theoretical modelling. However, bones are no longer the only evidence we can draw on. We now have a new weapon in our scientific armoury: molecular genetics.

The further we delve into the distant past, the more our interpretation of it relies on scientific innovation – indeed, revolution. Surrounded by exciting discoveries, one of the most stimulating things about being an archaeologist is that you never quite know where the next scientific revolution is going to come from, or how it will change the way we interpret the past. In the twinkling of an eye, yesterday's riddle can turn into today's accepted fact. Back in the 1960s and 70s it was the advent of radiocarbon dating and tree-ring dating that revealed just how ancient the distant past really was. Other scientific breakthroughs followed: advances in electron microscopy, scanning, geophysics, computer modelling and Big Data. But in the 1990s the real game-changer was the Human Genome Project: the sequencing and mapping of our entire genetic code.

Together with new techniques for rapid DNA sequencing, genetic analysis began to have a profound practical impact on archaeology. Theories of the origins and development of ancient languages, for instance, began to be correlated with the movements and migrations of ancient peoples, and with the spread of their technologies and ways of life. And as the genetic revolution extended its reach to our near relatives the apes and beyond, a new kind of archaeology opened up. This time it wasn't dependent on remains, or even on samples of ancient DNA. It was based on the genes and parts of genes preserved in the living genome that we and the other apes have inherited from our common ancestor, and it shows how tiny divergences, chemical changes here and there in the molecular chain, helped make us who we are today. Passed on to subsequent generations, these errors don't just mark steps in the processes of anatomical divergence: they are their root causes. By charting the way they happened, like people's names written into a family tree, we now have a whole new tree of life, and a whole new human backstory. Among the genes suspended within the long, coiled double helix of DNA, three have so far been identified as being linked in some way to language, speech and music. They are known as 'FOXP2', 'CNTNAP2' and 'SRGAP2'.

Printed on paper, with bright colours to distinguish its various elements, FOXP2 looks for all the world like a piece of modern abstract art. But the developments in human and animal behaviour that its structure represents are very ancient indeed. We share it with other mammals, birds, reptiles and even fish; but each has its own distinctive version.

Geneticists haven't yet determined all the different bodily functions to which FOXP2 contributes, but we do know that unfortunate things happen when it doesn't function correctly. Sadly, our genes do sometimes carry evidence of past damage, and when any human inherits faulty FOXP2 genes it has a detrimental impact on the development of their brain and lungs. One faulty parental FOXP2 gene in each cell is enough to cause speech problems in childhood; but when both copies are faulty, the outcome is even more serious.

All humans today share precisely the same FOXP2 gene, but this can't always have been the case. The FOXP2 of our nearest relatives, the chimpanzees and bonobos, differs from ours in the configuration of two links in the chain. The fact that human and chimpanzee FOXP2 genes are otherwise identical shows that we share a common ancestor not only in anatomical terms – which we worked out a long time ago by comparing skeletons – but also in our biochemistry; and yet in spite of their human-like FOXP2, chimpanzees are incapable of the levels of linguistic and vocal complexity that we take for granted, even in young children. Could it be that our tiny two-point mutation made all the difference? Could it be that the common ancestor of chimpanzees and humans was as incapable as a chimp of expressing complex, structured vocalisations and signs? If this is the case, and many scientists now think it likely, then we must wonder when, in our subsequent family tree, those two enabling mutations occurred. Was it when we parted company from the chimpanzee and bonobo line around five to six million years ago? Or was it much more recently?

No useful DNA has yet been recovered from the remains of *Australopithecus*. The extreme length of time, coupled with fluctuating conditions in the soils and rocks that embedded them, has degraded all complex molecules like DNA. In recent years, however, it's been possible to map the complete genomes of our more recent precursors, the Neanderthals, and substantial parts of those of their contemporaries, the Denisovans of eastern and southern Asia and the south-west Pacific. It turns out that both Neanderthals and Denisovans had precisely the same FOXP2 gene as us. To some students of human evolution this is a clue that speech could have been part of Neanderthal life some hundred and fifty thousand years ago, and that they were already becoming the communicative people that we are today. But if modern human FOXP2 is *not* a post-Neanderthal innovation, how much earlier should we imagine the two crucial changes occurring? And what might they tell us about the genesis of those other great mediums of vocal and gestural communication, music and dance?

The notion that there might be a gene or genes for music and dance as well as for language and speech has been given a boost by recent studies of the other two genes. CNTNAP2 is an enormously long gene that interacts with FOXP2 and carries mutations that appear to be implicated in susceptibilities to cancer, intellectual disabilities and language development disorders. SRGAP2 plays an important role in nerve development, especially in the cerebral cortex. Again there's no difference between our version of SRGAP2 and those of Neanderthals and Denisovans; but in 2012 scientists were able to suggest that it underwent two key mutations at around the time of the Australopithecines and the first appearance of *Homo*. Between two-and-a-half and three-and-a-half million years ago, according to geneticists' 'molecular clocks', it seems to coincide with both an expansion of the brain neocortex and the first evidenced use of stone tools. It's a promising start and, genetics being the fast-moving field that it is, further revelations are confidently expected. Indeed it can only be a matter of time.

Time: it's one of the sublime ironies of our archaeological past that this, the archaeologist's constant preoccupation, is seldom if ever seen in action. We see its results, but not its progress. The remains we find and the places where we find them never seem to record its actual passing, second by second; they merely express the fact of its having passed. We can see the stills but not the movie, so to speak. This is especially frustrating when what's at stake are those most transitory and time-critical of all human behaviours: speech and music, movement and dance.

The patterns of wear around the frets of a Renaissance cittern or the finger holes of a prehistoric bone pipe accumulate – but they don't form any helpful musical sequence. Like a worn doorstep, they betray time's passing after the event, by material reduction; but each set of actions tends to obliterate whatever went before. It's true that the growth rings in ancient wood and the temperature changes frozen into ice cores can give a sense of time passing, but they advance only in seasonal increments. They say nothing of the moments – the minutes and seconds – in which life is actually lived and things are said and done, danced and sung.

Yet sometimes, against all the odds, a discovery is made that has the capacity to replay a human activity in real time. We can see it in the long spiralling traces left by a potter's fingers on a wheel-spun bowl, or the tool marks left on a piece of wooden furniture that's been turned on a lathe. And perhaps the most astonishing, and so far the most ancient, of all real-time traces are to be seen in the marks left when, by accident or necessity, people found themselves walking across soft but hardening surfaces – surfaces that, like Thomas Edison's wax cylinders, were malleable enough to receive and preserve their imprints.

In 2020 Tommy Urban and Sally Reynold of Cornell and Bournemouth Universities published an account of an extraordinary set of

human tracks from White Sands in New Mexico. They are extraordinary for their immediacy and narrative power, for the soundscapes
that they conjure up in our minds, and for the purpose and rhythmic regularity displayed by the walker's stride patterns. Following
in their footsteps we can, in effect, replay them as a recording, in
real time. Might they offer us a glimpse of the future too – a glimpse
of what archaeology might some day be able to do for sound and
music?

The White Sands tracks were found in an area known as Alkali
Flats, close to where the first atomic bomb was detonated in July
1945. The ground is a smooth white clay surface, softened by ancient
rains and then baked hard by the sun, and in the interim something
has happened. From out of nowhere, a woman's footprints seem to
appear. The date is in the region of eleven to thirteen thousand
years ago, at around the end of the Last Glacial Maximum; and
here the footprints form a perfectly clear sequence. Like the scribe's
stylus on our Sumerian clay tablet, her bare feet have been pressed
into the wet surface of the clay. And as we follow her straight course
for maybe thirty minutes, she pauses to put down her load. It's a
small child. All around her are fresh prints of wild animals, including a large sabre-toothed cat. It's little wonder that she's pressing on
with such haste. What is she saying to comfort the child? Could she
be singing? There's a story here, of which we're glimpsing only the
merest phrase, and in all likelihood we'll never know what it means.
But for half an hour we've been walking there with her, out in that
vast white hostile desert.

A far older set of tracks, telling a similar kind of story, was found in
1976 at Laetoli in northern Tanzania, about fifty kilometres south of
Olduvai Gorge. They are recorded in a layer of fine ash ejected from
the volcano Sadiman, and it's proved to be the perfect medium for
capturing impressions of all kinds, even as small as raindrops. Over
the following seasons more were discovered. They are surprisingly
well preserved. And like the White Sands tracks they are heading pur-
posefully in a straight line towards the distant horizon.

Unlike the White Sands person, however, these people are very far indeed from being modern humans, Indeed, they are about as far as it's possible to get and remain balanced on two feet. Dating from about three and a half *million* years ago, they are australopiths. They are small, probably *Australopithecus afarensis* like the famous 'Lucy', and the scene their prints paint is no less touching. Three figures are resolutely traversing what must have been a drought-stricken and dystopian landscape. They are travelling close together – so close that they must be holding on to one another. The first figure is walking on the right, with the second, smaller, figure following in precisely his or her footsteps. The third figure, also small, is on the left of the group, and must be holding hands because its tracks echo the others' every slight meander. In one place the footprints on the left turn as if the figure is looking back. Maybe the others do too: their prints are unfortunately damaged at this point. But then they all continue on their way, until nearly twenty-seven metres from the first heel print, they finally fade from our sight.

There's something in their stride pattern that suggests a regular rhythmic habit that's quite remarkable, given their age and circumstances, and in a spirit of curiosity we might well wonder whether as they walked they too might not have been keeping time with their voices. But I don't believe that this is why I find them such a satisfying place to draw this exploration of sound and music to its close. It's really the perspective that they bring to our view of the remote past; the sense they offer us of an event, or part of an event, made physical and drawn out in the real-time way that we ourselves move and can understand. Could it be that one day, real-time sequences of a similar sort will hold clues not only to the way people walked? Might they also offer us a way of detecting changes in their senses of time, and timing, and rhythm: changes that would eventually take on modern symbolic meanings as music and dance?

While we wait to see what the next discovery may be, it's hard not to feel moved as these three small people walk away. We began our journey with a mechanical cutting stylus inscribing a real-time track of voices onto a cylinder of wax; we've eavesdropped on the traditional dances and processions of the Natchez of the Lower Mississippi; we've imagined the sounds of quills scratching on parchment and graffiti artists scratching on walls, and we've seen patterns of polishing left by musicians' fingers on their wooden fretboards and much-loved bone pipes. So perhaps it's appropriate to end with imagined sounds of something eerily similar. At any rate, this is where we leave them all, as they press on through the falling ash and rain, into their unknowable future – and the vastness of our still-to-be charted musical past.

The future of music's present

The present day

It's easy enough to see the differences between ourselves and our Australopithecine ancestors, four million years ago. They are as obvious in their limbs as they are in the shapes and capacities of their brains. There are contrasts too in how they used their bodies and engaged with their world. But they also hold some resonances. The most obvious is that we can no more foresee what our distant future has in store for us, for our civilisation and for our species, than they could see what the future had in store for them.

So as we watch them setting off to face the dangers and challenges that were no doubt ranged against them, we may find in their anxious journey a powerful parallel with our own predicament: a kind of kinship that's not so much biological as circumstantial. Of course, our knowledge of our world and of ourselves means that we're now able to hazard educated guesses as to what the coming months and years may bring. But it's hard to apply such musings to centuries and still longer spans of time, of the sort that we've been exploring while we've travelled deeper and deeper into the past.

Where will music be in a thousand, ten thousand or even a million years from now? What genres and styles will be in fashion? Will music even exist? We simply don't know. However, we can at least hope that someone will be around, in some human or at least hominin form; and if they are, then it's just possible that they may occasionally take time out to wonder about us, their ancestors, the people of the Anthropocene, and what it was that made us human.

If they are at all curious about our music, there *is* something we can confidently predict. It's that musical objects and traces will still be out there, hidden from sight yet waiting to be discovered.

Future archaeologists will be able to sift through cultural objects and remains of exactly the kind that fill our own archaeological museums today. There will be our equivalent of Palaeolithic painted caves. There will be undisturbed marine sediments to be sifted through for human debris, and other materials hidden in the ground – things that we will have left behind, either cast off casually or lost in various forms of disaster. And whatever of our time does survive, it would be strange if it doesn't include remains and traces of our music-making.

What exactly will survive? It's here, with the knowledge we've gained on our journey, that we can perhaps guess how much of a sound track we ourselves are leaving behind, and what any future investigator might be able to make of it. For what we have learned, I hope, is not just how ancient music evolved, but how the evidence of its evolutions travels through archaeological and geological time.

A large proportion of our musical hardware today is plastic, or cased in plastic, with plastic components, so it's unfortunate that the taphonomy of plastics – the way they are likely to change through time – covers only a hundred years. Plastic instruments might survive well in the controlled environment of a museum, but in average soil conditions – in cold, hard, compacted earth with variable humidity and acidic, alkaline or saline ground water – it's likely to be an altogether different story. Some may do reasonably well, like the fragment of a twentieth-century gramophone record recently excavated on Staten Island, New York. They may do still better in less hostile conditions of the sort that we've seen in deep-water shipwrecks similar to the *Titanic* and Ernest Shackleton's *Endurance*, recently located below the ice of Antarctica's Weddell

Sea. But most will likely deteriorate. Future archaeologists may have more luck with other materials – but like us, they'll have to decide for themselves how representative, how typical of our music-making, the musical hardware they find really was.

Having seen what four thousand years can do to bronze, I think we can be quite optimistic that a number of 'brass' instruments will survive for at least twice that length of time. Trumpets, and other sheet-metal instruments like cymbals, should do reasonably well too, given favourable conditions. Hot-metal castings like trumpet mouthpieces and bells of many kinds will do even better, provided that we haven't recycled them all. Keys and mechanical fittings from woodwind instruments and drums will fare similarly. But I doubt that brass wire strings will be so lucky, beyond a few hundred years, unless very special conditions prevail.

Heavier items of iron and steel should also be fairly future-proof, especially cast-iron piano frames like the ones abandoned in the music school at Pripyat – though with so many other parts missing it's not clear how far their survival will allow anyone to reconstruct the glories of a full-length concert grand. Drawn-steel piano strings and mechanical parts are unlikely to last more than a few centuries, even without the combined threats of vandalism, scavenging and recycling, while pressed steel units like the reed plates of harmonicas and concertinas may struggle to leave any trace, except perhaps as plate-shaped voids within crusts of corrosion.

The way instruments made from natural raw materials survive will inevitably vary, as it has in the past. Traditional musical instruments and children's toys are often made of wood, even today, though by now the more exotic and tropical timbers have mostly been replaced by less controversial alternatives. A modern acoustic guitar is unlikely to decay very differently from a Baroque fiddle or a Renaissance cittern, a Byzantine lute or a five-thousand-year-old Sumerian lyre. In the right conditions, wood can survive for hundreds of thousands of years. It will just be a matter of luck.

I suppose, in our favour, we do have a great deal of musical kit in circulation today, representing musical traditions that range from simple tourist drums and panpipes to magnificent church and theatre organs; and were all of it to survive it would paint the most vivid picture of twenty-first-century music in all its magnificent diversity. But this is never going to happen. We are too aware now of the value of their constituent materials, and likely to get more so as our present century wears on. Even in the ancient world, we saw that when things became obsolete and all other potential uses were exhausted, many would be melted down and reused, or burnt as fuel. Today more elaborate forms of recycling will take their toll of circuit boards for their gold and tin, while even the plastics that are currently going to landfill may eventually be mined and re-deployed. Virtual music technologies will simply vanish with them, unless as relics in cyberspace – assuming that cyberspace still exists.

One exception may be in so-called time capsules. It's notable how, of music's most spectacular archaeological discoveries, most have been preserved not by accident but by design. We saw it in the astonishing orchestra of bells, pipes, zithers and chimes found sealed in the tomb of Zeng Hou Yi at Leigudun. Such entombment doesn't eliminate decay and corrosion, but it can slow it down and render the evidence more recoverable.

There are of course less material ways in which we are unwittingly preserving our achievements. Over the last hundred years, for example, we've been projecting assorted debris and radio noise out into the vacuum of space. The first radio-frequency broadcast must already be more than a hundred light years from earth; no doubt attenuated far beyond the capability of any detection system that we have ourselves, but in theory still detectable somewhere, by someone. We've also left traces of our interest in sounds on the planet Mars, and on Saturn's moon Titan, where acoustic micro-phones are likely to bear indefinite witness. Then there are the things and documents that we've deliberately chosen to send.

It seems that the first actual musical instruments taken into space were a Hohner eight-note harmonica and a set of small jingle bells, carried aboard Gemini Six in 1965. The first Highland bagpipes to be played in earth orbit were taken to the International Space Station in 2015 by Danish astronaut Kjell Lindgren. And these are only three of several. Whether any of them are still up there I don't know, but two messages most certainly are. One is intangible: a NASA radio transmission of The Beatles' 'Across the Universe', which was transmitted on 4 February 2008 using the Deep Space Network, to mark the network's forty-fifth anniversary. Directed towards Polaris, the Pole star, and travelling at the speed of light, it's already completed the first fifteen years of its 431-year journey.

The second, travelling rather more sedately, is the so-called Golden Record, of which copies were attached to the hulls of two unmanned NASA spacecraft, Voyagers 1 and 2, in 1977. The tracks etched on these gilded copper discs include a range of traditional music and spoken-language recordings from around the world. The earliest in date was of the sixteenth-century English composer Anthony Holborne's 'The Fairie Round', performed by David Munrow and the London Early Music Consort. A written message from the then US president, Jimmy Carter, accompanied both Voyager craft. 'This is a present from a small, distant world,' he wrote, 'a token of our sounds, our science, our images, our music, our thoughts and our feelings. We are attempting to survive our time so we may live into yours.'

What any future human or indeed non-human archaeologist will be able to make of all these different materials, and the enormously varied musical traditions that they represent, is anybody's guess. They may be completely mystified. But, on the other hand, if they are anything like us, and are blessed with the same curiosity, ingenuity, imagination and persistence, they may just be able to find some clues among our sound tracks that will explain the kinds of people we were, and hoped one day to become.

Acknowledgements

Sound Tracks emerged from a career spent combining archaeological science with musical experiment and performance, and during its writing I have benefitted from the generosity and kindness of many friends, old and new. The idea of the book itself arose in discussions with my literary agent, Bill Hamilton of A. M. Heath & Co., and owes much of its present form to his enthusiasm and knowledge, as well as to the energy, skills and technical advice of all the good people at Penguin Random House: my publisher at the Bodley Head, Stuart Williams, my editor Jörg Hensgen, and my American publisher and editor Jonathan Segal. Of the Bodley Head team I should like to extend particular thanks also to Katherine Fry for her sterling copy-editing, to Kris Potter for the book's attractive design, to Rowena Skelton-Wallace for managing the editorial process, to John Garrett for the proofreading, and to Ben Murphy for taking on the onerous task of compiling the index.

Of the archaeological community, worldwide, I find myself indebted to many more friends and colleagues, past and present, than I can reasonably acknowledge here, and indeed am indebted to an extent far greater than I can begin to describe. But grateful mention must first be made of the army of excavators, conservators and post-excavation specialists with whom it's been my privilege to work over the years, and without whose tireless efforts all the science that we can now bring to bear on music's buried past would be of little avail. They know who they are, and I thank them all. Special mention must also be made of those academic colleagues whose pioneering researches have helped to bridge gaps in individual narratives. They are listed below, by name and specialism. I need hardly add that any shortcomings within the pages of this book are my own, and not theirs.

Valued collaborators and supporters have included especially Francesco d'Errico, Gisela Eberhardt, Ricardo Eichmann, Friederike Fless, Mark Geller, Klaus Geus, Mark Howell, Elke Kaiser, Gjermund Kolltveit, Cajsa Lund, Rosie Luff, Steven Plunkett and, last but by no means least, Francis Pryor – with whom I share a fen as well as a university and a passion for prehistory.

Finally, the book, and indeed much of my research, could never have happened had it not been for the early encouragement and wisdom of Denis Matthews and Benedict Sarnaker at Newcastle University, and of John Coles, Glyn Daniel, George Henderson and Laurence Picken in Cambridge. It was their vision and example that helped get me started. It's equally difficult to imagine it happening without the unwavering support of my family, especially my parents Jessie and Keith, and my wife Wendy who has lived through it all. In addition to checking and correcting the many drafts with unfailing cheerfulness, she helped me keep going with countless cups of tea and was there at the end to help me cross the finishing line.

To address a topic of this breadth and ambition has naturally involved some tough editing choices and deletions, so that the end result does not reflect the entire wealth, diversity and ambition of music's new archaeology today. Whole strands of vital research, together with many formidable intellectual breakthroughs and new finds, have had to be set aside in order to focus on the core journey. To any reader who notices something that I seem to have overlooked, I can only say 'there's always another day!'

Table of thanks (in alphabetical order of surname, with the chapters and specialist subjects to which they relate):

Cristina-Georgeta Alexandrescu (chapter 33, Roman music iconography); Maxime Aubert (50, Sulawesi cave art); Elizabeth Barham (26, Prittlewell lyre conservation); Lee Berger (50, 51, Rising Star Cave, *Homo naledi*, Sterkfontein caves); Martin Biddle (26, medieval resonating jars); Steven Birch (40, High Pasture Cave assemblage); Adje Both (22, Precolumbian music of the Americas); Dominique Buisson (48, Grotte d'Isturitz assemblage); Constance

Bullock-Davies† (12, medieval minstrelsy); Florence Calament (29, Antinoöpolis assemblage); Nicholas Conard (49, German upper palaeolithic assemblages); Ian Cross (51, music origins); Gabriela Currie (39, steppe harps); Paul Devereux (48, archaeoacoustics); Francesco d'Errico (48, 49, 50, taphonomy and micrography, Isturitz assemblage, Blombos cave); Ricardo Eichmann (29, 45, Antinoöpolis lute, Ancient Near Eastern music); Verónica Estevez (14, Lelystad citterns); Dean Falk (51, australopithecines, language and music); Lothar von Falkenhausen (38, Leigudun assemblage and bells); Jianjun Fang (16, 47, neolithic mouth harps); Xueyang Fang (38, Leigudun stone chimes); Peter Godman (28, Merovingian poets); Anna Gruszczyńska-Ziółkowska (30, Cahuachi panpipes); Garman Harbottle (47, Jiǎhú flutes); George and Isabel Henderson (20, early medieval art and culture); Martin Henig (17, Oxford assemblage); Christopher Henshilwood (50, Blombos cave); Peter Holmes (36, 42, 45, Tattershall *carnyx*, Iron Age trumpets, Bronze Age 'lurs', Charlesland pipes); Mark Howell (11, 22, Natchez and *La Belle* jingles, Precolumbian musical traditions); Raquel Jiménez Pasalodos (41, Iberian stelae); Dafydd Johnston (12, poetry of Iolo Goch); Gjermund Kolltveit (23, 31, European mouth harps, Dzhetyasar lyre); Aline Kottmann (26, Meschede, resonating pots); Anne Kilmer (44, Hurrian hymn, cuneiform music texts); Theo Krispijn (44, Hurrian hymn, cuneiform music texts); Rex Lawson (Prologue, piano rolls); Wendy Lawson (16, boatswains' calls); Mei Li (38, Leigudun finds); Alexandra von Lieven (37, 43, Egyptian texts and music, Tutankhamun's tomb); Cajsa Lund (Prologue, 13, 15, 'green music', *Kronan* music); Christophe Maniquet (36, Tintignac assemblage and carnyxes); Lisa Manniche (37, 43, Leiden lyre, Tutankhamun's trumpets); Claudio Mercado Muñoz (30, *chino* bands of Chile); Susanne Münzel (49, German upper palaeolithic pipes); Sebastian Núñez (14, Lelystad citterns); Simon O'Dwyer (27, 45, Irish wooden trumpets, Charlesland pipes); Christopher Page (17, Oxford musicians); José Pérez de Arce (30, *chino* bands of Chile); John Purser (27, 40, wooden horns, High Pasture cave, Scottish and Irish musical traditions); Susan Rawcliffe (24 Moche musical ceramics); Iegor Reznikoff (48, cave art and acoustics); Eleonora Rocconi (41, Greeks and Barbarian music); Susanne Rühling (32, Aquincum organ); Joachim Schween (42, Bronze Age 'lurs'); Dahlia Shehata (44, Ancient Near Eastern musical texts); Azilkhan Tazhekeev (31, Dzhetyasar lyre); Barbara Theune-Grosskopf (28, Trossingen assemblage and lyre); Rupert Till (48, archaeoacoustics); Christophe Vendries (29, 41, Antinoöpolis lute, Romans and Barbarian music); Angela Wardle (32, Roman *tibiae*); Xinghua Xiao (47, Jiǎhú flutes); Juzhong Zhang (47, Jiǎhú flutes)

List of Illustrations

Making a willow bark flute (© Wendy Lawson).

Steel reed-plate from a mouth organ, Antietam, United States (www.yankeerebelantiques.com, accessed 19 April 2021).

Norwegian children's toy whistle refashioned from an old clay tobacco-pipe (© Norges Teknisk-Naturvitenskapelige Universitet, Vitenskaps Museet, object acc. no. N23069; photograph by Aage Hojern)

Boatswain with whistle, from a Sicilian quilt, *c.*1380, showing scenes from the medieval tale of Tristram and Yseult (© Victoria & Albert Museum, London, no. 1391–1904, carousel-image no. 2006AG6902).

Fingerboard from a violin lost in the explosion that sank *Kronan* in 1676 (courtesy of Kalmar Läns Museum, Sweden; author's photograph).

Garland from the bell of a ruined trumpet, made by 'Lois Pesin' in 1567 (courtesy of the Thames Mudlarks; author's photograph).

Angels with straight trumpets from the Welles Apocalypse (© The British Library, London).

Mouth harp from medieval Lincoln (courtesy of Lincoln Archaeological Trust; author's photograph).

Singers' gallery in Lichfield Cathedral (courtesy of The Dean and Chapter, Lichfield Cathedral; author's photograph).

Electron micrograph of finger wear on a medieval flute (author's photograph).

Bone flutes found among craft residues in 11th-century Schleswig (courtesy of Schleswig-Holsteinisches Landesmuseum, Germany; author's photograph).

Musical experiment in an 11th-century manuscript (© Cambridge University Library).

Whistling bird on a Peruvian terracotta flask, 8th century (author's photograph).

Musical street art in 21st-century Italy (© Wendy Lawson; artist unknown).

King David composing the Psalms in an 8th-century English miniature (© The Dean and Chapter, Durham Cathedral).

The ghost lyre of Prittlewell, England, c.AD 600 (© Museum of London Archaeology).

Engraved scene on a lyre sound board, Trossingen, Germany, AD 580 (© Archäologisches Landesmuseum Baden-Württemberg).

Grave 58, Trossingen, Germany, AD 580 (© Archäologisches Landesmuseum Baden-Württemberg).

Lute from the tomb of a Byzantine woman, Egypt, 6th century (© Musée de Grenoble, France; photograph by J.-L. Lacroix).

Tibia from the River Thames, London, probably 3rd century (courtesy of The Museum of London; author's photograph).

Memorial to Lutatia Lupata, Mérida, Spain, perhaps 2nd century (Prisma Archivo/Alamy Stock Photo).

Milecastle 37 on Hadrian's Wall, England, early 2nd century (author's photograph).

Detail of a *carnyx* from the River Welland, England, probably 1st century, watercolour (courtesy of Lincoln City Library; author's photograph).

Carnyx hoard from Tintignac, central France, 1st century BC (Inrap/ Patrick Erneaux).

Lyrics added *c.* 250 BC to the back of an Egyptian lyre, *c.*250 BC (© Rijksmuseum van Oudheden, Leiden, Netherlands).

Niuzhong bells uncovered in a Chinese tomb, 6th–5th century BC (© Hebi City Museum, China).

Memorial stone from Zaragoza, Spain, 7th century BC (author's drawing).

Clay tablet (facsimile) with musical notes, from Syria, 14th century BC (author's photograph).

Waterlogged tubes buried in a wooden water tank, Charlesland, Ireland, *c.*2000 BC.

Sumerian lyre player pictured on the 'Standard of Ur', Iraq, *c.*3000 BC (courtesy of The British Museum, London; author's photograph).

Leonard Woolley, holding up his latest plaster cast, Iraq, 1927–8 (© The British Museum, London).

Crane-bone flutes from Jiāhúcun, China, *c.*7000 BC.

Traditional ringing stone with percussion marks, Brittany, France (© Wendy Lawson).

Swan bone pipe from Hohle Fels, Germany, *c.*8,000 years ago (© Universität Tübingen).

Vulture bone pipe from Isturitz, southern France, *c.*27,000 years ago (courtesy of the Musée d'Archéologie Nationale, St-Germain-en-Laye, France; author's photograph).

The author prepares to play a replica Isturitz pipe for a BBC television documentary (© Wendy Lawson).

Australopithecus footprints, Laetoli, Tanzania, *c.*3.5 million years ago (Images of Africa Photobank/Alamy Stock Photo).

Index